Books should be returned on or before the
last date stamped below

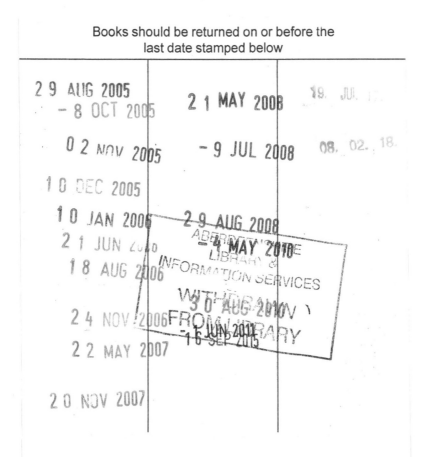

PIRATES
of the British Isles

PIRATES
of the British Isles

JOEL BAER

TEMPUS

First published 2005

Tempus Publishing Limited
The Mill, Brimscombe Port,
Stroud, Gloucestershire, GL5 2QG

© Joel Baer, 2005

British Library Cataloguing in Publication Data.
A catalogue record for this book is available from the British Library.

ISBN 0 7524 2304 5

Typesetting and origination by Tempus Publishing Limited
Printed in Great Britain

Contents

Abbreviations

BL   British Library
CO   Colonial Office
CSPA   *Calendar of State Papers: Colonial Series, America and West*
            Indies
CSPD   *Calendar of State Papers, Domestic Series*
GHP   Captain Charles Johnson, *A General History of the Pyrates*
            (London, 1724–28; edited by Manuel Schonhorn [attrib-
            uted to Daniel Defoe], 2nd ed., Mineola, New York:
            Dover, 1999)
HCA   High Court of Admiralty
HO   Home Office
NA   National Archives, London
NMM   National Maritime Museum, London
NPG   National Portrait Gallery, London
OIOC   Oriental and India Office Collection, British Library
SP   State Papers

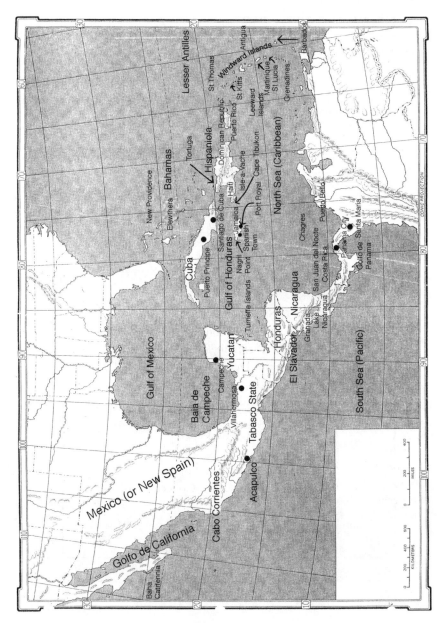

1 Central America and the West Indies

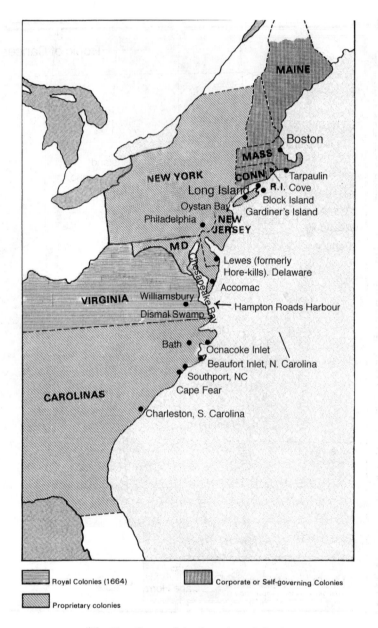

Royal Colonies (1664)

Corporate or Self-governing Colonies

Proprietary colonies

2 The East Coast of the American Colonies

Tropic of Cancer

Curacao

Cantagena
Lake Maracaibo Maracaibo

Venezuela Devil's Island

Columbia Surinam Cayenne
French Guiana

Isla la
Plata

Ecuador

Guayaquil

Porta

Peru

Brazil

Lima

Bahia
(Salvador)

Bolivia

Arica Potosi

Valparaiso

Juan Fernandez

Chile

Strait of Magellan Cape Horn

0   400   800
KILOMETERS

0   200   400   300
MILES

MODIFIED ORTHOGRAPHIC PROJECTION

3 South America

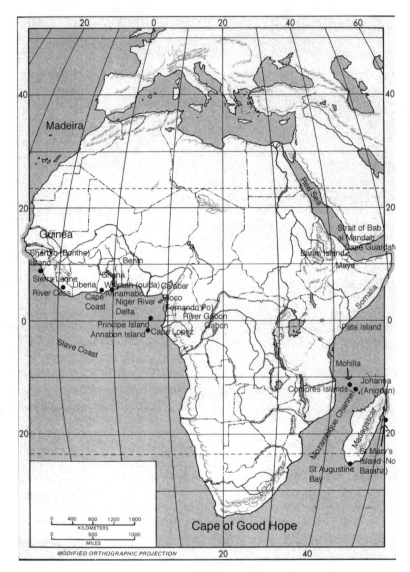

20   0   20   40   60

40

Madeira

Red Sea

20

Guinea

Strait of Bab
al Mandab
Cape Guardafi

Sherbro (Bonthe)
Island

Barim Island

Benin

Mayo

Sierra Leone

Ghana

Liberia

Wiydaah (ouida) Calabar

River Cess

Cape
Coast

Annamabo

Bioco
(Fernando Po)

Somalia

Niger River
Delta

River Gabon

Principe Island

Gabon

Annabon Island

Cape Lopez

Pate Island

Slave Coast

Mohilla

Johanna
(Anjouan)

Comores Islands

Mozambique Channel

Madagascar

St Mary's
Island (No
Baraha)

St Augustine
Bay

0   400   800   1200   1600
KILOMETERS
0   500   1000
MILES

Cape of Good Hope

MODIFIED ORTHOGRAPHIC PROJECTION   20   40

4 Africa

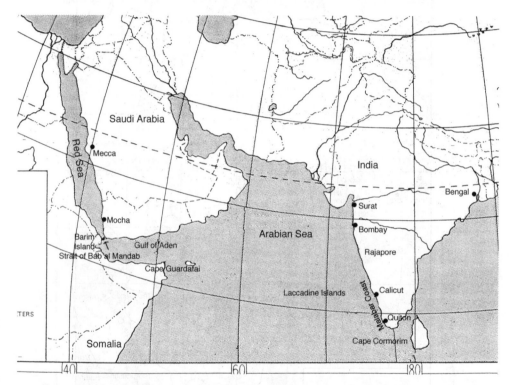

5 Arabia and India

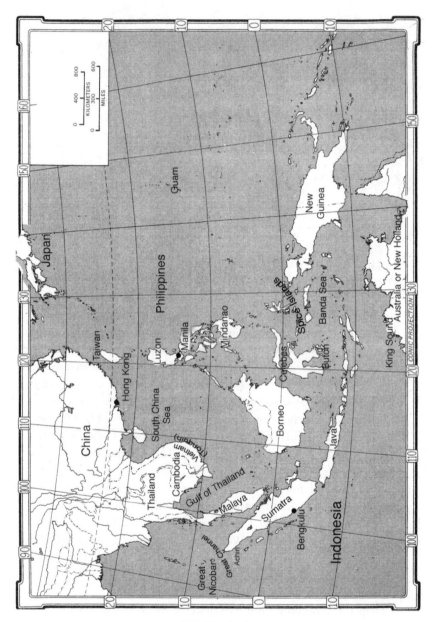

6 The East Indies

Preface

The genesis of this book was my curiosity about the ways in which the British law of piracy informed Daniel Defoe's novels of seafaring. My studies in this area have pulled me inexorably away from imaginative literature and towards the intersection between the history of piracy and of the law. Although the topic has led into abstruse areas where, like young William Dampier on a sugar plantation in Jamaica, I have found myself 'clearly out of my element', I have been blessed by the generous help of colleagues and friends. I am indebted to the cheerful and tireless labours of Macalester College librarian Jean Becone and to the staffs of the University of Minnesota libraries – especially Carol Urness, former curator of the James Ford Bell Library, and Tim Johnson, current curator of the Rare Books Collection – the National Archives, British Library, Guildhall Library, and Pepys Library (Magdalene College, Cambridge).

I am grateful for the valuable counsel of Paul Alkon, Manuel Schonhorn, and Lauren Benton in America; David Marley in Canada; and Anton Gill, D.W. Jones, David Starkey, Diana and Michael Preston, and Roy Palmer in England. What started as fruitful professional relationships have developed over the years into warm friendships with Marcus Rediker at the University of Pittsburgh and James Derriman, Christopher Ware, and James Kelley in England.

Help has also come from Macalester College in the form of two research grants and a subvention for the acquiring of illustrations, and from the encouragement of colleagues Alvin Greenberg, Giles Gamble, James Stuart, Juanita Garciagodoy, David Itzkowitz, and Peter Weisensel whose interest in my endless stories of the pirates is greatly appreciated.

I wish also to thank friends outside the academy: Shirley Anderson for her energy and research skills; Don Enerson for persistently asking the right questions; Fred Rohlfing for his zeal in rooting out errors and helping to fit all the parts together; and my wife Edwina Nagahashi for her longstanding patience.

This book is dedicated to the memory of my parents, Bella and Solomon Baer.

Introduction:

Gentlemen of Fortune

Pirate – even today the word has a sudden and threatening sound, despite sentimental boys' fiction and romantic movies. Before Douglas Fairbanks Jr and Johnny Depp, before Robert Louis Stevenson and Gilbert and Sullivan, before nation states and commercial shipping, there was the pirate. He was an ancient plunderer of coastal villages, a hunter and gatherer of other people's goods to supplement the livelihood of his own family and village. Some believe that he had a hand in inventing trade, carrying with him goods for barter when theft was inconvenient or dangerous.

In the ancient world, he was often respected as a bold warrior, the Greek word for pirate deriving from the verb *peiran*, 'to attempt or attack'.

So far from being a disgrace, and an illegal occupation, [piracy] was considered an honourable calling, and looked upon much in the same light as deeds of arms in the days of chivalry. We find the Homeric heroes boasting of actions which in later times would have sent them to the gallows'.[1]

By the time of Thucydides, the pirate had begun to be looked upon with reproach, a feeling intensified during Caesar's day when he was branded as a destroyer of the peace for opposing Roman hegemony in the Mediterranean and Adriatic Seas. Cicero, for example, considered the pirate 'the common enemy of all with whom neither faith nor oath is to be kept'. (*De Officiis*, 3.29.107). The lawmakers' fear of him has come down to modern times in the phrase 'the common enemy of the human race', Sir Edward Coke's epithet for the pirate, and so effectively has he been demonised that, as late as the eighteenth century, British law permitted his captors, if need be, to hang him 'at the Main-yard-End... without any Solemnity of Condemnation'.[2]

From the mid-seventeenth to the early eighteenth century, an epidemic of piracy swept across the world's oceans, caused by the instability and opportunism of the new age. This was the time when men like Henry Morgan, William Kidd, and Edward Thatch (Blackbeard) established the legends from which has flowed so much popular entertainment, but more importantly, it was a time of profound change. The growth of a new commercial aggressiveness and the globalisation of trade, the race for empire among the European powers, and the frequent continental and colonial wars destabilised the traditional relationships among seaman, merchant, and king. Out of necessity, frustration, greed or rebelliousness, thousands of European sailors broke the traditional bond of loyalty between worker and master and became pirates.

This book recounts the lives of six extraordinary British figures from the heyday of piracy with special emphasis on the struggle to bring them to justice. Most were daring, resourceful warriors; a few were charismatic leaders who gave posterity the image of a pirate chief. Two led their men to capture princely treasures against enormous odds, the crimes of another nearly brought down a British ministry, and one wrote the most celebrated book of travel in English before Captain Cook. While the exploits of two were thought honourable, even heroic, by the English, most were harshly treated as national policy swung towards 'zero tolerance', a mood expressed in radical reform of the law of piracy.

Fascinating as they are in their own right, their stories provide an outline of pirate history from 1660 to 1722, which falls into three phases:

1660–1690, state-sponsored piracy: Henry Morgan raids the towns of Spanish America under the legal authority of colonial governors and is followed by William Dampier and others who do the same with fraudulent commissions as state-sponsored plundering degenerates into simple brigandage.

1690–1700, Indian Ocean piracy: Henry Every and William Kidd prey on Muslim shipping in the Indian Ocean and Arabian Sea after Spain, France and England begin to suppress the West Indian buccaneers.

1700–1722, 'at war with all the world': Edward Thatch and Bartholomew Roberts throw off the last remnants of patriotic restraint and attack ships of all nations off Europe's Atlantic colonies and along the coast of Africa, earning reputations for cruelty, terror and suicidal bravado. (See Illustration 1)

Three critical events provide convenient landmarks in this history: Morgan's taking of Panama City in 1671, the passage of William III's reform law of piracy in 1700, and the mass trial of Bartholomew Roberts's crew in 1722. Morgan's greatest victory ironically undermined the state's tolerance for the plundering of the Spanish colonies and set the stage for an organised campaign against the pirates. The 1700 law promoted their downfall by creating throughout the world special piracy courts severely tilted against the accused, a boon to the empire's merchant adventurers. Captain Roberts's destruction was the single most dramatic effect of the new law and put an end to the reign of the pirates in Caribbean and Atlantic waters.

To flesh out the above outline, let us first look briefly at what motivated seamen of the period to risk the extraordinary dangers of pirate life. An eyewitness to the famous mutiny in 1694 by which Henry Every became a pirate chief provides a convenient starting point.

At Corunna [Spain] the men demanded their pay which was to be paid them by contract every Six months, which not being paid them... Henry Every Master of the Charles the 2nd. went up & down from Ship to Ship & perswaded the men to come on board him, & he would carry them where they should get money enough.[3]

The success of Every's rebellion speaks not only to the discontent of seamen during this period, but also to the opportunities for those bold enough to sail under the black flag. (See Illustration 2) Discontent and opportunity are central to the eruption of British piracy after the restoration of the Stuarts in 1660. Withheld wages was the prime source of unrest among merchant sailors, followed closely by harsh treatment at the hands of captains, arbitrary changes in the route of voyages, the loss of traditional perquisites and sources of compensation, and, of course, bad food. Seamen in the navy complained most of long delays in pay, largely the result of perennial under-funding. They rarely mutinied aboard Royal Navy ships, but rather carried their grievances with them when, like Henry Every, they were discharged and returned to the merchant service. In the 1690s the mutinous spirit reached even to the decks of East Indiamen, the ships of Britain's most prosperous and disciplined trading company. (See Illustration 3)

At the same time, the sea offered more opportunities for the labourer during the early modern period than did the land. The work was often brutal and there were many ways to die, but wages – especially in wartime – were high and an enterprising tar could sometimes put in a small stock of exotic goods for sale at home while privateers and men-of-war held out the possibility of shares in loot from prizes (captured enemy ships). It is no wonder, then, that the ship was the setting for a well-known rags-to-riches story in which a young man works his way up to captain or even higher, a story promised by the title of the first prose narrative based on Henry Every's adventures: *The Life and Adventures of Capt. John Avery grown from a cabin boy to a King.* (London, [1709])

In fact, some mariners did travel from forecastle to quarterdeck based on their skill – witness the naval careers of Admirals Sir John Narborough, Sir Cloudesley Shovell, and Sir William Myngs (who liked to boast that his father was a shoemaker and mother a hogman's daughter).[4] The sturdy men who went to sea during this period grew to have higher expectations than landsmen and less patience for abuse or periodic unemployment. After all, they had touched the bundles of wealth with their own hands and knew that there was a fortune to be made aboard ship. It was all a throw of the dice, of course – the sea was ruled by Dame Fortune, a place of death and dreams, of long odds and lucky strikes. The merchant gambled that his ship would come in.

No one knew the odds better than the pirate, who gambled that he would take the merchant's ship before it came in. The seventeenth and eighteenth centuries were good times to be 'a gentleman of fortune' – a contemporary euphemism for pirate – for the vast expansion of seaborne trade during this period dramatically increased the sheer number of targets. Moreover, in contrast to bulk items like coal and fish shipped for centuries along Europe's coasts, blue-water traders were now more likely to carry precious metals, exotic spices, or rare manufactured goods like fine china or Indian silks, cargoes that promised to 'make the voyage' of lucky pirates. Instead of limiting themselves to the coasts as before, Europe's merchant navies now ventured far from home into lonely and unpoliced waters.

The temptation of many rich, unprotected targets was increased by the intense and bloody competition among Europeans for goods, markets and trading bases. It was the political wisdom of the time that 'there is no trade without war and no war without trade'. When national treasuries could not sustain the costs of naval warfare – which by the mid-seventeenth century had become global – all the maritime powers commissioned private men-of-war to take up the slack. Privateersmen became skilled at capturing the enemy's merchant ships in order to weaken its war effort, and they often became outright pirates despite oaths, bonds, and procedures for 'condemning' prizes.[5] When war ended, unemployed Caribbean privateersmen turned *en masse* to piracy, giving rise to the general belief that privateering was the 'cradle of piracy'.

Most of the privateers who went 'on the account' (i.e., agreed to payment by share of the plunder rather than monthly wages) did so to profit from uncontrolled hostilities in the Caribbean. Spain's authority to exclude foreigners from its new world empire was based on the Treaty of Tordesillas (1494) by which the Pope recognised Spain's claim to all the land west of 48 degrees west longitude, an entire hemisphere. French raiders hotly contested that claim into the 1550s, when war between France and Spain was settled by the Treaty of Cateau-Cambrésis (1559). During the treaty negotiations, Spain informally agreed to include North America in the peace but reserved its monopoly over all the lands south of the Tropic of Cancer and west

of the longitude of Flores Island in the Azores. What was at stake was
not only control of land but also access to trade with Spain's Central
and South American colonists. The effect of such shortsighted diplo-
macy was a permanent, undeclared war in the excluded areas against
French, Dutch and English privateers, or, to use the contemporary
phrase, 'no peace beyond the line'.[6] (See Illustration 4)

In this legal grey zone – no peace but no declared war – raiders like
Henry Morgan and William Dampier proliferated, and precarious
British colonies tolerated their excesses because they were the only
force capable of holding the Spanish, French and Dutch at bay. As
soon as an invasion of a British colony was rumoured, they were
granted privateering commissions, which they used to rob ships and
pillage towns under the pretext of intelligence-gathering or disrupt-
ing the enemy's mobilisation. If they were captured for taking British
ships, they usually had to be tried in London under old laws inadequate to the threat they posed. If by chance they were prosecuted in
the rare colony with qualified courts, juries acquitted because they
brought cheap goods and money to settlers hamstrung by England's
restrictive Navigation Acts.

British privateers found Spanish America an erratic and vulnerable
enemy. Spanish professional officers were often brave and skilled but
the colonials they commanded were poorly trained and badly
equipped. The blitzkrieg tactics of the raiders required their prey to
be self-reliant, agile and resourceful, qualities not fostered by Spain's
over-centralised imperial system. Conditioned to shy from independent initiative, Spanish colonists, even when augmented by Indian and
African slaves, were often routed by the shock of a buccaneer charge.
With vast holdings in Asia and the New World, the Spanish empire
was so overextended that its colonists sought arms and equipment
from European smugglers, the very merchants whom imperial policy
sought to shut out. The privateers' victories in the 1660's and 1670s
demonstrated to the world that the Spanish empire was rich but weak.

In the next chapter we will see how the privateers of Jamaica succeeded in navigating the grey zone until the mid-1670s. But when
crown colonies such as Jamaica and Barbados were ordered to arrest
them, they went for protection to the Bahamas, the Carolinas, Rhode

Island or Pennsylvania, proprietary colonies governed by an individual or a consortium of charter holders less responsive to the political breezes at London. Chronic neglect and under-funding of the proprietaries made them especially vulnerable to attack and encouraged their settlers and governments to collude with the pirates. It was not until the second decade of the eighteenth century that Whitehall brought them in line with its anti-pirate crusade.

By the early 1670s the tide began to turn against the 'pirateers', as contemporaries sometimes called them.7 The reasons for this shift in England's policy range from the need to court Spain in the run-up to the next European war to the desire to win the Asiento, the exclusive right to supply slaves to Spain's colonists. The first shot in the war against the pirates was fired in 1670 on the diplomatic front; England sought to destroy their *raison d'être* by negotiating a treaty with Spain that would for the first time apply to the Caribbean. In the following decades, the government brought the Royal Navy to take more vigorous and sustained action against them in the Caribbean, Atlantic and Indian Oceans. It pressured sitting colonial governors to stiffen their resistance to them, cashiered the known bad actors, and put the proprietary colonies on notice by rescinding the charter of the Bahamas, the most corrupt. In response to harassment in the Caribbean, many veteran pirates sailed into the Indian Ocean, the jealously guarded realm of the British East India Company, where they targeted Muslim commerce. Their early successes triggered unmerited reprisals by the Indian authorities against the company, which, in turn, brought pressure on Whitehall to take action. Some warships were dispatched but the most effective response was overhaul of the antiquated laws by which pirates were defined and prosecuted.

The legal history of piracy is rarely discussed in pirate biographies, but it is long and intriguing. The crime of piracy is generally understood simply to be robbery at sea, but we have seen that many pirates of our period might hope to have their actions understood as a kind of armed 'taking' validated by the special conditions of settler life in the Caribbean as well as by colonial commissions. In his authoritative study *The Law of Piracy*, Alfred P. Rubin demonstrates that from antiquity to

early modern times, piracy has been anything but a simple legal concept. To the Greeks and Romans,

> the word *peirato* and its derivatives... applied not to brigands or others
> outside the legal order, but to small communities including fighting men
> who were regarded as capable of forming alliances and participating in
> wars as they were fought between acknowledged political leaders within
> the legal order of the time.[8]

These men were, in effect, what would in the early modern period be
called authorised privateers.

The most famous *peiratos* of antiquity were the Cilicians of the
eastern Mediterranean, who for centuries before Christ had included
armed takings at sea in their economy. When Pompey fought them
in 68–67 BC, it was not for their criminality but rather their defi-
ance of Roman power, and they were vilified as 'something like
rebels'. The Cilicians bear a resemblance to the Barbary pirates of
the seventeenth century, in that both peoples lived near waters that
sustained a 'lively and dangerous commerce and conflicting claims
to authority' and both exacted the equivalent of a tax on passing
merchants 'with capture of the vessel, confiscation of its cargo, and
the enslavement of the crew the penalty for tax evasion'. Both peoples shared a similar fate: they were subjugated when there was no
longer room for 'an antiquated way of life in the new commercial
and political order that could not countenance interference with
trade in the Mediterranean Sea'.[9] The West Indian buccaneers, too,
formed communities that survived on a mixed economy of hunting, light agriculture and piracy in hotly contested seas and were
criminalised by a nascent empire grown intolerant of actions it had
once encouraged.

The term *pirate* shifted during the centuries until, in the sixteenth, it
took on for the first time a precise meaning in British law, one whose
takings at sea have not been licensed by a recognised authority, a complete reversal of what it had meant in antiquity. It is no accident that
English lawyers saw fit to define the term just as their nation was
about to vie with the Netherlands, Spain and France for global

markets and empire. For Rubin, the history of the term supports the general notion that law is constructed in response to state policy rather than to facts, moral or religious principles, or the dictates of reason.[10] An empire based on commerce cannot be sustained by workers who, rejecting the 'discipline of the sea', destroy trade and dominion to satisfy their personal appetites.

Some of the most powerful thinkers of the seventeenth century took a different view of law. Alberto Gentili, Hugo Grotius, Samuel Pufendorf, John Locke, and a host of other philosophers, searched for something less ephemeral than political or economic policy upon which to ground the law. They came to believe that nature taught us the principles of law and parliaments should attempt to codify those principles. They encouraged global exploration and trade because they brought back information about diverse peoples that demonstrated the universal laws of human social organisation. While their theories liberalised attitudes towards non-European peoples, their rationalistic and universalising habit of mind also justified the casting aside of local traditions and social orders. For example, since piracy is a deterrent to the wholesome interchange between all peoples, it is the duty of all to bring pirates to justice, anywhere on the seas and regardless of the victims' or miscreants' nationality or the parochial claims of foreign states.

Natural law theory greatly stimulated the growth of international law, including the rules of war and the law of the sea. Most relevant to us is that under its influence the British in the sixteenth and seventeenth centuries asserted the right to prosecute pirates of all nations, a radical departure from medieval practice. *Pirate*, Rubin contends, 'had acquired a meaning as a vague basis for ever expanding English assertions of jurisdiction'.[11] Pirates would not only be the shock troops of empire, they would also help to provide its legal rationale. A good example of this expansion of British jurisdiction occurs in the trial of Captain Bartholomew Roberts's crew in Chapter 6.

The evolution of the modern law of piracy begins in 1536 with the Offences at Sea Act (28 Henry VIII, c.15). Since 1361 piracy had been considered a form of petty treason prosecuted like high treason under the civil law without a jury, a procedure that mandated specific kinds of evidence difficult to obtain for crimes at sea. Because circumstantial evidence was not permitted, either a confession or the testimony of two 'indifferent' eyewitnesses to an overt act of piracy was required for conviction.

> In all Criminal Matters and especially in this of Pyracy the Rules of the Civil Law are, that before Judgment of Death can be given against any Offender he must either Confess his Office or it must be plainly and directly proved by two Witnesses that saw the Offence Committed. [12]

Moreover, there was a rigid, pre-established mode of weighing evidence in felony trials under the civil law. 28 Henry VIII, c.15 kept piracy a crime at admiralty (i.e. civil) law, but circumvented these restrictions by mandating the use of common law procedure in piracy trials. Henceforth the accused would be indicted by a grand jury, tried, like other felons, before a twelve-man petty jury of their peers, and convicted by unanimous vote. Free from specific criteria of guilt, common law juries could weigh the evidence in whatever manner they saw fit, 'which the Civil Law admits not of'.[13] Such juries, it was thought, would be more prone to convict pirates than judges diligently applying the evidentiary requirements of the civil law.

Henry VIII would probably never have allowed such a major change if he did not trust in his judges to coerce juries into doing the state's bidding. Under the Tudors the English jury had lost much of its vaunted independence; judges could and would fine or imprison jurors who delivered the wrong verdict.[14] This practice ended in 1671, but late-Stuart and Georgian judges found other ways to persuade juries into acceptable verdicts. Their power did not wane until the rise of the defence lawyer in the late eighteenth century.[15] Nearly every piracy trial we will look at illustrates the ways in which the bench supported the prosecution and helped to shape a narrative of events highly prejudicial to the accused. The trials at London of Henry Every's men (1696) and of Captain Kidd (1701) offer the means of observing piracy proceedings under the 1536 statute, although as show or state trials, they were atypically long and courteous to the defendants and displayed features – such as counsel for the state – absent from more routine exercises.

Early in Charles II's reign, it became obvious that Henry VIII's piracy law provided inadequate protection to merchants and settlers at the growing points of the empire. Attempts were made in the 1670s and 1680s to bring colonial prosecutions in line with the law, but the colonists, fearing expansion of crown authority, steadily resisted the importation of admiralty courts and the civil law. The result was that piracy trials – rare occurrences at best – varied in procedure from colony to colony, were sometimes staged to acquit the defendants, and might be overturned by the High Court of Admiralty in London. The Privy Council's directive to have all the colonies adopt a 1681 Jamaica law that closely followed 28 Henry VIII, c.15, was largely ignored; in 1684 it was undermined by a finding that under the statute colonial courts lacked the jurisdiction to try pirates. While the prohibition was temporarily waived for colonies with a version of the Jamaica law, this finding shifted focus from colonial initiatives to radical reform from the centre. The next step was passage of the Navigation Act of 1696 requiring the colonies to set up courts of vice-admiralty, answerable to the High Court in London; their primary goal was to protect the king's revenues, but they would also provide the venue for future piracy trials.[16]

Finally, the Board of Trade began in 1696 to consider a new, comprehensive piracy law. A bill was draughted with advice from the East India Company by 'one of the leading civil lawyers of his generation', High Court of Admiralty judge Sir Charles Hedges.[17] Hedges and his allies seized the moment in the name of national security to bring back certain trial procedures abandoned in 1536 and obnoxious to most Anglo-Americans. The bill, made law in March 1700 (11-12 William III, c.7), created two standards of justice for those accused of piracy, one for the colonies and another for the home country. The law's provisions are examined at length in Chapter 5, its effects upon three important trials in Chapters 6 and 7.

If you could go back in time and watch a piracy trial at the Old Bailey in 1700, the experience would be filled with dissonances. The judge, the defendant, the jury, the oath promising the truth, the whole truth, and nothing but the truth, the examination and cross-examination of witnesses, the judge's charge to the jury – these would give you the comfort of recognition. But it would be a false comfort, for other elements of the trial – the judge's frequent questioning of the witnesses and expressions of opinion, the absence of lawyers, the breathtaking speed of the proceedings, and the expeditious pronouncing of the death sentence – would signal that you were, indeed, in another time and a different country. My intent in scrutinising piracy trials is to illustrate the workings of the most potent weapon in the war against the pirates but also to observe the differences between criminal justice in the heyday of piracy and in our own time.

We shall see in the following chapters that the law was never far from the pirates' consciousness although, to cope with the terrors of imprisonment, trial and execution that became more common as the empire mobilised to destroy them, some pirates adopted a devil-may-care attitude, jested about death, and even embraced it on the very gallows itself.[18] For most onlookers, an execution was a spectacular entertainment, for some an opportunity to hawk their wares or pick pockets. From the authorities' point of view, the last scene in the drama of justice was meant to frighten living seamen from taking the pirates' course but also to bring the condemned to repentance and faith in the promise of salvation. The judge's behaviour in the trial of Captain Bonnet in Chapter 6 and the horribly botched hanging of Captain Kidd in Chapter 5 gives occasion for a look at the varied faces of execution.

Anyone attempting to study pirate history discovers the difficulty of finding full and accurate information about the subject. Of the hundreds of accounts published since the events, few are accurate and well documented, most are rehashes of Alexandre Olivier Exquemelin's *De Americaensche Zee-Roovers* (Amsterdam, 1678), Basil Ringrose's 'The voyages and adventures of Capt. Bartholomew Sharp and others in the South Sea'[19], and Captain Charles Johnson's *A General History of the Pyrates* (London, 1724–28). (See Illustration 6) These works are invaluable but themselves contain many exaggerations and inventions that have been passed uncritically from writer to writer. I have come to rely, instead, on books and articles published mainly since the 1960s and founded on research in the archives, especially the National Archives (formerly London Public Record Office) and the British Library[20] In addition to the records of the home government, the East India Company and the Royal African Company, these archives hold reports of most piracy trials held in the colonies after 1700. The chapters on Henry Every and William Dampier are supported by my own research published earlier in journals.

What cannot be found in the documents is often waiting seductively in the pages of the *General History*. Its unknown author, 'Captain Charles Johnson',[21] was a lively writer with a dramatic flair and an ear for the language of his contemporaries. He brings the story of the pirates to life as few others have done, but often at the expense of historical truth. Since it is impossible at times to know if he is inventing or faithfully rendering information from manuscript or oral sources, I am inclined to doubt what is not otherwise corroborated. After a long struggle of conscience, however, I have come to understand it is morally impossible not to borrow from Johnson, and a disservice to the reader. I have therefore taken pains to identify all citations from the *General History* so that readers may, if they will, take the passages with a grain of sea salt.

Henry Morgan:

'More Used to the Pike than the Book'

In the language of the sea, to sail 'close to the wind' is to proceed into the wind by skilful steering and arrangement of sails, a manoeuvre to keep the ship on course in the teeth of adverse weather. Those who sail too close will lose headway and fall behind, but those who succeed stand to win the race. Henry Morgan made a career and a fortune by sailing close to the wind. For more than a decade he successfully contested the power of Spain, the Spanish lobby in London, and the English law of piracy. After many attempts and when he was at the height of his popularity in Jamaica, his enemies succeeded in having him arrested and sent to England where they trusted he would stand trial for his life.

Morgan was born in 1635 near Tredegar, Wales, into a family distinguished since Elizabeth's reign by its genius for military command. Two of his paternal uncles became major-generals, one on each side of the Civil War. Edward Morgan remained loyal to the crown at the head of his troops in Wales and later became Lieutenant Governor of Jamaica. Thomas Morgan, a master in the use of artillery and siege tactics, was so respected by George Monck (the Commonwealth general whose support would assure the restoration of Charles II) that he was made governor of Jersey to defend against an expected French invasion. Henry later wrote that his childhood prepared him not for governance but for soldiering. 'I left school too young to be a great proficient in [admiralty] or other laws, and have been more used to the pike than the book'.[1] Early in his twenties he came to the Carribean to make his fortune, possibly in the the force that Cromwell raised in England and the West Indies to initiate his 'Western Design' for conquering Central America. The first target was Hispaniola, but the poorly organised and commanded expedition failed miserably. To save face and make some conquest, the fleet under Admiral William Penn (father of the founder of Pennsylvania) and General Robert Venables seized Jamaica on 16 May 1655. This undeveloped island was to become Morgan's home and base for his operations throughout Spanish America.

'Our great enemy is the Spaniard', thundered Cromwell in the year after Jamaica was captured. 'He is a natural enemy, by reason of that enmity that is in him against whatever is of God'.[2] While the depth of Henry Morgan's religious feelings are unknown, Cromwell's call for a holy war strongly affected the British West Indian colonists and explains, in part, their stubborn antagonism towards 'the Spaniard' for the next three decades, an antagonism sustained by fears of Spanish invasion and lust for Spanish treasure. Jamaica was to become the lever of that antagonism. To strengthen their defences, the new rulers of the island invited French and Dutch buccaneers at Tortuga and Hispaniola to relocate and mobilise as privateers against an enemy counter-attack.

'Privateer' is a legal term denoting, in the seventeenth century, a person empowered during wartime by royal commission to capture enemy vessels and, once they have been condemned by a court of admiralty, to receive the bulk of their value, the rest going to the King (ten per cent) and the Lord High Admiral (fifteen per cent). 'Buccaneer', on the other hand, is a sociological term denoting an inhabitant of the West Indies who lived in informal and international communities away from the centres of state power by hunting, subsistence farming, taking merchant ships (mainly Spanish) and raiding coastal towns. The term comes from the buccaneers' manner of roasting meat on wooden spits called *boucans*. They were also called 'cow killers' and, more flatteringly, 'the brethren of the coast'.(See Illustration 7)

The buccaneers were composed largely of refugees and renegades from all nations – criminals, castaways, debtors, runaway slaves and apprentices, deserters or discharged soldiers and seamen – who shared a love of liberty and contempt for conventional society. They were first drawn to Hispaniola by the herds of wild cattle Columbus and Spanish colonists had introduced before 1600. In their settlements on the island, they practised a crude kind of socialism by which they jointly sold meat to passing ships. To escape attacks by the Spanish, many buccaneers retreated to the island of Tortuga off the north coast of Haiti and petitioned for French help, which arrived in the early 1640s. Thus was established the first buccaneer stronghold in the Caribbean. (See Illustration 8)

The first English commanders to make effective use of the buccaneers were Edward Mansfield, leader of the privateers, and Christopher Myngs, Admiral of the Royal Navy squadron at Jamaica. Their combined raids on the rich coastal towns of South America were so profitable – some say their booty in 1659 was worth £300,000, or, in current money, nearly £26,983,000 – that they established a 'pattern of pillage' Morgan and others would follow. The crusade against the Spanish received a shock, however, upon word in July 1660 that the Commonwealth had fallen. Evidence of a more conciliatory policy towards Spain came swiftly enough, but although Charles II might announce in February 1662 the end of war with Spain in Europe, he aquiesced in Governor Edward Windsor's commissioning of privateers after Spain refused to open its colonies to English merchants.[3]

The precise legal status of relations between Spanish and British colonists beyond the line was unsettled well into the eighteenth century. The Spanish considered duly commissioned British privateers criminals rather than combatants in war, and the British authorities after 1660 sometimes supported and sometimes harassed them. For example, Christopher Myngs was arrested and sent to England to defend the legality of his descents on the Main, but in 1662 was returned to his post in Jamaica. Such an equivocal response by Whitehall only encouraged the raiders. How far could they go before the law would crack down on them? Myngs and Morgan would shortly test the limits more dramatically than ever before.

When in 1662 an invasion of Jamaica from Cuba was imminent, Henry Morgan, then an officer in the Port Royal Regiment, was among the first to receive a privateering commission from Governor Windsor. In a ship probably owned by him and his friends, he joined Myngs's fleet of eighteen ships and 1,500 men, which in October took Santiago de Cuba, the island's second largest city. This British victory whetted the privateers' appetite for plunder so that four months later in February 1663, Myngs took the town of San Francisco de Campeche in New Spain (Mexico). An order to desist was sent from London, but the King's 'dislike of all such undertakings' was sporadic and difficult to honour.⁴ In 1664 the new Governor of Jamaica was Thomas Modyford, a follower of General Monck, now Duke of Albemarle; his Lieutenant Governor was Henry Morgan's uncle, Edward, come to Jamaica to recoup his fortune. At first, Modyford sought to comply with the King's order, but he soon perceived the danger of recalling the privateers, about 1,500 men in twelve ships. The fear was that if he did so, they would turn to the French or Portuguese for commissions, simultaneously stripping Jamaica of its defences and making it their prey.

While Modyford was settling into his new role, Henry Morgan was beginning to make his mark by an epic raid into regions where no other force of British had gone before. After returning to Jamaica early in 1663 with Myngs, he and two other captains had sailed out again in December with about 200 men. Excited by what they had seen at San Francisco, they steered west for Bahia de Campeche off New Spain's Tabasco province, still bearing their commissions from Governor Windsor. Myngs had targeted coastal towns; Morgan and his crews boldly marched into the jungle fired by tales of cities paved with gold. Guided by Indians hostile to the Spanish, they approached Villahermosa, the largest city in Tabasco, via a circuitous, swampy route of 300 miles. Just as they had hoped, the town was caught by surprise, captured, and plundered. With their loot and 300 prisoners, they returned north to the coast only to be opposed by a Spanish naval force in control of their ships. Although outnumbered, they held this force off until they could escape in various small vessels. Morgan learnt here never to place his ships in harm's way during a land campaign.

The second leg of their voyage took them eastward to the Spanish Main where they launched a deep penetration to within a few miles of the Pacific. At the south end of Bahia de San Juan del Norte, they found the river that today marks the border between Nicaragua and Costa Rica. Struggling against the current, they paddled their canoes thirty-seven leagues towards the great Lake of Nicaragua. What happened next appears in the brisk report Modyford sent to London.

> Riding by day under keys and islands and rowing all night, by the advice of their Indian guide, they landed near the city of Gran Granada, marched undescried into the centre of the city, fired a volley, over-turned 18 great guns in the Parada Place, took the serjeant-major's house, wherein were all their arms and ammunition, secured in the Great Church 300 of the best men prisoners, abundance of which were churchmen, plundered for 16 hours, discharged the prisoners, sunk all the boats and so came away.

The intruders marvelled at the size and cultural richness of Granada – 'This town is twice bigger than Portsmouth with seven churches and a very fair cathedral, besides divers colleges and monasteries, all built of freestone, as also are most of their houses' – but they also took special note of Spanish vulnerability:

> They have six companies of horse and foot besides Indians and slaves in abundance. Above 1,000 of these Indians joined them in plundering, and would have killed the prisoners, especially the churchmen, imagining that the English would keep the place, but finding the English would return home, requested them to come again, and in the meantime have secured themselves in the mountains.[5]

The assistance of 1,000 Indians helps to explain how Morgan's small force could subdue the town, but theirs was still a tale of great determination, endurance, and military skill. By rough count, Morgan and company had sailed, marched or paddled over 3,700 miles, much of it steamy, rugged terrain.

When they returned to Jamaica in September 1665, the raiders had little to say in defence of their actions except that they were taken under Windsor's commission and that they did not know about the new policy towards the Spanish, a ruse Morgan used repeatedly in his career. Given the present threat to Jamaica – and Morgan's connection with Lord Albemarle through the governor and his uncle Thomas – these excuses were enough.

For Modyford, the Nicaraguan raid was a delight and a curse. At mid-century he had supported Cromwell's aggressive stance towards the Spanish. But as governor he was charged to control the privateers, which the example set by Morgan had just made even more difficult. The choice between alienating the privateers or antagonising the King became intolerable so that on 22 February 1666 the council prepared a resolution arguing cogently for a complete reversal of London's policy. Five days later, Modyford proclaimed that Jamaica would once again freely grant commissions against the Spanish. Simultaneously, he sent the King stories of Morgan's raids which, he observed, found the Spanish 'in all places very weak and very wealthy'.[6]

Not everyone in Jamaica that night drank a toast to the governor and 'the sweet trade of privateering'. The old opposition between Commonwealth men and Royalists was giving way to one between those who profited from pirateering and those who did not. Prominent among the latter were entrepreneurs who looked for the time when Spain would grant England the Asiento. On the other hand, Jamaica's planters and petty merchants eagerly anticipated the goods pirateers brought in and sold at cut-rate. Thomas Lynch, Provost-Marshal and member of Modyford's council, was the leader of the pro-Spanish faction and hence chief antagonist of Modyford and Morgan. He would have to bide his time until the pendulum swung again.

In the two and a half years between the Nicaragua raid and his next expedition, Morgan worked to establish himself in Jamaica. From the sale of Spanish prizes and booty, he was now a man of some means. A recent biographer depicts him in his early thirties as:

... wide-shouldered, slim and powerfully built, with a sallow complexion partly hidden by a pointed black beard worn in the style of Drake and Raleigh. Deeply tanned, he appeared the typical swashbuckling adventurer...(See Illustration 9)

But Morgan did not simply look the part. He possessed a 'strong and forceful personality and quick intelligence at a time and place when they, and known bravery, were the main elements of leadership'.

... a man then less than thirty years of age who could lead several score desperadoes of various nationalities for hundreds of miles across marshes and arid pampas, along dangerous coasts in canoes and then up strange rivers, and at the end have those men boast about it all as 'Harry Morgan's Way', had that indefinable and very rare magnetism which in any age will make him famous.[7]

And win him a desirable mate. In the period from 1666–68 he married his uncle Edward's daughter, Mary Elizabeth, in what appears to have been a love match, supervised the rebuilding of Port Royal's decayed fortifications, and commanded the town's militia, the Port Royal Volunteers. A gregarious man, he was already a frequent guest at the wicked town's many pubs; he was later to suffer greatly from drinking and to be known in our own day – unfairly – for little else, thanks to Captain Morgan's Original Spiced Rum.

After war began in 1667 between france and spain, England lined up against Louis XIV by reaffirming its peace with Spain and joining with the Netherlands and Sweden in the Triple Alliance (1668), an accord that, once more, failed to recognise Britain's dominion over Jamaica or include areas 'beyond the line' in the terms of the peace. The old fear of attack from Cuba still haunted the Jamaican colonists and set in motion the privateers' next major raid.

In spring of 1668 Modyford appointed Morgan admiral of a fleet of ten ships and 500 English and French buccaneers charged with getting intelligence of Spanish plans. The terms of his commission reputedly limited him to taking enemy ships, but Morgan concluded from experience that if he could succeed in gathering information, Whitehall would forgive his raiding Spanish towns. His first target was Santa Maria de Puerto Principe, the second wealthiest town in Cuba, which yielded about £10,000, a modest prelude to Morgan's next attempt, the taking of Puerto Bello.[8] (See Illustration 10) This city on the northern coast of Panama received goods and specie passing overland between Spain's Atlantic and Pacific colonies and was defended by a strong garrison and three imposing castles equipped with heavy artillery. Puerto Bello had for nearly seventy years withstood all efforts to take it; the incomparable Drake had declined the attempt and died in its bay.

Too weak to assault from the sea, Morgan used a strategy that became his trademark: surprise and a furious, disciplined charge from the land side. With his ships anchored safely over a hundred miles to the west, his force of 422 set out towards Puerto Bello on 10 June in twenty-eight canoes. They landed next morning at three o'clock, marched silently through the sleeping town, and before the alarm could be sounded, stormed 'the Iron Castle'. According to one of his captains, the garrison had thirty cannon but it was caught shorthanded. Its 130 men fought courageously for three or four hours before being overwhelmed, and when the buccaneers gave them the opportunity to surrender, they chose to fight to the death: 'the garrison, all of which refusing quarter were either killed, wounded, or cut to pieces'.[9] Gloria Castle across the bay put up less of a resistance and the third, St Geronimo, none at all.

While Morgan's men were enjoying their victory, the Viceroy of Panama City, Don Juan de Guzman, was setting out to cross the isthmus with an army of 3,000. Five days later he engaged Morgan's much smaller force – reduced now by sickness and injuries to about 300 capable of fighting. They fought stubbornly, however, and when Guzman failed to dislodge the raiders, he ransomed the town for 100,000 pieces of eight in addition to the booty already seized, in all more than £70,000.[10] The share for the rank-and-file started at about £120, a noble sum for a common merchant seaman used to fifteen or twenty shillings a month.

Morgan kept his promise not to destroy the town, but upon his return to Jamaica he had to defend himself against 'the usual scandals' circulated by the Spanish and their allies. He was so far from abusing female prisoners, he wrote, that:

> several ladies of great quality... were proffered their liberty to go to the President's [Guzman's] camp, but they refused, saying they were now prisoners to a person of quality, who was more tender of their honours than they doubted to find in the President's camp among his rude soldiers, and so voluntarily continued with them till the surrender of the town and castles, when with many thanks and good wishes they repaired to their former houses.[11]

The evidence suggests that he did, indeed, restrain his men more effectively throughout his career than other commanders of buccaneers. He was therefore galled that charges of torture, rape and murder were widespread and that he was personally accused of making nuns and priests into human shields at Puerto Bello.

English journalists and historians, of course, extolled Morgan for his victories. He was framed in an English edition of *De Americaensche Zee-Roovers* as 'Our English Jamaican Hero', his history 'so much remarkable in all its Circumstances, as peradventure nothing more deserving Memory, may occur to be read by future ages'. His fighters were celebrated as 'the truest patterns of undaunted and exemplary Courage, that ever [England] produced'.[12] Two incidents in the Puerto Bello campaign were especially ripe for this treatment. Exquemelin's first English translator made his speech before Porto Bello echo that of Shakespeare's Henry V at Agincourt: 'If our number is small, our hearts are great. And the fewer persons we are, the more union and better shares we shall have in the spoil'.[13] Morgan's relations with the Viceroy were made to project 'our English Jamaican Hero' as an exemplar of chivalry. When the Viceroy wrote to ask for a sample of the pistols used to master Puerto Bello, he obligingly invited Guzman to keep the pistols for a year, 'after which time he promised to come to Panama and fetch them away'.

> The Governor of *Panama* returned the Present very soon unto Captain *Morgan*, giving him thanks for the favour of lending him such Weapons

as he needed not, and withal sent him a Ring of Gold, with this Message: *That he desired him not to give himself the labour of coming to* Panama, *as he had done to* Puerto Vello; *for he did not certifie unto him, he should not speed so well here as he had done there.*[14]

This anecdote is probably apocryphal, yet it captures the spirit of the age, an iron fist in a silken glove.

As might be expected, the sack of Puerto Bello only increased the threat of an invasion of Jamaica. Old Spain reacted to the news by dispatching a squadron of six warships to assault the buccaneers. Ignorant of this danger, Morgan returned to Port Royal in August 1668 with intelligence of a large force assembling at Cartagena, Colombia, the most strategic market town on the Spanish Main. If this force were to be disrupted, he told Modyford, there was no time to waste. The governor reluctantly agreed, the word went out, and a few weeks later in September, Morgan sailed with a fleet of twelve ships and 900 men to Ile-à-Vache, an island off the south-west coast of Hispaniola, to rendezvous with other buccaneer crews. Here at a council of war on 2 January 1669 disaster struck the fleet: Morgan was at supper with his captains aboard the *Oxford* when the magazine blew up, killing more than 200 men and sinking his most powerful ship. Morgan escaped death by inches.

Although shaken by the accident, he managed to refit and revise his plans. Cartagena was now out, but he would strike inland once more, an action that exceeded his authority to disrupt a Spanish invasion. On 9 March 1669, with a force reduced to eight ships and 500 men, he entered the narrow strait that leads into Lake Maracaibo, Venezuela. (See Illustration 11) Cannon fire from the bastion guarding the straits stopped the buccaneers' advance, but by evening the garrison had pulled out. Morgan was relieved but puzzled as he inspected the fort until a burning fuse revealed that the fort was a trap and the magazine about to explode; someone – possibly Morgan himself – yanked the fuse and prevented another horrible slaughter. After spiking the Spanish guns, he entered Maracaibo to find that it too was deserted so that he had to scour the adjoining countryside for fleeing citizens and their wealth. Three weeks later, he targeted Gibraltar near the southern end of the vast lake, an assault that ended, as usual, with the plundering and ransoming of the town.

The most perilous part of the raids was yet to come: the withdrawal from Lake Maracaibo. When he returned to the strait on 17 April, he found the fort re-armed and the narrow exit blocked by three of the six warships sent from Spain after his victory at Puerto Bello. Faced with an enemy force of 500 men and seventy-eight cannon, Morgan offered to surrender his prisoners in return for free passage, but Admiral Don Alonso del Campos y Espinosa in the *Magdelena* responded that they would be allowed to pass only if they gave up everything they had taken. This was too much for his men, who told Morgan they had 'rather fight, and spill the very last drop of bloud they had in their veins than surrender so easily the Booty they had gained with so much danger to their lives.'[15]

Morgan and his men contrived two deceptions that saved them from annihilation at Campos's hands. The first was to set loose on the enemy a ship rigged with upright logs dressed as seamen, 'with Hats and Montera caps'.[16] Only upon boarding did the Spanish realise it was a fire ship about to ignite and take the *Magdalena* down with it. Terrified by this disaster, the crew of a second ship ran it aground and swam to the fort, and the third was boarded and taken by the buccaneers while in the channel. (See Illustration 12) Morgan now ordered a frontal assault upon the last obstacle to his escape, but the fort's cannon drove the raiders back. It was time for his second stratagem: what the Spanish saw when they scanned the enemy's position was the shuttling of men to where they could attack the fort from the land, but in reality all of Morgan's men returned to the prize ship lying in the bottom of their canoes. The defenders were fooled into lugging their big guns to the land side, allowing the buccaneers to ride the ebb tide past their position and into the clear.

Morgan returned to Jamaica late in May 1669 with an estimated 250,000 pieces of eight – about £62,500 – besides booty, cattle and slaves; his losses, about fifty comrades felled by bullets or disease.[17] The revelry in Port Royal when Morgan's ships came in was in sharp contrast to the mood at Government House. Whitehall was taking the Spanish ambassador's protests more seriously than ever before and insisting, in no uncertain terms, that Modyford curb the privateers.

The governor complied by selectively withdrawing privateering commissions, distributing land grants to high-ranking captains, and
encouraging others to become planters and merchants. He knew full
well, however, that with the present their fever, the best he could
achieve would be an illusion of control. Colonel William Beeston, a
future Lieutenant Governor of Jamaica, dryly remarked in June 1669
upon Modyford's efforts: 'nevertheless the privateers went in and out
but not with commissions'. [18]

Harry Morgan had no difficulty accepting this swing of the pendulum for he prospered greatly from the land grants – some might
call them bribes. True, he had lost his commission for exceeding his
authority, but on 30 November 1669 he received 836 fertile acres in
Clarendon parish, south Jamaica, entrenching his family even more
deeply in the island's ruling class. He and Mary Elizabeth set about
establishing a sugar plantation on this land, but when the tasks of
home building, estate management, and overseeing of slaves grew
tedious, Harry could muse upon his next campaign against the
Spaniard. The time was sure to come.

It came more swiftly than he had a right to expect. Wary of a
British government that talked peace but accepted twenty-five percent of the privateers' take, the Spanish began to build a large fleet
of West Indian privateers that, reinforced by men-of-war from Spain,
would revenge their humiliation at Puerto Bello by strangling the
trade of the French and English, raiding their colonies, and destroying their pirates. Jamaicans' fears were renewed by the capture of
documents revealing Spain's new policy as well as by the sharp
increase in Spanish attacks at sea and, more ominously, on Jamaica
itself. These fears escalated when Manoel Rivera Pardal in the
summer of 1670 plundered and burnt settlements on the north-west
coast and challenged Morgan to single combat in a message he nailed
to a tree:

> I come to seek General Morgan with two ships of 20 guns and, having
> seen this, I crave he will come out upon ye coast and seek me, that he
> might see ye valor of ye Spaniards. [19]

The Spanish were turning the tables on British Jamaica.

As hazardous as it was to his career, Modyford saw no other way to save Jamaica than to unleash Morgan, the only man he knew who could unify and command the privateers. On June 29, the planter-dominated council concurred in appointing him admiral of Jamaica's naval forces and granting him

> power to Land in the enemies Country as many of his men as he shall think needful; and with them to march to such places as he shall be informed the said Magazines or Forces are, and then accordingly take, destroy and dispose of; and to do and perform all manner of exploits which may tend to the preservation and quiet of this Island.

Morgan's forces would be paid according to the Jamaica discipline, i.e. 'the old pleasing Account of no purchase no pay', but he was limited by his commission to raid only Spanish towns that were or might be involved in preparing for war.[20]

Modyford understood that his new policy might not pass muster in London, even though it allowed the state better to judge whether the buccaneers' takings on land were legal. Therefore, he instructed Morgan to govern his men by naval law and prevent the slaughter of Spanish colonists. He was also given the power to arrest commanders or seamen who deserted and to appoint lieutenants 'for the better keeping of the soldiers and seamen to their obedience'.[21] By imposing traditional naval discipline upon the new fleet, he hoped to counter the charges of brutality raised against the buccaneers by the Spanish lobby in London.

Lacking airmail and e-mail, the governor did not know how determined His Majesty's government had become to forestall war with Spain. On June 12 Lord Arlington had sent him instructions to keep the privateers just as they were, but above all to 'oblige them to forbear all hostilities at Land' (the privateers, of course, preferred attacking cities to avoid sharing their plunder with King and Admiralty). The letter that reached Jamaica on 18 August ended with Arlington's opinion that:

> the Spanish men-of-war attacking Capt. Barnard and others in the Bay of Campeachy is not at all to be wondered at after such hostilities as your

men have acted upon their territories, and, because this way of warring is neither honourable nor profitable to his Majesty, he is endeavouring to put an end to it, and Modyford shall be timely advertised of the progress of the negotiation.[22]

Modyford put on a happy face in his reply, but the governor must have felt a chill pass over him upon reading these words. He could hardly recall the fleet of eleven ships and 600 men now on its way to another rendezvous at Ile-à-Vache. It was going to be a winter to remember – and perhaps to repent.

By the terms of the Treaty of Madrid (July 1670), Spain won the de-commissioning of the pirateers and the prohibition of trade except under 'particular licence' in return for recognition of British Jamaica and a blanket amnesty for offences on both sides since 1660. For Morgan, this meant amnesty for all crimes committed as far back as Myngs's expeditions of 1662–63. Even though the treaty was not published in Jamaica until spring of 1671, it is likely that Morgan knew in general of its contents while volunteers from throughout the Caribbean came to Ile-à-Vache. When he sailed on 6 December for Cape Tiburon, a second rendezvous point on Hispaniola, peace with Spain was probably the last thing on his mind. Morgan commanded the largest privateer fleet ever mobilised against Spanish America, thirty-eight ships and over 2,000 men. Most were English from Jamaica and the West Indies followed by French and Dutch from Tortuga and Hispaniola. The target was Panama City on the Pacific side of the isthmus, second only to Cartagena in importance to the Spanish. (See Illustration 13)

Key to the raiders' strategy was control of the Chagres River, which would allow them to navigate half the way to their goal. Consequently, an advance party, led by the infamous Rok Brasiliano and Erasmus Reyning, was sent to take the imposing fort at the mouth of the river, the castle of San Lorenzo de Chagres. (See Illustration 14) The defenders fiercely resisted the siege until the fort was breached and buccaneers rushed in with a violent charge. The ensuing two-day battle and loss of thirty-two comrades forced the buccaneers to admire 'the valour of the Spaniards'. With the fort in his hands, Morgan started up the Chagres River on 8 January 1671, forty-three small vessels and 1,400 men strong. He hoped to catch Panama City off guard, but the jungle hid hundreds of spies who relayed his progress and strength to his old adversary, Don Juan de Guzman.

It was hard work following the twisting river as it climbed into the hills, enduring the heat, the humidity and the plague of mosquitoes, flies and tics. After four days, they left their boats to bushwhack towards the 'King's Road', the well-worn trail between Puerto Bello and Panama City. Two hundred men would guard the boats, leaving 1,200 to conquer Panama. Veterans of jungle warfare, they carried their muskets well smeared with lard and wrapped in greasy cloths, their powder in corked bottles and their slow match coiled in glass jars against the torrential rain.[23] Fortunately, inflated rumours of their strength spread up river and caused the garrisons of several defensive positions to flee in terror back to the city. The Spanish resistance consisted of sniping at the extended column – galling but not fatal. Meanwhile, Guzman was fuming at the failure of his troops to do their duty. If the garrison at Venta de Cruces at the head of the King's Road did not stop Morgan, only he could save Panama. Guzman reinforced the garrison and, with his remaining 800 men, withdrew to Guiabal, a few miles north of the city. Time would tell if he could trust his many native and black troops to stand and fight. The retreating Spanish scorched the earth, evacuating everything useful and torching every shelter from the rains. This policy had begun to fray the buccaneers' resolve. Desperate for food, they accused Morgan of leading them into a death trap, but he continued to project confidence, and when they took Venta de Cruces without a fight and found the going easier on the King's Road, the grumbling subsided. When they could see the Pacific from a nearby hilltop, their confidence soared. The trail now took them through the vast grassland fronting Panama City, where they found cattle to roast on the *boucan*.

The mood of the city's defenders at Guiabal was not positive. Even before they had seen a single pirate, most had deserted the Viceroy in order to save themselves and hide their valuables. Guzman now believed defeat likely because it would be very difficult to block Morgan any closer to the unfortified city. Nevertheless, he retreated, assembled a new army of 1,500 infantry, 200 cavalry and a secret weapon, and positioned himself at Battaglia just outside the city. The Spanish were in a compact and symmetrical line with cavalry on either side, a good formation to receive a frontal attack, but Morgan was not about to comply. He began the battle by sending his left flank to harass the enemy's right and break up their line. Platoons of Guzman's cavalry and infantry opposed this manoeuvre but were turned back by musket fire, and when Morgan's men followed in pursuit, the Spanish right bolted.

With mostly unseasoned soldiers, Guzman wanted to stay planted in tight formation rather than charge the enemy himself or wheel to the right to counter Morgan's feint. He held to this strategy but also launched his secret weapon at Morgan's flanks – two troops of 1,500 cattle apiece. But Morgan's best sharpshooters were ready for the stampede so that, before it could disorder his men, the cattle were dispersed in every direction, many running into the defenders' lines. The mayhem thus created led to a route and a great slaughter of the fleeing Spanish.

Morgan marched into Panama City on 18 January, but he had little time to enjoy its beautiful architecture and abundant warehouses. While he was busy subduing the last pockets of resistance, the city was set on fire – ravaged, Guzman believed, by slaves and their owners, and not, as Exquemelin tells it, on Morgan's command. The buccaneers, in fact, tried to control the fire and save the wealth it was about to destroy, but without success. Morgan would later elegise the city in his report to Modyford:

> thus was consumed the famous and ancient city of Panama, which is the greatest mart for silver and gold in the whole world, for it receives all the goods that come from Spain in the King's great fleet, and delivers all the gold and silver that comes from the mines of Peru and Potozi.[24] (See Illustration 15)

The pirates lost much by the fire and even more by the escape of *La Santissima Trinidad*, a galleon into which the city's residents had carried 'an immense treasure in Silver and Gold'.[25] The *Trinidad* was later spotted in Panama Bay by one of Morgan's ships, but the captain could not rouse his drunken crew to go after it!

If most of Panama's treasure was spirited away, much still remained. When Morgan exited the town on 14 February, it was in a train of 175 mules laden with 'silks, linens, gold and silver lace, plate, [and] jewels,' as well as £30,000 in specie. Nevertheless, its value was well below the legendary treasure supposed to have crowned his greatest victory.[26] As admiral, Morgan was entitled to one percent of the specie and a similar share of the goods, in toto less than £1,000, but many did not find their shares – perhaps as little as £20 apiece – sufficient for what they had suffered in the quest. Morgan's division of the profits and the discipline he had imposed on men forever proud of being masterless caused much suspicion and bitterness among his troops, feelings reflected in privateer Captain Charles Swan's plot to seize the ships and cruise in the Pacific.

The plot was foiled and the buccaneers returned to Jamaica where they delighted tavern-keepers and merchants with their free spending. For Modyford and his faction, however, Morgan's greatest victory spelled disaster. Whitehall had decided to remove the popular governor in December 1670, but wisely kept it secret until the arrival of his successor. In July 1671, two warships, HMS *Assistance* and *Welcome*, rode at anchor in Port Royal Bay to ensure the colony's loyal submission to its new leader, Sir Thomas Lynch. Seven weeks later Modyford was sent on his way to London and the Tower, while Morgan, suffering from what a contemporary described as 'a lingering Consumption',[27] was spared arrest until 1672 when England needed to secure Spain as an ally in its new war against the Dutch. His request to be tried in Jamaica where he could find defence witnesses and a pro-buccaneer jury was denied, and when HMS *Welcome* set sail with the afflicted admiral on board, the rout of the war party was complete.

Morgan arrived in London in August 1672, and may at first have been kept in the Tower, but as time passed he was treated with growing favour, especially after advising Charles II in the summer of 1673 about the best way to defend Jamaica from the Dutch; the King was growing disillusioned with Lynch, but he was impressed by Morgan's reputation and knowledge. Although still the King's prisoner, he was subsequently welcome among the intellectual and political élite where, in the autumn of 1674, at Baron Berkeley's house, he lectured his host, Governor Modyford, and the author John Evelyn on the vulnerability of Spanish America. He told them that 10,000 men would easily conquer all the Spanish Indies, they were so secure...They were so supine & unexercis'd, that they were afraid to give fire to a greate gun.[28] It is almost certain that he also met with General Monck's son Christopher, second Duke of Albemarle, whose influence with the King and the Lords of Trade may have saved him from a state trial. Instead of suffering under ignominious exile, he was publicly celebrated as 'Panama Morgan'.[29]

On 23 January 1674, after eighteen months of exile, the King knighted and made him Lieutenant Governor and ordered him back to Jamaica to serve under the Earl of Carlisle, recently named to replace the ineffective Lynch. When Carlisle declined the post, John Vaughn, Earl of Carberry, was appointed in his place. Nearly fourteen tedious months passed before Sir Harry arrived at Port Royal on 5 March 1675, a vindicated man more respected and well connected than ever before.

The rift between Morgan and the buccaneers stemming from disappointment over the Panama booty was deeper than it appeared. Encouraged, perhaps, by his second grant of land in September 1676 – 4,000 acres in St Elizabeth parish, south-west Jamaica – he had come to believe with Lynch that 'planting, and not privateering, is the true interest of England in this island'.[30] Moreover, his roots were in the officer class where hierarchy, discipline and obedience were everything while the buccaneers arose, in good measure, from the displaced and disaffected common soldiers of Europe's wars. They had made a life on the margins not simply to escape the restraint of civilised society.

In their enterprises at least, they practised notions of liberty and equality, even of fraternity, which for most inhabitants of the old world and the new remained frustrated dreams, so far as they were dreamt of at all – more than we usually suppose, perhaps.[31]

One of William Dampier's biographers goes further in labelling

> the rise of the buccaneers... a considerable movement, almost a rebellion,
> of men of all nations – former slaves, criminals, adventurers and what not
> – against the Spanish authority... an insurrection of all the discontented
> elements of the West Indies.[32]

Above all, they secured their freedom through a loose society that was
anti-royalist and egalitarian. The phrases associated with them –
'brethren of the coast', 'no purchase, no pay', 'no peace beyond the
line' – echo their stubborn independence, fraternal spirit and alienation from European notions of order. Morgan had for a brief time
corralled them into an alliance that advanced British power in the
Caribbean; after Panama, he would increasingly release his hold on
their admiration and loyalty.

GovernorVaughn's tenure was tumultuous in part because he lacked
the flexibility and tact of Modyford. From the start the new governor
was suspicious that Morgan was out to upstage him and subvert his
hard line towards the privateers. Even though no new commissions
were being issued at Jamaica, Vaughn had to grapple on one hand with
the rising number of Jamaican ships taken by the Spanish, and on the
other with French privateers manned by English seamen coming into
Port Royal to provision or sell their plunder. Ironically, Morgan, who
professed ignorance of admiralty law, was early in 1676 made president of the Court of Vice-Admiralty, which oversaw many cases
involving privateers. When accused by Vaughn of collusion with them
and obstruction of justice, Morgan protested in August 1676 that:

> as God is my judge and witness I have never entertained a thought in my
> life but what hath been really devoted to His Majesty's service and inter-
> est nor never will.

In truth however, he kept Port Royal open to Spanish traders throughout the late 1670s, if they bore valid foreign commissons and paid his
office the appropriate duties and fees.[33]

In the summer of 1677 another raid on the Spanish Main undermined tolerance for the pirateers and provoked a chain of events that
would put his proud words to the test. The Jamaica assembly with the
support of the planters presently passed a law making it piracy for
Jamaicans to serve under foreign commission against nations at peace
with England. Nine men who had participated in the raid and subsequently sold 150 black slaves to the planters became the first condemned under this law. Wishing to maintain the Royal African
Company's slaving monopoly as well as suppress piracy, Vaughan badly
overplayed his hand however, he denied their captain James Browne
habeas corpus and had him quickly tried and executed, an arrogant
measure that alienated the privateers, the planters, the judiciary and
the assembly. He also lost the confidence of the king's counsellors who
decided that he would go and Morgan stay. Thus, as admiralty judge
and later as acting governor, Morgan was willy-nilly placed at the
helm in the campaign against the pirates.

Vaughn left unceremoniously for England in March 1678. The Earl
of Carlisle this time accepted the post and received the Great Seal
from Morgan in July. Two tasks immediately confronted Carlisle: suppressing the privateers and gaining acceptance of the Crown's plan to
write Jamaica's laws and have them enacted 'by and with the consent
of the General Assembly'. The assembly itself led the battle against this
radical change in the colony's governance, refusing to rubber-stamp
laws sent over from England: 'they will submit to wear, but never consent to make chains... for their posterities'. As ludicrous as this sounds
from men who tended the chains of black and Indian slaves in the
tens of thousands, the assemblymen 'were so highly incensed that they
were near questioning the king's power and authority to do it'.[34] Even
Carlisle's council fumed at the royal instructions, but Morgan was not
among the disobedient; he stood by Carlisle on the constitutional
issue, continued to oversee the colony's defences, and joined with
those eager to suppress the pirates. With no apparent irony, he
declaimed in 1680, 'May God love me no longer than I love justice'.[35]

Carlisle was so frustrated by resistance to his policies that he left
suddenly for home in the spring of 1680 after making Morgan his
deputy, a post he would retain for nearly two years. While Carlisle,

Vaughn and Lynch were conspiring against each other in London, Morgan was confronting the issues of defence, governance and piracy. The commodore who won a fortune by not knowing about the Treaty of Madrid, now begged Whitehall for copies of the latest treaties 'for my guidance'. He brokered a compromise between the King and the assembly that appeared to solve the constitutional crisis, greatly strengthened Port Royal's fortifications to a total of 116 cannon, and brought to trial several pirates, some former comrades in arms. Perhaps because he was himself notorious as a freebooter, he fought the war against the pirates with singular energy: 'I use the utmost severity of the law against them'.[36] He expressed no bad conscience over this turnaround, but maintained that his raids on the Spaniard were fully authorised by King and governor. His letters to Whitehall were deferential but frank, vigorous and incisive. Morgan was emerging as the most effective governor of Jamaica since Modyford.

Although he had profited from the colony's hatred of the Spaniard and Modyford's tilt towards the privateers, by the early 1680s he was ready to follow Carlisle in branding them as destructive to Jamaica's prosperity: he called them 'ravenous vermin', who 'discourage the Spaniards from private [i.e. clandestine] trade with us, which would otherwise be considerable'. Moreover, they reduced the ranks of poor labourers essential to Jamaica's growth:

> Nothing can be more fatal to the prosperity of this Colony than the temptingly alluring boldness of the privateers which draws off white servants and all men of unfortunate or desperate condition.

He seems finally to have understood the dangerous economic consequences of privateering, not least because it was an attractive alternative to the body- and soul-crushing fate of the labouring classes in plantation society. As a privateer captain, Morgan had worked and fought by the side of brave apprentices, indentured servants, slaves, 'runaways and debtors'[37]; as a member of the educated military and social élite, he must now take the long view and see them simply as 'labour', or, in today's parlance, an economic 'asset'. He is well known for being a convivial man who would drink with any good fellow, but this did not make him forget his interest as a landowner – he had amassed more than 6,100 acres by 1682, much of it arable – and as political caretaker of a commercial machine.

Morgan was not an original legal thinker, but by the 1680s he had become proficient in admiralty and other laws. His stint as Judge Admiral, for example, had schooled him in the Navigation Acts and the difficulty of upholding them in the colonies. In his cups he probably loved to embelish this story about the venality of colonial juries:

> a ship from Ireland came here with several casks of Irish soap and was seized by His Majesty's Receiver. The case was tried in the Court of Common Pleas, and the jury found for the defendant with costs. One witness swore that soap was victuals and that one might live upon it for a month, which the jury readily believed and found the aforesaid verdict.

He knew that the prohibition on Jamaicans taking privateering commissions against Spain and cruising against England's allies was a necessary but insufficient response to the current threat. As governor, therefore, he pressured the assembly to mandate the death penalty for Jamaicans who 'serve in a hostile manner in America, under any foreign prince, state, or potentate' but also to grant pardons for English who give up their foreign commissions. These measures would go a long way towards locking 'men of unfortunate or desperate condition' into Jamaica's labour system. Morgan also signed a bill 'declaring the laws of England to be in force in Jamaica', a bold lunge at equality with the home country that was promptly struck down by the King.[38] Most important of all was a 1681 law that applied the provisions of 28 Henry VIII, c.15, to piracy cases in Jamaica, a law that England soon tried to force on its other New World colonies.

Despite all of Morgan's efforts, depredation at sea was even greater at the end of his time as governor. It was just as Modyford had predicted: when English commissions were revoked, the rovers turned upon English shipping under foreign commissions or crossed the line into outright piracy with no inhibitions. Sir Thomas Lynch estimated Jamaica's losses by the end of 1682 at £40,000–50,000.[39] Especially ominous were the activities during the 1680s of a new wave of English rovers who carried outdated or bogus commissions. Their favourite targets were Spanish coastal towns in the Caribbean but also treasure galleons from Manila and Peru in the Pacific. In 1680 Morgan found himself in the curious position of signing arrest warrants for Captains Bartholomew Sharp and John Coxon who had just led a successful raid on Puerto Bello twelve years after he had done the same with impunity.

The alarming rise in piracy and Sir Harry's loud bouts of drunkenness gave Lynch and Vaughn the leverage they needed. By the middle of 1681 they had convinced Whitehall to sack him and send Lynch back for a second term. He arrived in Jamaica on 14 May 1682 and quickly swept Morgan's circle – self-styled 'the Loyal Club' – from most of their government positions.

Morgan retired to his great house on the northern coast of Jamaica near Port Maria – fortified to withstand pirate attack – where he supervised his plantations, entertained friends, and worked sporadically for the reinstatement of his allies. During this last period of his life, he grew increasingly concerned with his legacy and the perpetuation of his name. In 1685, he sued the publishers of the first two English translations of Exquemelin's *Americaensche Zee-Roovers* for libel, asking each for £20,000 in damages for asserting that his father was a yeoman farmer, that he himself had been indentured to a Barbados planter, and that he had abused and murdered defenceless Spanish during his raids.[40] The suits were brought for honour not money, however, and were settled out of court in return for retractions in the next editions and about £200 apiece; they led, therefore, to the first public acknowledgement of the book's many errors and fictions.

Near the end of his life, he enjoyed two final forms of vindication. Thanks to yet another swing of the pendulum, his Tory faction was restored to power with the assumption of Christopher Monck to the governorship, and on 12 July 1688, he once again took his seat on the council. Sir Harry's appearance there would not be repeated; he died on 25 August of congestive heart failure probably brought on by tuberculosis and intemperance. Morgan's death coincided with the last days of buccaneer power in the Caribbean. He, above all, was the warrior who had focused and extended that power and the governor who had most resourcefully worked to destroy it. It is not surprising that even admirers of Morgan conceded the paradoxes of his career. Bryan Edwards, an early nineteenth-century biographer reported that 'some of Sir Henry Morgan's private letters... manifest such a spirit of humanity, justice, liberality, and piety, as prove that he was either been grossly traduced or that he was the greatest hypocrite living.'[41]

Disturbing contradictions in Morgan's character might be brushed aside, as Edwards finally does, by attributing them to Spanish propaganda. Or they might be absorbed in the popular tale of the young gentleman who leaves his father's home to become rascal or outlaw but eventually reforms and claims a place of social power. Shakespeare's Henry V and Defoe's Robinson Crusoe are notable examples of this character type; a twentieth-century variation is found in John Steinbeck's first novel, Cup of Gold (1929), where 'Henry Morgan' pursues a romantic ideal of greatness until his greatest triumph, Panama, leaves him disillusioned and he smothers at Jamaica under the roles of husband and judge.

A close look at the real Harry Morgan, however, has exposed more continuities than contradictions. He was an officer reared in an age when to plunder the enemy's towns was honourable because it was politic: looting paid the soldiers and reduced the enemy's ability to wage war. Morgan was careful never to be without a commission and outside the legal bounds of his society. He could not return to respectability because, in his view, he had never shrugged it off. What is equally true is that the 'bounds of society' were flexible where colonial politics were concerned. The law of piracy could be applied rigorously to the buccaneers or ignored altogether, especially in cases of attacks against the Spanish. Piracy was, in effect, determined by policy. The English used their pirateers to seize, develop and defend land that they then ruled under English and international law.

Jamaica's survival and later evolution into the empire's 'crown jewel' was rooted in the soil of these all-too-common ironies.

3

William Dampier:
'That Old Pirateing Dog'

By the time William Dampier came to seek his fortune in Jamaica, the colony's most valuable item of export after sugar was 'logwood' (*Haematoxylon campechianum*), a rare tree that yielded a deep purple dye highly prized by makers of fabrics.[1] Before 1675, it was harvested by Indians for Spanish merchants, but when political pressure restricted the commissioning of English privateers, hundreds of the unemployed pushed their way into Bahia de Campeche, the prime area for logwood in Mexico. A caprice of history would thus link Europe's best-dressed lords and ladies with the coarse and turbulent men who had terrorised Spanish America and marched with Morgan on Panama.

It was through his experience among the logwood cutters that Dampier came to join the brethren of the coast and make himself a name that terrified the Spanish almost as much as Morgan's. Dampier's most fearsome weapons, however, were not cannon and sword, but knowledge and the pen. (See Illustration 17)

Dampier's story is one of the poor young man who fights his way out of poverty, obscurity and outlawry by the exercise of his 'exquisite mind'.[2] He was born at East Coker, Somersetshire, in August 1651 into a large family of tenant farmers, and, after the deaths of his parents, was taken under the patronage of William Helyar, the lord of the manor. During his childhood on the farm, Dampier learnt to look closely at nature, of which, he recalled, 'I had a more than usual Knowledge for one so young; taking a particular delight in observing it'.[3] Between the ages of eighteen and twenty-two, his field of observation widened dramatically during service on merchant ships and a man-of-war before Helyar sent him to assist the manager of Bybrook, his Jamaica sugar plantation. (Bybrook in St Catherine's parish was adjacent to Angels, Sir William Modyford's 20,000-acre estate near Spanish Town.) Dampier took up residence there in 1674, but, after violent arguments with the manager, soon quit for a similar position at a plantation in St Ann's parish to the north. Recognising that here, too, he was 'clearly out of my element', he shipped in February 1676 aboard a small merchantman trading supplies for logwood.[4]

Once at Campeche, there was little about the rich natural environment and the society of logwood cutters that escaped his eye or journal. He observed the area's topography, variations in soil, patterns of vegetation, and coastal features, especially those critical to navigation. He studied many kinds of edibles, including several unknown in Europe: the Sapadillo fruit, 'long and very pleasant', the Coco-Plum, 'white, soft and woolly, rather fit to suck than bite'; the 'extraordinary sweet' gar-fish that

> dart themselves with such Force that they strike their [long bony] Snout
> through the sides of a Cotton-Tree Canoa; and we often fear that they
> will strike quite through our very Bodies

and the dark flesh of the giant curlew. Dampier recorded such outlandish oddities as the Mountain cow (tapir), sloth, ant-Bear and armadillo, and thrilled at the sight of the jaguar 'so very stately and fierce'.[5]

He was just as curious about the human world he found in the bay. He recorded the absurd figure made by the buccaneers on their weekly hunt for cattle:

When they have kill'd a Beef, they cut it into four Quarters, and taking out all the Bones, each Man makes a hole in the middle of his Quarter, just big enough for his Head to go thro', then put it on like a Frock, and trudgeth home.[6]

In contrast, Spanish cowboys have more sophisticated ways: they hunt on horseback, bringing cattle down by hoxing – cutting their tendons with knives lashed to long poles – and protect their supply of salt to cure the beef by firing the top surface of a salt mound into a hard, black layer that keeps out the tropical rains. Like other Englishmen before him, he sympathised with the Indians, a generous and peaceful people whose sufferings under a caste system where they were placed even below African slaves '[make] them very melancholy and thoughtful'.[7]

When Dampier tried his hand at cutting logwood, the difficulty of the work, sickness and a disastrous storm frustrated his efforts, and in desperation he turned to the common alternative of piracy. His first cruise 'on the account' was with men who had no legal commission, but in his writings he obligingly calls them privateers. In a year's time his share of plundering in the bay was enough for him to return to England (August 1678) and take a wife, Judith, a servant of the Duchess of Grafton. But only a few months later, early in 1679, he was drawn back to Jamaica.

The future most decisively struck for him when he went partners with a merchant named Hoby who planned to trade with the Moskito Indians of Honduras and Nicaragua. Before they were to sail, all of Hoby's men except Dampier deserted to join a buccaneer fleet of nine ships and 500 men forming at Negril Bay. After three or four days alone with Captain Hoby, he too 'ran', setting himself on a course that would, after many painful turns, lead him to success. (See Illustration 18)

The fleet's admiral was Captain John Coxon, a Jamaica privateer that Governor Vaughn had tried to capture in 1676. His principal consorts were Captains Bartholomew Sharp, another recalcitrant Jamaica privateer, and Richard Sawkins, who had been arrested in 1679 for piracy but had escaped from Port Royal gaol. The legal justification for their enterprise was 'a mixture of outdated French and English commissions, including "let passes" from Governor Carlisle "to go into the Bay of Honduras to cut Logwood"'.[8] They would now attempt nothing less than a reprise of the buccaneers' two greatest victories. (See Illustration 19)

They started well in 1680 with the quick seizure of Puerto Bello, easy pickings after Morgan's reduction of it in 1668. Some buccaneers were disappointed with the take, £40 per man, but it was double what most of Morgan's men had earned at Panama. Their next target was Santa Maria in south-eastern Darien (Isthmus of Panama) where gold from nearby mines was collected three times a year for shipment to Spain. On 5 April the raiding party of 331 men landed near Golden Island, south-east of Puerto Bello, and marched over the Darien mountains; the way was steep, wet and exhausting, but they were guided by Cuna Indians always ready to help enemies of the Spanish. Santa Maria was a great disappointment. Its valuables had been carted off before their arrival and they had missed the spring gold shipment – 300 pounds of it – by a mere three days! All that was left was to canoe wearily down the Santa Maria River into the Gulf of San Miguel and plot the downfall of New Panama City (built after Morgan's raid). With the last of their energy, they paddled across the Gulf for eight more days until the city appeared in their spyglasses.

As the pirates came closer, their pleasure at having reached the objective faded, for in the harbour were eight Spanish warships, and three were sailing out to meet them. They were small but carried more than 220 men, three times the number in the pirates' vanguard. The pirates' strategy was to position canoes on both sides of an oncoming warship and rake its decks with crossfire. The first ship to run the gauntlet lost several men and sailed off, but the second, carrying eighty-six and commanded by Don Jacinto de Barahona, stalled when its helmsman was shot and its sails 'lay aback'. The pirates now came up quickly under the enemy's stern where they could avoid its cannon and prevent the Spanish from regaining control of their ship; every time a man came aft to take the helm, he was shot dead by their marksmen until, after sixty-one were killed, Barahona finally surrendered. Meanwhile Captain Sawkins's canoe lay close by the third warship whose crew of seventy-seven African slaves under Don Francisco de Peralta had three times repelled the pirates. Suddenly a series of explosions on the ship allowed the invaders to board and end the battle. The pirates admired their Captain Harris who had entered Barahona's ship with wounds in both his legs, but honoured even more the valour of Peralta who, when the first explosion blew some of his men into the water, had

> leaped overboard, and, in spite of all our shot, got several of them into the ship again, though he was much burnt in both his hands himself.[9]

The victors counted their casualties, eighteen dead and twenty-two wounded, and pressed their captives for information about the remaining warships. These were manned by skeleton crews and gave up without a fight. The greatest prize was the 400-ton *La Santissima Trinidad*, the very same ship that Morgan's men had a decade ago allowed to escape with the riches of Panama. But when a head count revealed that deaths, injuries and defections had reduced the pirates to 250, too few to attempt New Panama City, the expedition began to break up. Some returned to the 'North Seas', as the buccaneers called the Caribbean. Dampier went with the faction under Captains Sharp and Watling that continued operations in the Pacific – the 'South Seas' – his motive a passion for discovery no less than for Spanish gold and silver. What happened on this cruise would only intensify that passion.

Sharp's force in the prize, renamed *Trinity*, numbered 107 Europeans. His subsequent cruise off the western coast of South America was notable more for internal wrangling and badly managed raids than for plunder. In February 1681 the pirates' last hope for a windfall disappeared at Arica in present-day Chile where the silver from Potosi and other Andean mines was gathered for shipping. (See Illustration 20) The raid was so badly executed that Captain Watling and many other pirates were killed, and in April, fifty-two men, including Dampier and his friend Lionel Wafer, the crew's surgeon, deserted to retrace their steps across the Isthmus. Dampier's other 'ingenious Friend', Basil Ringrose, a self-educated Londoner who was also keeping 'an exact and very curious journal of all our voyage', remained with Captain Sharp.[10]

After stocking their canoes with chocolate made by kneading cocoa with flour and sugar, Dampier and company sailed due north some 2,100 miles into the Gulf of San Miguel, about 100 miles south-east of Panama City. Here they abandoned their boats and marched across the Isthmus via a route twice as long as their first crossing but with the advantage of greater secrecy. The company was helped along the way by two different indigenous peoples, the Moskito and the Cuna. Dampier gives us a vivid picture of the Moskito, natives of the Nicaraguan and Honduran coasts but often found aboard English privateers and pirates throughout the West Indies. He much admired their dexterity, courage and hunting skills and the ease with which they adapted to English ways, becoming excellent marksmen and brave comrades against both the French and Spanish.

Included in Dampier's company were two Moskito men who hunted turtle, fish, hog and monkey for them, but the Cuna Indians of the Isthmus were their greatest support. (See Illustration 21) They guided them through the pathless forest, sold them a variety of cultivated foods – plantain, yams, potatoes, sugar, fowl, eggs – and doctored the lame or sick. The most to benefit from Cuna hospitality was Lionel Wafer, whose knee was shattered by an accidental explosion of gunpowder. Unable to walk without great pain, Wafer and four others (including the 'ingenious' and scholarly pharmacist Richard Gopson) stayed among the Cuna nearly four months, during which time he methodically recorded many aspects of their world, sometimes participating like a modern anthropologist in their daily life and rituals. At first he was treated poorly by the Cuna, who 'look'd on us very scurvily, throwing green Plantains to us, as we sat cringing and shivering, as you would Bones to a Dog'. But when Wafer cured the fever of the paramount chief's wife, 'the Indians... in a manner ador'd me'.[11] The book he wrote about his Darien experience is among the most comprehensive and objective ethnographic reports of the early modern period and still a valued source on seventeenth-century Cuna society. (See Illustration 23)

Dampier and Wafer must have been great comforts to one another even before the re-crossing of the Isthmus. They shared the same intellectual interests, habits of observation, and even prose style, the 'unadorned' style recommended for scientific communication by the Royal Society. Their 'field notes' took the form of journals systematically recording events, locations and phenomena. To protect these precious journals, Dampier put his in 'a large Joint of Bambo, which I stopt at both ends, closing it with Wax'. This precaution was justified by the torrential rains,

> tho' whether it rained or shined it was much at one with us, for I verily believed we crost the Rivers 30 times this Day: the Indians having no Paths to travel from one part of the Country to another.[12]

Clearly, Ringrose, Dampier, Wafer and Gopson prove that not every buccaneer was an unthinking brute. Unfortunately this literary circle disbanded when Ringrose left with Sharp, Gopson died, and Wafer left Dampier to join another splinter group. Bartholomew Sharp's later career would be a mix of great highs and miserable lows. His fortunes were sinking after the disaster at Arica, but his luck improved as the *Trinity* sailed towards Cape Horn. In the *Rosario*, the richest prize he took off the coast, he found a small treasure in silver and gems but missed a large cache of silver bars disguised as tin; his most auspicious booty was a Spanish *derrotero*, a secret book of charts of the entire west coast of South America. He returned to England in the spring of 1682, but instead of enjoying his wealth was arrested on charges of piracy and murder brought by the Spanish ambassador incensed at the loss of yet another *derrotero* (Morgan had brought one home from Panama).[13] The ambassador would not be comforted by the course of English justice: historians suspect that Charles II agreed to fix the trial in return for Sharp's help in copying and interpreting the *derrotero* before it was returned to Spain. Not only was he presently acquitted when the judges threw out the damning testimony of Indian and black eyewitnesses from his own crew, but he was also offered command of a navy sloop preparing to salvage a Spanish wreck in the Caribbean. He declined the position, however, and returned to the West Indies to engage in legal and criminal activities at Bermuda, Nevis, Anguilla and St Thomas. These activities led to his second escape from the noose at a 1687 piracy trial in Nevis. But next year his luck finally ran out when he was sentenced to life in prison by the Danes at St Thomas. Crippled and penniless, he probably died there sometime after 1699.[14]

After Dampier's company returned to the Caribbean, they cruised without 'purchase' from Costa Rica to Venezuela until, attracted by the northern colonies' permissive attitude towards pirates, twenty of them, including Dampier, sailed to Virginia where they arrived in July 1682. We know little of his thirteen-month stay there except that he was living at Point Comfort at the mouth of the James River when Captain John Cook, a veteran of the descent on Puerto Bello under Coxon, came to recruit for a new 'adventure' in the South Seas.[15] When articles were drawn up to regulate the adventurers' behaviour and, above all, forbid drunkenness on ship, Dampier signed on, happy to find Wafer and other old companions among the crew. In command of seventy men in a ship of eighteen guns called the *Revenge*, Cook sailed from Accomac, Virginia, in August 1683.

The *Revenge* sailed east to pick up the Guinea and Brazil currents that would drive it back across the Atlantic and along the coast of South America. The pirates' first landfall was the Cape Verde Islands where they careened[16] and took on provisions, including the all-important salt for food preservation. They captured their first prize here, a Dutchman going to sell slaves at Virginia in violation of the Navigation Acts. The pirates' justification for taking his wine and food was that 'they might as well rob him as he the King, he being bound to rob the King of his duties'.[17] Their second prize was another slaver, a Danish ship of thirty-six guns taken at Sierra Leone which, under the name *Batchelor's Delight*, became their flagship on the voyage towards Cape Horn.

Of the torments suffered by sailors rounding the Horn, a recent biographer of Dampier has this to say:

It could take months from the last port of call, and when it was completed the ship could be a mess, soaking and stinking; the supplies could be used up or spoiled to such an extent that the ship's rats would prefer to nibble the toes of the sailors as they slept than eat what was left of the food in the barrels. The sense of solitude was dreadful, and the idea of losing one's masts in the storms that blew here was unendurable, because in that event a ship would be as good as lost.[18]

Ships coming from the east faced the added difficulty of going into the very teeth of the Roaring Fifties. After a miserable and frightening passage, the *Batchelor's Delight* made for Juan Fernandez, a favourite rest stop for freebooters almost 400 miles west of Valparaiso, Chile. (See Illustration 24)

This was Dampier's second time on the island; during the first in 1681, his captain had forgotten that William, a Moskito, was still hunting in the woods when they put to sea. Would they find him now, after a lonely three-year struggle to survive? Dampier and those who knew William doubtless scanned the shoreline on 23 March 1684 as the *Batchelor's Delight* nosed into the bay on the island's south side. 'By God, there he is on the shore, our William!' the sailors would have shouted. Dampier, who is usually unsentimental, cannot recall without emotion the pleasure of that reunion:

> when we landed, a Moskito Indian, named Robin, first leap'd ashore, and running to his Brother Moskito Man, threw himself flat on his face at his feet, who helping him up, and embracing him, fell flat with his face on the Ground at Robin's feet, and was by him taken up also. We stood with pleasure to behold the surprize, and tenderness, and solemnity of this interview, which was exceedingly affectionate on both sides; and when their Ceremonies of Civility were over, we also that stood gazing at them drew near, each of us embracing him we had found here, who was overjoyed to see so many of his old Friends come hither, as he thought purposely to fetch him.[19]

Then William treated them all to a celebratory feast of goat cooked in cabbage. Readers of Defoe's *Robinson Crusoe* will recall a similar emotional reunion between Friday and his father on a remarkably similar 'desert island'. (See Illustration 25)

Because a pirate alert had sounded along the coast, Cook steered well out to sea on his way to their next source of provisions, the Galapagos Islands. In this biologically isolated place, Dampier found much to wonder at and record. A century and a half later, his published notes on the islands would nourish Charles Darwin's interest in their unique ecosystem. From the Galapagos the pirates seem to have been directed by random bits of information rather than a grand design. Hearing of rich and 'safe' targets on the coast of present-day El Salvador, they proceeded due north, but Cook died before they could reach Cape Blanco (Costa Rica), and with Dampier's friend Edward Davis at the helm, they landed on the island of Ampalla, where the Indians greeted them with song and music.

Dampier's reflections upon this encounter once again reveal his usually well-hidden capacity for empathy:

> All the Indians that I have been acquainted with who are under the Spaniards, seem to be more melancholy than other Indians that are free; and at these publick Meetings, when they are in the greatest of their Jollity, their Mirth seems to be rather forced than real. Their Songs are very melancholy and doleful; so is their Musik: but whether it be natural to the Indians to be thus melancholy, or the effect of their Slavery, I am not certain: But I have always been prone to believe, that they are then only condoling their misfortunes, the loss of their Country and Liberties: which altho' these that are now living do not know, nor remember what it was to be free, yet there seems to be a deep impression in their thoughts of the Slavery which the Spaniards have brought them under, increas'd probably by some Traditions of their ancient Freedom.[20]

In this time, before the concept of 'race' was widely accepted, it was still possible for an Englishman who had tended a Jamaica sugar plantation to empathise with the plight of slaves. It helped, of course, that the slaves were those of 'the Spaniard'.

The moment of inter-cultural friendship ended with a pistol shot: one of the pirates, in a spasm of paranoia, killed a high-ranking Indian, the only native who spoke a language the visitors could understand.

The *Batchelor's Delight* was put hastily to sea on a course for the friendly island of La Plata off Ecuador. There it was joined in October 1684 by the *Cygnet* under Captain Charles Swan, he who had commanded the tiny *Endeavor* in Morgan's raid on Panama and then conspired unsuccessfully against the admiral. Now he was employed by London merchants to trade with Spanish colonists on a cruise proposed by Basil Ringrose after his return to England with Sharp. Dampier must have been happy to be again with Ringrose, who was aboard the *Cygnet* as agent for the merchants. Captains Davis, Harris and Swan now sailed together, raiding Paita and Guayaquil where from several prizes they captured an abundance of Quito cloth and about 1,000 African slaves.

Dampier was a buccaneer with a vision, frequently at odds with his company's aims. He calculated that with such a company of slaves and the support of the Cuna, they could set up a pirateer outpost at Santa Maria in Darien ideally positioned to control the area's gold mining and to trade with the North and South Seas.

> In a short time we should have had assistance from all parts of the West-Indies; many thousands of Privateers from Jamaica and the French Islands especially would have flockt over to us; and long before this time we might have been Masters not only of those Mines (the richest Gold-Mines ever yet found in America), but of all the Coast as high as Quito... But these may seem to the Reader but Golden Dreams.

Here is the pragmatic Dampier concerned not for the sensibility of slaves but for the main chance – 'there was never a greater Opportunity put into the Hands of Men to enrich themselves than we had'.[21]

Dampier's mates were in no mood to settle down, however. After their recent victories, they thought only of the gold standard of success as a pirate, intercepting the plate fleet from Lima to Panama. This fleet sailed every three years with about 24,000,000 pieces of eight (£6,000,000), a treasure equivalent in 2002 to the purchasing power of £685,520,000. Unmoved by the chance of suddenly becoming rich beyond his wildest golden dreams, Dampier was bitterly disappointed when the company rejected the Santa Maria scheme, took onboard only seventy slaves, and sailed into Panama Bay. After a few weeks, more English and French were drawn to the bay by the scent of silver until the raiders numbered nearly 960 men in ten ships with sixty great guns.

At last, on the morning of 28 May 1685, the royal fleet of seven ships, 154 cannon and 1,430 men came into view and appeared ready to defend itself. Despite their prey's superior strength, the pirates came out at three o'clock in the afternoon confident that, being upwind, they were positioned to control the battle. But both sides were unwilling to come 'board-to-board' so that the afternoon was spent firing at long distance. As night fell, the pirates continued to chase the Spanish flagship, whose light would curiously go off for a time and then suddenly reappear in a new direction. Next morning Davis saw with disgust that the pirate ships were scattered but their prey rode in formation and to windward. From this he understood that the Spanish had lured them into following several decoy lights, not only the one aboard the flagship. As the enemy bore down on them, the pirates

> ran for it, and after a running Fight all day, and having taken a turn almost round the Bay of Panama, we came to an Anchor again... in the very same place from whence we set out in the Morning.[22]

Instead of pursuing their advantage, however, the Spanish now broke off and went into New Panama, putting an end to the raiders' dream of boundless silver. They learnt later that they had been on a fool's errand; the Spanish admiral had stashed his cargo on the west coast of the Gulf of Panama before venturing to chase them.

Their defeat was not costly, but it was demoralising. All the French soon left and there were words between Davis and Swan. Davis and Wafer sailed for England via the Straits of Magellan while Captains Swan and Francis Townley continued in the Pacific. Among those who stayed with Swan were Ringrose and Dampier, the latter explaining,

> I came into these seas this second time more to endulge my cureosity than to gett wealth, though I must confess at that time I did think the trade lawfull.[23]

Like other intelligent and usually careful persons, Dampier could be wilfully self-deluded.

If one of the pirates' golden dreams died at Panama, another was born on the decks of the *Cygnet* – the dream of taking a Manilla galleon. Every year two great ships sailed in tag-team fashion between Acapulco and the Philippines, with trade goods and silver going west and silk, spices, porcelain and jewels going east. It had been a century since an English corsair had seized one of these fabled ships. On 25 August 1685 Captains Swan and Townley headed north to ambush the galleon, due around Christmas, and in mid-December they took up positions north of Acapulco at Cape Corrientes. They trusted that the galleon would follow its historic route, south along Baja California, across the mouth of the Gulf of California, and past the Cape. Their plan and timing were excellent; the galleon was, in fact, dead on course to fall into their trap. The thoughts of the old, pirating dogs turned to the rich goods they would fence... the jewels they would stitch into their great coats... their proud homecomings in Jamaica, London, New York. They had made only one error Dampier could think of – neglecting to stock up on enough food to ride out the ambush. But Townley had provided forty bushels of maize on 28 December, and a day after celebrating the new year, Swan and Townley landed to search for cattle.

During their five-day hunt, the galleon slipped past them into the safety of Acapulco.

The aftermath of this their third major failure was the usual – discontent and blaming followed by break-up of the fleet. Townley's company went south to cruise along the coast of Peru. Swan went north with the hope of looting mining towns, but to keep Dampier as his navigator, he promised to take the *Cygnet* to the East Indies. His force of 200 easily repelled several attacks by Spanish militia but at Santa Pecaque, a village north-west of Guadalajara, their luck ran out. Fifty men were killed here, including Basil Ringrose, who was deeply mourned by Dampier. The captain was now fed up with pirating and, on 31 March 1686, ordered the *Cygnet* and its tender to begin the long haul across the Pacific. Swan wanted to return home by this course, Dampier to continue his discoveries, and the crew to cruise for prizes in the Philippines. (See Illustration 26)

Good weather and the prevailing north-easterly winds allowed the ships to make excellent progress, but the further west they sailed on short rations, the angrier the sailors became, to the point of plotting to kill – and eat – the proponents of the voyage. The danger passed when land was sighted on 20 May, so that Captain Swan might jest, 'Ah! Dampier, you would have made them but a poor Meal; for I was

as lean as the Captain was lusty and fleshy'. Thanks to Dampier's navigation, the ships came to an anchor at Guam as planned, sailing more
than 6,800 miles in a remarkable fifty-two days.[24] To their great relief,
the Spanish governor was happy to sell them food and supplies, and
not surprisingly, Dampier rhapsodised about the island's coconuts,
limes, breadfruit and hogs. But fate was to disturb their comfort with
one more absurd joke at the pirates' expense. The second Manila
galleon, laded with silver at Acapulco, was now within sight of Guam.
Suspecting the worst of his guests, the governor secretly warned its
captain to stay out of sight, yet when the pirates heard from the natives
of its being near, Swan would not go out. 'There is no Prince on
earth', he privately told Dampier, 'able to wipe off the Stain of such
Actions'.[25] Had they done so, they would have had easy pickings, for
the galleon was stuck on a nearby shoal.

Their next stop was Mindanao, where the *Cygnet* anchored on 22
June 1686. Dampier was so pleased by its climate, fertility, proximity
to the Spice Islands, and freedom from Spanish domination that he
was later to promote its use as a British trading base. Here he made
copious notes about the plants and animals and learnt from the native
peoples 'to wash Morning and Evenings in these hot countries, at least
three or four Days in the Week'.[26] Swan was even more taken with
the place on account of the natives' hospitality. The Mindanaoans
were not exactly gentle lotus-eaters, but their land seems to have cast
a spell over the usually forceful English commander. After six and a
half months of doing nothing, his men had divided into drunken fac-
tions, and Swan's control of them had so deteriorated that it would
not take much to set off a mutiny. The spark was the sailors' accidental discovery of Swan's journal and the harsh things he had written
about some of them.

Led by Josiah Teat, captain of the tender, ninety of the crewmen –
including Dampier – seized the *Cygnet* and set out on 14 January 1687
to hunt for prizes off Manila. Dampier had not been active in the
mutiny, but going with Teat was, he thought, the lesser of two evils.
(His way was always to '[to keep] his mind to himself until he had to
take one side or the other', an attitude that no doubt afforded the
freedom to observe and record what he had seen, but did little to

develop in him the art of commanding men at sea.[27]) Teat's plan was
to hunt off the Asian mainland until the Acapulco ship for 1687
approached Manila. Consequently, the *Cygnet* arrived in mid-March
at the Condore Islands (Con Son) about sixty miles from the Mekong
Delta (current-day Vietnam) and then cruised in the Gulf of Thailand.
Command had by this time shifted to John Read, an old logwood
cutter, but he was no more successful at crew control than Swan or
Teat. Dampier and some others were soon 'sufficiently weary of this
mad Crew' and 'willing to give them the slip'.[28]

After four weeks at Condore, the *Cygnet* made a great loop around
the South China Sea ending at Luzon in October, very educational
for Dampier but, with no booty of consequence, a waste of time for
the others. Captain Read, with Dampier as his navigator, then took
them along the east coast of the Philippines, steering past Mindanao
and Celebes and into the Banda Sea. Here in the heart of the Spice
Islands, they were plagued by tornadoes, served cockles each large
enough to feed seven men, and hosted by the sultan of Butong. He
entertained them with praise for British justice and censure for the
abusive Dutch, a common litany among the Indonesian peoples.
Dampier tells of a peaceful moment on their departure from Butong
when they passed five intensely green islands from which they heard
drums and suspected that the natives 'were making merry, as 'tis usual
in these parts to do all the Night, singing and dancing till Morning',
images from a South Sea island paradise yet to possess the European
imagination. [29]

By 27 December they had threaded the maze of islands between
Celebes and Timor *en route* to New Holland (Australia) 'to see what
that Country would afford us'. Alas, in the King Sound region where
they anchored on 5 January 1688, they found a harsh, dry country and
'Indians' with nothing to recommend themselves. Nevertheless, they
stayed until 12 March, resting, looking around, attempting in vain to
clothe the aborigines and make them into drawers of water. To
Dampier, who measured a people by their houses, farms, technology
and work ethic, these were 'the miserablest People in the World',
without 'Herb, Root, Pulse nor any sort of Grain for them to eat, that
we saw; nor any sort of Bird or Beast that they can catch, having no

Instruments wherewithal to do so'.[30] His uncharitable comments probably signal disillusionment with the enduring European myth of an hospitable *Terra Australis Incognita*.The company was so irritated by his nagging them to leave for the nearest British outpost that they nearly marooned him here. (Ironically, Dampier's most enduring claim to fame is as the first Englishman to explore Australia.)

Read decided to sail north-west towards the Arabian Sea where, he had heard, one could make one's voyage by preying on Muslim shipping.The entrance to the Red Sea was especially attractive because of its volume of trade and the natural choke point at the Strait of Bab el Mandab. (English pirateers had operated there sporadically since the early 1600s, but their numbers had increased dramatically towards the end of the century as the authorities made the West Indies inhospitable and the Spanish improved their defences in the Pacific.) Adverse winds blew the *Cygnet* too far to the east so that early in May it was off the island of Nicobar, north of Sumatra, the crew surviving poorly on rice steeped in coconut milk. Although suffering with the rest, Dampier was secretly pleased to be at Nicobar because he knew of an East India Company 'factory' (trading station) within striking distance at Achin (Banda Aceh), Sumatra. While his mates were busy finding food and careening, he was planning his deliverance. For some time, Captain Read had suspected Dampier of disloyalty and feared that if he deserted, he would reveal the *Cygnet's* course and intent. But Nicobar was separated from Sumatra by the Great Channel, 130 miles of turbulent sea.Thinking the Channel impossible to navigate without a sizable ship, Read allowed Dampier and seven others to stay on the island. The *Cygnet* departed on 6 May 1688, and the marooned men prepared to do the impossible.

With his journals in their stoppered bamboo container, Dampier now began what he would remember as the worst voyage of his life.[31] The men embarked for Achin on 15 May 1688 in an outrigger canoe and seemed to be making good progress by sail and oar until Dampier realised on the third day that they had been thrown back by a strong southerly current. Next day, the canoe was hit by a fierce gale, a 'Sumatra', which hurled it violently off course towards Malaya. In the evening, the Sea was already roaring in a white Foam about us; a dark Night coming on, and no Land in sight to shelter us, and our little Ark in danger to be swallowed by every Wave; and, what was worst of all, none of us thought our selves prepared for another World.

Dampier's account of his religious awakening on the night of 18 May is unique in his journal for personal revelation and rough eloquence:

> The Reader may better guess than I can express, the Confusion that we were all in. I had been in many imminent Dangers before now, some of which I have already related, but the worst of them all was but a Play-game in comparison with this. I must confess that I was in great Conflicts of Mind at this time. Other Dangers came not upon me with such a leisurely and dreadful Solemnity. A sudden Skirmish or Engagement, or so, was nothing when one's Blood was up, and push'd forwards with eager Expectations. But here I had a lingring View of approaching Death, and little or no hopes of escaping it; and I must confess that my Courage, which I had hitherto kept up, failed me here; and I made very sad Reflections on my former Life, and look'd back with Horror and Detestation, on Actions which before I disliked, but now I trembled at the remembrance of. I had long before this repented me of that roving course of Life, but never with such concern as now. I did also call to mind the many miraculous Acts of God's Providence towards me in the whole Course of my Life, of which kind I believe few Men have met with the like. For all these I returned Thanks in a peculiar Manner, and this once more desired God's Assistance, and composed my Mind, as well as I could, in the hopes of it, and as the Event shewed, I was not disappointed of my hopes.[32]

The terrific wind and numbing rain at last abated, they returned to a southerly course and, on 20 May, landed east of Achin, where they were nursed by kindly Malay fishermen.

Dampier vividly conveys both the severity of his illness and his frustration at this time: he writes of being:

so distempered, that I could scarce stand, therefore I whetted and sharp-
ened my Penknife, in order to let my self Blood; but I could not, for my
Knife was too blunt.

The invalids were at last carried to Achin and treated by a Malay
doctor who prescribed laxatives so strong that he 'had above 60 Stools
in all before it left off working'.[33] Against all odds, he survived the
cure but afterwards suffered from bouts of fever and dysentery for a
whole year.

The man's great resilience and powers of concentration were not
diminished, however. Despite his illness, he would not rest quietly, but
for the next two years, from July 1688 to June 1690, served aboard vessels that visited Malaya, Tonquin (Vietnam), Cambodia and India.
During these voyages he acquired half share in Jeoly, a tattooed
Philippine prince, whom he hoped to show for profit in England. In
the summer and fall of 1690, he worked as gunner at the East India
Company's fort in Bencouli (Bengkulu), Sumatra, but, the fort's governor proving 'brutish and barbarous', Dampier escaped one night to
the company ship *Defence* that resumed its homebound voyage on 25
January. When the *Defence* anchored in the Downs on 16 September
1691, there was little of obvious value for Dampier to take off the ship
so that he was forced to sell Jeoly to raise cash. (The prince's new
owners showed him in London and Oxford before he died of small-
pox, probably late in 1692.) Yet there was something else, a modest-
looking object that would make his fortune – the hollow bamboo
stoppered with wax.

It is likely that Dampier had been planning a book at least since
Panama when he had served alongside the journal writers Ringrose,
Wafer and Sharp. What he needed now was time to look over his
journals, to select, rearrange and write, but after greeting his wife
Judith and his family, he was obliged to go back to sea to earn a living.
We know the details of only one voyage he took in the six years
between his return and the publication of his first book, a voyage from
which would emerge the most successful British pirate of the 1690s.
In August 1693 Dampier went second mate aboard the *Dove*, one of
four merchant ships bound for the West Indies. The story of the

'Spanish Expedition Shipping' will be told fully in the next chapter, but it suffices here that a mutiny at the Spanish port of Coruña ruined the expedition and that the flagship (renamed the *Fancy*) was taken on a legendary pirate cruise commanded by Henry Every. But Dampier, who had had enough of roving, declined to join Every and remained at Coruña in the *Dove* until his contract expired in February 1695.

A month and a half after returning to England, Dampier and fifty-eight others from the failed enterprise brought a civil suit in admiralty court claiming that the owners had improperly withheld most of their wages. The defendants counter-charged that the plaintiffs had aided and abetted the mutineers and therefore, according to the printed contract each had signed, were not owed anything. This proved a winning strategy when, in January 1696, admiralty judge Sir Charles Hedges dismissed the suit for lack of evidence, a ruling uncharacteristic of admiralty wage cases in the late seventeenth century, but the status and connections of the defendants may have overborne the court's usual interest in appeasing able seamen, especially during war.[34] The dismissal implied that Dampier was complicit in Every's crimes, a charge supported by his loyalty to six of the *Fancy*'s men prosecuted in 1696: Dampier testified on their behalf and raised bail for one of them.

One supremely good thing may have come out of his nearly seventeen idle months at Coruña: it is likely that he took his journals out of their container and began to write the first draft of his adventures. This draft seems to have given him an *entrée* into learned society once he returned to London, for he reports that he discussed Jamaican agriculture with Morgan's old enemy Governor Vaughn, a past president of the Royal Society, and that his work had been 'Revised and Corrected by Friends'.[35] In 1697 *A New Voyage Round the World* was greeted by enthusiastic reviews and its author hailed as the first Englishman to circumnavigate the world since Cavendish.(See Illustration 27, 28)

The book is understandably silent about crimes its author had committed aboard the *Batchelor's Delight*, *Cygnet*, and other buccaneer ships, but it contained enough incriminating evidence to raise any attorney general's eyebrows. True, it would be hard to find eyewitnesses to support a piracy indictment, but Dampier was also protected from prosecution by the scientific élite for whom his book was, in substance and style, a model of natural history writing, exactly the kind of book they had encouraged travellers to write. In addition, statesmen and merchants praised it for advocating British penetration of the Pacific and offering detailed sailing and survival instructions to mariners. His standing as scientist/navigator was further enhanced by a second book, *A Supplement of the New Voyage* (1699), featuring a lavishly detailed description of Campeche and the invaluable 'Discourse of Winds, Storms, Seasons, Tides, and Currents in the Torrid Zone'. Although Dampier did not make navigating the Pacific seem easy, speculation in the 'South Seas' trade shortly to grip England (and culminate in the 'South Sea Bubble' that burst in 1720) was encouraged by the *New Voyage*.

Dampier's life was transformed by the success of his book. He was now a guest at the tables of gentlemen and scholars like Samuel Pepys, Hans Sloane (naturalist and future physician to Queen Anne), and John Evelyn, who found him 'a more modest man' than the rough buccaneer he had expected.[36] His powerful new friends got him a sinecure in the London Custom House, and the Board of Trade invited him frequently to testify about Panama and piracy. (See Illustration 29, 30) Most important of all, the Admiralty gave him command of HMS *Roebuck* to explore the entire coastline of *Terra Australis Incognita*, 'the first... voyage planned for the deliberate purpose of scientific exploration'. [37] (See Illustration 31)

Although the voyage of the *Roebuck* (1699–1701) is important in the history of science and Australia and gave rise to Dampier's third book, *A Voyage to New Holland* (1703), it failed in its mission and brought Dampier's brief naval career to a shameful end. The captain had three problems, each of which was potentially fatal: he was ignorant of naval command, the ship was decrepit, and the crew was inexperienced. To compensate for the last and establish his authority, Dampier placed in critical positions three men he had known from the Spanish Expedition Shipping. The preferential treatment he gave to them angered his lieutenant, George Fisher, a veteran career officer; exasperated by the captain's neglect of naval protocol and decorum, Fisher openly disparaged his seamanship and accused him of planning to run away with the ship, publicly referring to him as 'that Old Pirating Dog'.[38] Evidently either Fisher or others aboard the

Roebuck knew of the revelations in the *New Voyage* and, worse yet, his three old friends could link him with the arch-pirate Every, still thought to be active in the Indian Ocean.

As the *Roebuck* approached Brazil, Dampier lost his patience with Fisher during an argument over the broaching of a cask of beer, hit him with his cane, and had him put in irons. After the voyage, the Admiralty convened a court martial which heard evidence of Dampier's actions and bad character, including a report of his protecting three of Every's men found at Bahia, Brazil. The captain had reported them to the Portuguese governor and requested that they be sent to England on the next inbound warship, but the most violent of them, Every's former carpenter John Guy, may indeed have been given a second chance for his special skills: his name appears on the paybook of the *Roebuck* as an able seaman.[39]

On 8 June 1702 the court martial, chaired by Admiral of the Channel Fleet Sir Cloudesly Shovel, found 'that the said Capt. Dampier is not a Fitt person to be Employ'd as com[mander] of any of her Ma[jesty's]ships'. Such a stinging judgement would normally ruin a career, but in no way diminished his reputation as England's premier navigator in the Pacific. In October 1702 he was put in charge of the privateers *St George* and *Cinq-Ports* and instructed 'to cruize upon her Ma[jesty's] Enemys in such parts of America where no attempts have been yet made'.[40] Dampier was to fight the French and Spanish in the War of the Spanish Succession (1701–1714) on this, his first cruise with a valid privateering commission. He might well have felt vindicated when, on 16 April 1703, he was introduced to Queen Anne by her husband and Lord High Admiral, Prince George, perhaps at the request of the Prince's friends in the naval and scientific communities.

The record of the privateering cruise makes it apparent that Dampier was losing his focus, for its only success came on 7 May 1704 when, off Garanchinè in the Gulf of Panama, he took a large Spanish trader. Soon after, Dampier's consort, the *Cinq-Ports*, absconded with the loot and proceeded to Juan Fernandez where its quartermaster Alexander Selkirk was voluntarily marooned after arguing with Captain Stradling. Meanwhile, Dampier had received word that the

Manila galleon, *Rosario*, was approaching Acapulco – his third chance of a lifetime. When he came upon it on 6 December, he had to board quickly before the big ship rolled out her guns and hammered the *St George* to pieces. Dampier delayed, took a crushing shot to his stern, and ran. Convinced that their commander was not only arrogant but a drunk and a coward from whom they could expect nothing more, thirty-five men mutinied in January 1705 and sailed away in the Spanish prize, one of them taunting him gallingly at the end, '*Poor Dampier, thy Case is like King James, every Body has left thee*'.[41]

The captain and twenty-seven loyalists soon abandoned the worn-out *St George*, seized another Spanish ship, and made for home. When he reached London late in 1707, Dampier hardly had time to lick his wounds before a former midshipman aboard the *St George* attacked him in print. The brief pamphlet war that followed would encourage the heir of one of the investors to sue him and others for fraud in 1712, but by 1708 he had again gone to sea. Astonishingly, Dampier became a leading figure in an ambitious new privateering expedition directly after his last had ended in infamy. True, he would never again be trusted with command, but as pilot his counsel would be invaluable. To compliment their great 'sea artist', the investors chose as Admiral the Bristol mariner Woodes Rogers who, although he could not boast Dampier's knowledge of the South Seas – no one could – was strong where Dampier was weak: 'it was his steadiness, his sense of duty and his natural talent for leadership which recommended him'.[42]

The voyage of the *Duke* (Captain Rogers) and *Duchess* (Captain Courtney) from August 1708 to July 1711 accomplished nothing less than what Sharp, Swan, Dampier and other English freebooters had failed at since Sir Thomas Cavendish in 1587 – the capture of a Manila galleon. On 22 December 1709, after a battle in which he sustained agonising wounds to his jaw and knee, Rogers took the *Nuestra Señora de la Encarnacion Desengaño* on its approach to Acapulco. After this victory and the sack of Guayaquil, Ecuador, the fleet returned to England with nearly £150,000 in goods and money, an enormous success. Rogers also returned Alexander Selkirk from Juan Fernandez where he had lived alone for nearly four and a half years after being marooned by the *Cinq-Ports* in 1704. (Selkirk's experiences were to provide

Daniel Defoe with the inspiration and setting for *Robinson Crusoe*
(1719)). We will meet Rogers again when he appears in Chapter 5 as
the reform governor of the Bahamas, a key figure in the campaign
against the West Indian pirates. (See Illustration 32)

Dampier had played a critical role in the expedition's success, but
there had been some embarrassing memory lapses and odd judge-
ments. Nevertheless, his reputation outlasted his personal vitality, and,
when the fleet put in at Amsterdam (as a precaution against seizure by
the East India Company for interloping, that is, violating a chartered
company's trading monopoly), a British agent there eagerly sent good
news to the prime minister, 'Dampier is alive'.[43]

His wife Judith had probably died before he came home for good
and went to live in retirement with his cousin and executor, Grace
Mercer, in Coleman Street, St Stephen's parish, London, comfortably
sustained by his Customs House sinecure and by loans in anticipation
of what the investors in the *Duke* and *Duchess* owed him. The ships
were still at Amsterdam when lawyers from London came aboard to
solicit clients and nearly all their men signed up to sue the owners.
The schedule of wages, shares and plunder was especially complicated
and the suits dragged on for years. No stranger to the civil law, Dampier
also claimed a place in line, but he died early in 1715, two years before
a final settlement with his estate.[44]

William Dampier emerged from the mass of restless, unruly men
that Henry Morgan ended by repudiating, yet they were alike in several ways. Both were energetic, combative, ambitious – unwilling to
live safe, conventional lives. They were intelligent and resourceful men
who used piracy as a stepping-stone to fortune and respectability.
Both were masters of their trades, which they plied fearlessly at the
physical and moral frontiers of their era, and each left behind a legacy
of achievement for others to build upon. They are, moreover, the only
subjects of this book known to have died in bed.

1 A popular woodcut used to represent various British pirate chiefs throughout the eighteenth century. Captain Charles Johnson, *History and Lives of the Pyrates* (London, 1725).

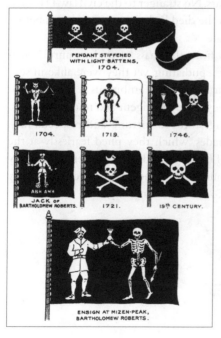

2 Versions of the Jolly Roger. Francis Boardman Bradlee, *Piracy in the West Indies* (Salem Mass., 1923).

3 *Left:* Arms of the Old East India Company. George Birdwood, ed., *Report on the Old Records of the India Office* (London, 1891).

4 *Below:* No Peace Beyond the Line: the area excluded from continental peace treaties in a fanciful map of Central and South America. A.O. Exquemelin, *Bucaniers of America* (London, 1684–85).

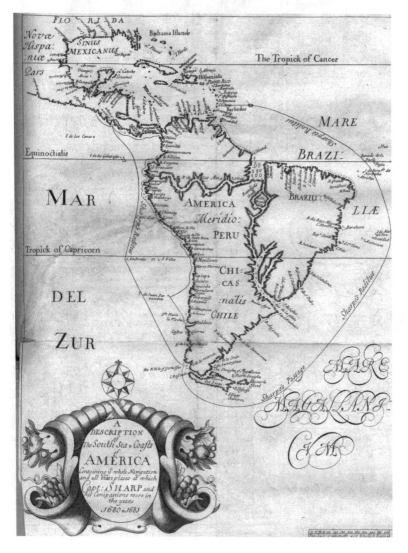

5 Buccaneers attack a
Spanish ship. A.O.
Exquemelin, *Historie der
Boecaniers van America*
(Amsterdam, 1700).

6 The first great compilation
of pirates' lives. A.O.
Exquemelin, *De
Americaensche Zee-Roovers*
(Amsterdam, 1678).

7 Scenes of
buccaneer life. A.O.
Exquemelin, *Histoire
Des Aventuriers
Flibustiers* (Trevoux,
1775).

8 Buccaneer fort at
Tortuga. Jean
Baptiste du Tertre,
*Histoire Generale Des
Antilles* (Paris,
1667–71).

9 Portrait of Morgan. A.O. Exquemelin, *De Americaenche Zee Roovers* (Amsterdam, 1678).

10 Buccaneers assault Puerto del Principe, Cuba. A.O. Exquemelin, *Piratas de la America* (Cologne, 1681).

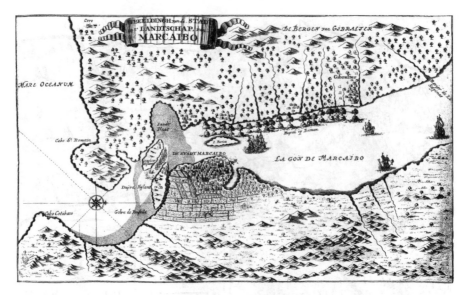

11 Map of Lake Maracaibo, Venezuela. A.O. Exquemelin, *De Americaenche Zee Roovers* (Amsterdam, 1678).

12 Morgan fights his way into Lake Maracaibo. A.O. Exquemelin, *Bucaniers of America* (London, 1684–85).

13 *Above:* Map of the Isthmus near old Panama City. A.O. Exquemelin, *Histoire Des Aventuriers Flibustiers* (Trevoux, 1775).

14 *Right:* Terror of 'the Spaniard'. A.O. Exquemelin, *Bucaniers of America* (London, 1684–85).

ROCK. BRASILIANO

15, 16 'Thus was consumed the famous and ancient city of Panama'. A.O.
Exquemelin, *Piratas de la America* (Cologne, 1681).

17 Captain William
Dampier. Thomas
Murray c.1697.

18 The cockpit of the privateers. William Dampier, *A New Voyage Round the World* (London, 1697).

19 *Above:* 'The Author's Entrance into the South Seas'. William Dampier, *A New Voyage Round the World* (London, 1697).

20 *Right:* Perilous silver mining techniques in New Spain, *c.*1698. Giovanni Francesco Gemelli Careri, *A Voyage Round the World* (London, 1745).

Maniere de Pêcher la Tortue.

21 Buccaneers 'striking' for sea turtles. A.O. Exquemelin, *Histoire Des Aventuriers Flibustiers* (Trevoux, 1775).

22 Sea Cow and Calf. A.O. Exquemelin, *Histoire des Aventuriers qui se sont Signalez dans les Indes* (Paris, 1686).

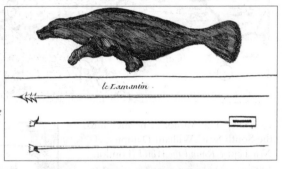

le Lamantin.

The Indians marching upon a Visit, or to Feast. P. 140.
Lacenta. his Lady. Attendants.

23 The buccaneers' ally: a party of Cuna Indians, Panama. Lionel Wafer, *A New Voyage and Description of the Isthmus of America* (London, 1699).

24 The rugged highlands of Juan Fernandez, the inspiration for Robinson Crusoe's island. Richard Walter, *A Voyage Round the World... by George Anson* (London, 1748).

Laudatur et Alget.
Juven. Sat. I.

25 Portrait of Daniel Defoe in 1706. Defoe, *Jure Divino* (London, 1706).

26 First edition of *A New Voyage Round the World* (London, 1697).

27 Dampier's route in the East Indies. William Dampier, *A New Voyage Round the World* (London, 1697).

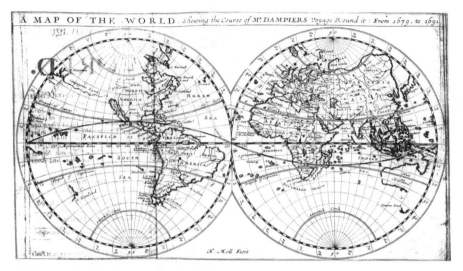

28 The world according to Dampier. William Dampier, *A New Voyage Round the World* (London, 1697).

29 The London Custom House (Christopher Wren, *c.*1668), site of Dampier's one and only desk job. Engraving by John Harris (1714).

162

1697.
July 6th
Account of the Isth-
mus of Darien

Trade Forreigne.

Account of the Isthmus of Darien
and parts adjacent in America presented to the Board by Mr. Dampier,
and Mr. Wafer.

Journal B, 147

An Answer to Queries proposed by the
Honble Committee of Trade.

Your Honours are pleased to propose Two
Queries, the first is, How much of the Country, in or
near the Isthmus of America is possessed by the Wild
Indians independent of the Spanyards.

Our Answer to this is, That on the North Sea
Coast the Spanyards had no settlement (when we were
there) from the Bastamentos, which lye to the Eastward
of Portobel, till you come about 10 leagues Eastward of
the mouth of the River of Darien; all that Coast of the
Continent being possessed by the Indian Natives, who
were under no subjection to the Spanyards, but some
of them had some Commerce with the Spanyards, and
others of them were at War with them, inviting the
Privateers to their assistance against them. In the
Islands are no Inhabitants of any sort, but they are
visited as well by the Indians from the Continent, as
by the Privateers.

On the South sea Coast the Free Indians have a
much longer Tract of Ground, for from the River of
Cheapo, to about half a degree South of the Equator
(making in a strait line, without reckoning the bendings
of the Coast, 9 or 10 degrees of Latitude, and near upon
600 Italian Miles) there are no Spanish settlements, except
them very small; one about the River of Sta Maria in
the Good River in the Gulf of St Michael, another

30 Wafer and Dampier's report
on Darien for the Board of
Trade, 6 July 1697.

D:us Hans Sloane Baronettus

31 Sir Hans Sloane, Queen Anne's
physician and scientific virtuoso.
Engraving by John Faber Jr (1729)
after Kneller (1716).

ESPIRITU SANTO *on* SAMAL, *one of the Phillipine Islands, in the latitude of 12:40 N° Bearing W S W distant 6 leagues* .... *the* CENTURION *engag'd and took the Spanish Galeon call'd* NOSTRA SEIGNIORA DE CABADONGA, *from* ACAPULCO

32 *Above:* Taking the fabled Manila galleon: battle between Anson's *Centurion* and the *Nostra Seigniora de Cabadonga.* Richard Walter, *A Voyage Round the World… by George Anson* (London, 1748).

33 *Left:* The employment contract of William May, steward of the *Charles II.*

4

Henry Every:

'I am a Man of Fortune, and Must Seek my Fortune'

For more than a decade after the autumn of 1696, Henry Every, a career seaman born in 1659 at Newton Ferrers near Plymouth, held centre stage in the public imagination as the boldest and most successful of pirates. At one stroke, he had won for each of his men far more than the great Morgan or the lesser Captains Sharp and Swan had done for theirs; enough, in fact, for the prudent to become gentlemen of property. Every was also popular with seamen in general for punishing oppressive owners by running away with their merchant ship. He is the only pirate we will consider of the many who were created by rebellion of the ordinary sailors, or, in the sea language of the time, the 'people' of the ship.

Every's story begins in 1693 with the launching of the Spanish Expedition Shipping, a venture that outfitted the *Charles II, Dove, James,* and *Seventh Son* to trade with Spanish America and, more importantly, to bring up treasure from galleons sunk in the West Indies. The venture was speculative, but it was well organised and funded by a large number of savvy London investors led by Sir James Houblon, an eminent importer of Spanish wines and groceries. According to the terms of the Treaty of Madrid, Houblon acquired a trading and salvage licence from Carlos II, after whom he named the flagship. The *Charles II* was a ship to be proud of, a fast, agile 'ship of force' newly built in London that, with forty guns mounted, was capable of defending whatever it might bring up from the deep. Houblon found some of the best 'sea-artists' that money could hire for the expedition. Every was made sailing master of the flagship, probably because of his service against France in the War of the Grand Alliance (1689–1697) where he rose to chief mate of HMS *Albemarle*, a great ship-of-the-line. Every's captain, John Strong, achieved fame as second in command to Sir William Phipps, who in 1687 salvaged an immensely rich wreck near Hispaniola (the same that Bartholomew Sharp had declined to hunt for in 1682). William Dampier, perhaps England's best, but as yet unheralded, navigator, was second mate of the *Dove*. The fleet was commanded by Sir Arturo O'Byrne, an Irish Catholic nobleman with long service in the Spanish Marines. (See Illustration 33)

Despite thorough preparations, the project ran into trouble when the House of Trade that administered Seville's commercial monopoly throughout the West Indies blocked the ships' passage from Coruña.[1] To save money while lobbying the authorities for passes, the owners began to skimp on the men's food and other 'necessaries', triggering bitter complaints. 'I never eat worse Beef than at the Groin', Dampier recalled later.[2] The most serious complaint was that Houblon was withholding the men's wages and starving their families. The mood aboard all four ships grew ugly.

When the expeditions' managers in London ignored desperate calls for help, the suspicion of the crews deepened. Ethnic and religious hatreds drove their fears that the Irish and Spanish on the expedition might betray them to the French or sell them 'into the King of Spaines Service to Serve him... all dayes of their lives'. To make matters worse, Captain Strong died and his replacement, Charles Gibson, was championing the sailors' cause and defying O'Byrne. According to John Fishley, the business agent, Gibson perswaded [the crew of the *Charles*] to oppose the Generall, & not to lett him come onboard them saying yt if they would stand by him he would stand by them to secure ym theire wages.[3]

William Phillips, a trooper on the *Dove*, later attested that at this time Henry Every began to go

up & down from Ship to Ship & perswaded the men to come on board him, & he would carry them where they should get money enough.[4]

On 1 May 1694, all the ships' intrigues came to a head: with the expedition's officers and men on the deck of the *James*, the admiral proposed a compromise which the men rejected with one voice, declaring that the ships would not leave Coruña 'unless they had first all their pay to that day'.[5] To end the strike, O'Byrne sent Fishley to London to beg the owners for eight months wages, about £5,000 (today, £535,680). Houblon did not have time to respond, for at nine o'clock on the evening of 7 May, about sixty-five men seized the *Charles II* and steered it towards open water. The quiet of the bay was broken by cannon fire from the *James* and the two Spanish forts, but Every and his men vanished safely into the night.

The next morning, Every called a general meeting and proposed that they cruise for prey in the Indian Ocean. All but his inner circle were surprised at this; he had hinted before the uprising that he would take the ship home. The debate before the mast is a set piece in dramas of rebellion at sea, ending predictably in loud huzzahs and chants of 'A Gold Chain or a wooden Leg, we'll stand by you!' Every was the kind to command a crew's attention, a tall, strongly built man with a dark complexion and gray eyes, whose dignity was enhanced by 'a light coloured Wigg'.[6] Unfortunately, the debate was not recorded, but given the situation and the recent history of mariners' grievances, it may be possible to reconstruct his chief points. He might have begun by justifying the seizure of Houblon's ship in lieu of the men's suffering at La Coruña and their back pay which, if they returned to England, they would probably forfeit – along with their lives – before courts dominated by the great merchants. He might have reminded the many veterans among them of the blood they had shed at the Boyne and Beachy Head only to be enslaved at the hands of King William's 'New Lords' and surrendered to their former enemies.[7] Rising from sweet revenge to golden promise, he might have congratulated them on a good ship, a battle-hardened commander, and intelligence of the best places to wait in ambush for Indian traders, current intelligence from the expedition's own officers. Moreover, it was a good time of year to depart for India, and, with the navy preoccupied by the French, they could anticipate little English resistance.

He would have promised that the Indian Ocean was filled with prizes richer by far than could be found in the West Indies, reminding them of Captain Thomas Tew's capture just a year ago of treasure worth more than £200,000. In possession of such wealth, one could buy immunity from prosecution in the colonies or England itself. And it was no more wrong to cruise against the Muslim of India than the Spaniard beyond the line, for were they not both infidels of rich but rotten empires, by custom and faith the fair prey of English seamen? Those who called it wrong, notably the grandees of the East India Company, would deprive them of their ancient liberties as Houblon and O'Byrne had deprived them of just wages and decent food.

Every might have ended by declaring the proposed cruise the last chance for some to earn security for their families. Looking out over the company, he could identify several who were married and others, like William May, Gibson's steward, who knew that it was 'a great grief... for an aged man [to go to sea]', being

> little better than a slave, being always in need, and enduring all manner of misery and hardship, going with many a hungry belly and wet back, and being always called "old dog", and "old rogue", and "son of a whore"'.[8] Instead, in the spirit of our betters whose lust for sunken treasure had floated the *Charles*, we should seize this opportunity to make good fortune ours – and ours alone.

After loud huzzahs, eighty-five men agreed to take their chances with Every, while fourteen or fifteen were allowed to return to Coruña. The loyalists were about to enter the boat when Every went down to speak with Gibson, sick with a fever in his cabin. The chief mate attempted to explain himself and reconcile with his captain:

> I am a man of fortune, and must seek my fortune. Says captain Gibson, I am sorry this happens at this time. Says he, If you will go in the ship, you shall still command her. No, says capt. Gibson, I never thought you would have served me so, who have been kind to all of you; and to go on a design against my owners orders, I will not do it. Then, says Every, prepare to go ashore.[9]

Henceforth, Every would be the only master of the ship, which the crew renamed *Fancy*.

Stories of Every, his deeds, and his *Fancy* – a few of them true – would soon travel around the world. By early August 1694 report of the mutiny had arrived in London and been turned into a street ballad that celebrated the bold pirate and his wonderful ship.(See Illustration 34)

> Her Model's like Wax, and she sails like the Wind,
> She is rigged and fitted and curiously trimm'd,
> And all things convenient has for his design[10]

In fact, the *Fancy* was more than 'convenient'. It sailed like the wind because it was well designed and had just been careened. Moreover, it had been laded with 150 large tubs of bread, 100 small muskets, and over 100 barrels of gunpowder in preparation for sailing. A newly minted pirate chief could not have asked for better accommodations.

Before setting out for the Cape of Good Hope, the men agreed that the captain would take two shares of the plunder and each adult mariner one, a more equitable distribution than that aboard privateers. While it would be some time before the final sharing, the *Fancy*'s first plunder was not long in coming. In three weeks, the *Fancy* arrived at the Cape Verde Islands, where Every abducted the Portuguese governor to ensure that he would be given 'what victuals they had a mind to'. After taking on fish, beef and salt, his men searched three English ships from Barbados for other 'necessaries'. Joseph Dawson, their quartermaster, gave the victims 'bills for what he took of them' – an indication that the company was still reluctant to commit itself to downright piracy.[11] In addition to provisions, Every welcomed nine volunteers from the Barbadian ships, increasing his strength to ninety-four, a complement still below ideal fighting strength. (Pirates, like the period's battleships, required large crews. It took from six to fifteen men to man each of the great guns so that more than 200 would be needed to fire a broadside, sail the *Fancy*, deliver small arms fire, and board the enemy.)

From the Cape Verdes, Every sailed south-east along the Guinea coast, flying British colours to lure aboard local merchants.

When they came aboard, they surprised them, and took their gold from them, and tied them with chains, and put them into the hold.[12]

The five pounds of gold dust the pirates took were less useful than the slaves who could be sold or bartered anywhere along the coast and would help give them the cover of an interloper against the Royal African Company, a disguise that would explain their furtive behaviour. The *Fancy*'s next stop was Fernando Po (Bioco), a large island in the Bight of Benin due south of modern-day Nigeria. Here, its hull was again cleaned and major changes made to its upper works. The changes are not described in the documents, but they probably included removing stern castle, quarter and poop decks to reduce wind resistance and allow the ship to shed water more efficiently in heavy seas. A flush-decked, galley-like profile would render it less 'leewardly', faster and more manoeuvrable than the ships most likely to oppose it in the Indian Ocean.[13] Another result of these changes might have been the reduction of distinctions between the officers and people; unlike merchant or naval commanders, Every probably had no great cabin to mark his rank.

The *Fancy*'s first overt act of piracy came in October 1694, near Principe island, where they challenged two Danish privateers on the pretence that England was at war with Denmark. When Every proposed to let them go free in exchange for provisions and their money, the Danes refused, shouting back that they were a 'thin [Scheet] & they did not fear us'.[14] After an hour-long fight, however, the Danes surrendered, and the pirates took forty pounds of gold dust, chests of fabrics, small arms and fifty large casks of brandy. Victory and brandy made them so expansive that they gave away seven of the slaves at Principe and welcomed seventeen Danes into their ranks.[15]

Every's last landfall in the Atlantic was the island of Annobon, 250 miles south-west of Principe. Here he took on provisions – water, oranges and about fifty hogs – paying for them with money and small arms. He now decided for Madagascar, probably via the traditional route – Vasco da Gama's – south-west to the coast of Brazil and then, in the latitude of Buenos Aires, south-east into the powerful West Wind Drift by which he would clear the Cape. This course would allow him to avoid the southerly currents along the African coast and keep the *Fancy*'s location unknown to the Dutch and Portuguese. Early in 1695, they arrived at south-western Madagascar, probably near Augustin Bay, a favourite stop since mid-century for European ships *en route* to the Indies. The area afforded good water, abundance of edibles, and a populace happy to supply the English; in return for small arms and powder, the pirates took a hundred bullocks. After a voyage of about 4,300 miles from Annobon, in a crowded ship and through the tropical summer, it was time to feast – on Danish brandy and the roast beef of Madagascar. Later there would be time to clean the *Fancy*'s hull in preparation for the pursuits and escapes to come.

The feast ended a month later when Every sailed for the Comores off the north-west tip of Madagascar. Sometime after stocking up on water, fresh fruits, vegetables and hogs at Johanna (Anjouan) and taking forty volunteers from a French 'pirating junk', he was told by the natives that three East Indiamen had come to anchor on the other side of the island. Suddenly, in the words of the cabin boy John Elston

two of [them] appeared in sight and both came within two gunn shot which made us to sigh and run from thence.[16]

Every ran for the open sea; they gave chase, but the improvements made at Fernando Po allowed the *Fancy* to outsail its pursuers. He now ranged to the north-west as far as Kenya and then returned to Johanna. This two-month period of going and coming appears, at first glance, a sign of aimlessness, but Every had a plan. He expected the Muslim treasure fleet to emerge from the Red Sea in August to catch the westerly monsoon winds. Until then his task was to preserve ship and crew.

In mid-spring, 1695, he ended the period of waiting. After increasing his forces to 162 with fifty-two French volunteers taken on in the Comores, he sailed north towards the Red Sea. A month later the *Fancy* appeared off Cape Guardafui at the entrance to the Gulf of Aden, a voyage of 1,800 miles, nearly out of provisions but on the verge of fulfilling the purpose of its cruise. (See Illustration 35)

Meanwhile, the East Indiaman *Benjamin* had come into Johanna and found an extraordinary open letter left there by Every:

> To all English Commanders lett this Satisfye that I was Riding here att this Instant in ye Ship fancy man of Warr formerly the Charles of ye Spanish Expedition who departed from Croniae ye 7th of May. 94: Being and am now in A Ship of 46 guns 150 Men & bound to Seek our fortunes I have Never as Yett Wronged any English or Dutch nor never Intend while I am Commander. Wherefore as I Commonly Speake wth all Ships I Desire who ever Comes to ye perusal of this to take this Signall that if you or aney whome you may informe are desirous to know wt wee are att a Distance then make your Antient Vp in a Ball or Bundle and hoyst him att ye Mizon Peek ye Mizon Being furled I shall answere wth ye same & Never Molest you: for my men are hungry Stout and Resolute: & should they Exceed my Desire I cannott help my selfe.
>
> as Yett
>
> An Englishman's friend
>
> At Johanna February 28th, 1694/5 HENRY EVERY
> Here is 160 od french Armed men now att Mohilla who waits for Opportunity of getting aney ship, take Care of your Selves.[17]

One commentator has characterised this letter as a 'curiously muddled compound of patriotism and piratical bravado'.[18] I think it, rather, a shrewd tactic to avoid conflict with the only force in the Indian Ocean capable of effectively opposing the *Fancy*, the heavily armed ships of the East India Company. The letter also conveys the commander's distance from his men; his fear of losing control over them reflects the caution and moderation he had shown so far in the cruise of the *Fancy*.

Near Cape Guardafui, Every's company was supplied by the natives with food and drink. As the ship moved west along the coast of present-day Somalia, however, they encountered resistance. When the people of Mayd refused to do business with them, the pirates burnt their town and, in an act of religious bigotry that began a pattern of outrages against Muslims, blew up their mosque.[19] (The Cape of Good Hope, it was said, was where an Englishman leaves his conscience.) Not long after Mayd, the *Fancy* met two small privateers fitted out in the American colonies and bent on the same game. Captain Richard Want was an 'old sportsman' determined to recoup the money he had squandered in Carolina and Pennsylvania after his last pirate cruise. Bearing a commission against the French from the notoriously corrupt Governor Cadwallader Jones of the Bahamas, he had left Delaware early in January 1694 with sixty men in the sloop *Dolphin*.[20] Captain Joseph Faro in the *Portsmouth Adventure* was from Rhode Island also with a crew of sixty. Every, Want and Faro agreed to sail together to the Strait of Bab el Mandab, there to wait in concert for the 'Moors'.

In June 1695 the pirate squadron anchored at Barim, or 'Bab's Key', an island in the middle of the Strait. Here Want sent twenty-two French crewmen aboard the *Fancy*, bringing its strength to 184. In one or two days, three more small pirate ships – all from the American north-east – arrived at Barim. William Mayes, bearing a legitimate commission against the French, commanded the *Pearl*, a brigantine out of Rhode Island with thirty to forty men. Thomas Wake, a seasoned pirate once pardoned in King James II's reign, came up in the *Susanna* fitted out in Boston and Rhode Island with ten guns and seventy men.[21] The most renowned of Every's fellow captains was Thomas Tew in the sloop *Amity*, eight guns and sixty men. After his great Red Sea robbery of 1693, Tew had enriched his Rhode Island backers and secured another privateering commission the following year from Governor Benjamin Fletcher of New York. The pirate captains 'agreed on and signed Articles to share & share alike', but despite Tew's fame and experience, it was Every they chose as admiral.[22] He would command six ships and over 440 men.

The flotilla waited patiently at Barim to ambush the ships returning from Mocha (on the coast of present-day Yemen) to Surat, India,
'a prosperous city with the largest commercial marine in the Indian
Ocean'. Every year a host of Indian and Portuguese merchants bearing fabrics, indigo, spices, tobacco, medicines, fine porcelains, '[ivory]
ornaments, figurines, and other bric-a-brac', would travel across the
Arabian Sea and through the Strait of Bab al Mandab. Their mission
was to carry pilgrims to Mecca and to trade with the Turks, Arabs and
Armenians who, for a century, had come each spring to Mocha. The
Mocha fleet took home great amounts of specie in gold and silver,
elephant tusks, quicksilver, aloe, myrrh, frankincense, saffron, dates,
almonds and other fruit.[23] Trading ended in August so that the merchants might take advantage of the south-west monsoon winds on
their return home. The fleet was most vulnerable during this voyage
as each ship sought to be first with its wares at Surat and other Indian
ports. Spread out for hundreds of miles in open water, they could not
be protected by the few well-armed ships.

After waiting anxiously for a month, the pirates got word that the
convoy had already sailed, passing them in the night! The pirate captains
met hurriedly and voted to pursue, but first they ordered their ships
more efficiently. The leaky *Dolphin* was burnt and its crew of sixty sent
mostly to Every, increasing his company to about 240. The *Fancy* sailed
so well that even with the *Pearl* in tow, only Faro's *Portsmouth Adventure*
could keep pace with it. They never saw Tew and the *Amity* again,
although the *Susanna* managed to come up late in the battle.[24] (See
Illustration 36) It took the pirates two weeks to catch up with their
prey. Uncertainty, short provisions, and the stench of hundreds in tight
quarters had made the pursuit a test of will. Finally, on 7 September
1695, the *Fancy*, *Pearl*, and *Portsmouth Adventure* outran part of the fleet
off Cape St John north of Bombay, struck sail, and waited.

Next day, in the mists of early dawn, the *Fath Mahmamadi*, a ship of
two to three hundred tons, passed innocently 'within about a pistol
shot' of the *Fancy*, an easy mark for its primed and hungry crew. The
Fancy opened with a broadside and small shot, the *Fath Mahmamadi*
answered with three rounds, but then thought better of it, struck its
colours, and was carried towards Cape Diu. According to John Dann,

a mariner from Rochester, they found in her silver and gold worth £50,000–60,000.[25]

Pleased as they were by this treasure, what happened next must have taken their breath away: shortly after coming to anchor, a look-out spotted the *Ganj-i-sawai*, an enormous trader owned by none other than the Grand Mughal Aurangzeb, emperor of Muslim India. At 1,600 tons, with eighty guns, 800 returning pilgrims, and 400 soldiers, the *Ganj-i-sawai* surely inspired equal parts joy and fear.

Once in range, the *Ganj-i-sawai* began the battle by firing her chase guns at the *Fancy*. Then it turned to fire broadsides, but because of the great disparity in size, its cannon balls sailed harmlessly over the English ship. The *Fancy* responded with its own broadsides aimed at sails and rigging and soon disabled the Indian's mainmast. Every continued for more than an hour to bombard the enemy at long range until he realised that the *Pearl* and *Portsmouth Adventure* were afraid to board the huge ship according to his plan; he would have to do it alone. He did not relish this – Indian soldiers were renowned for their swordsman-ship. As Every came board-to-board with the *Ganj-i-sawai*, however, the *Pearl* took heart and advanced too. The Indians raked them with their muskets '& threw fireworks into us to set our sails &c on fire'.[26]

Before they could climb its steep sides, the pirates heard a tremen-dous explosion on the imperial ship. One of its cannon had burst, sending shrapnel in all directions, instantly killing many. While the survivors struggled to put out the fires or ran below in terror, the pirates took advantage of the confusion, scrambled aboard from port and starboard, and subdued the remaining defenders. To those who were hiding, they shouted promises of 'good Quarter'.[27] Twenty-five of the Indians were killed, twenty wounded; on the pirates' side none were dead and only one or two wounded.[28] (See Illustration 37)

This astonishing victory by fewer than 250 pirates was profoundly humiliating to the Mughals. They explained it by accusing Captain Muhammad Ibrahim of cowardice, reporting that he had run below in the thick of the battle and urged his concubines to don turbans and fight like men. On his own part, Ibrahim had an equally fanciful excuse for his failure: he claimed that he was attacked by 1,200 pirates but resisted for five to six hours and that 'many of the enemy were sent to hell'. That hell was the place from which this enemy came was the lesson of the battle's aftermath. Passengers were stripped and tortured to reveal their wealth and women were raped.

> there happened to be a great Umbraws Wife (as Wee hear) related to the king, returning from her Pilgrimage to Mecha, in her old age. She they abused very much, and forced severall other Women, which Caused one person of Quality, his Wife and Nurse, to kill themselves to prevent the Husbands seeing them (and their being) ravished.[29]

The contemporary historian Muhammad Hāshim Kāfi Kāhn was told that the pirates held the *Ganj-i-sawai* for a whole week, a report factually wrong but, if it came from a survivor, psychologically understandable. The pirates' atrocities are consistent with their earlier brutality towards the 'Moors'. They were no doubt motivated by religious and racial bigotry as well as revenge for their bad reception on the Somali coast.

We do not know precisely what happened during the two or three days the pirates ransacked the *Ganj-i-sawai*. According to the records, young John Sparkes was the only pirate publicly to express regret for his cruelties aboard the great ship. In the behaviour of the pirate commander, however, we may be able to find a glimmer of decency. The thirteen-year-old cabin boy, Philip Middleton, reported that '...all the *Charles's* men, except Every, boarded [the *Fath Mahmamadi* and *Ganj-i-sawai*] by Turns'.[30] It would have been out of character for him to join in the crew's bestiality, for he would need their respect in the long voyage home. If Every stayed aboard the *Fancy*, he must have recalled his earlier words, 'my men are hungry Stout and Resolute: & should they Exceed my Desire I cannott help my selfe'. (See Illustration 36)

Now that the *Fancy* had 'made its voyage', they needed to get out of harm's way. To secure their wealth – probably about £200,000 in gold, silver and jewels (currently, about £18,477,000) – Every advised that they sail for the Bahamas where they might buy protection. Consequently, the *Ganj-i-sawai* was released on 11 September, and the fleet went to Rajapore, 160 miles south of Bombay, to refit, provision and divide the booty. It appears that a full share was £1,000, but some men received £600 or £500, 'according as the company thought they deserved'.[31] To men used to wages of less than £2 per month, this sharing was a wondrous thing indeed, even for boys like Phillip Middleton and John Elston, who were given £100 apiece. Every had kept his promise to 'carry them where they should get money enough'.

After Rajapore, the *Fancy*, *Pearl* and *Susanna* left for the Cape of Good Hope, putting in first at the Diego Royes Islands and then, in November 1695, at the French island of Réunion (or Mascareen). Here the French and Danes left the *Fancy* and Every resumed the disguise of an interloper in the slave trade by buying nearly ninety slaves. Pirates sometimes used slaves to do the heavy work aboard ship, and their value as 'the most consistent item of trade' ensured that the pirates could buy what they wanted in the New World without using their 'Arabian gold' and betraying themselves as 'Red Sea men'.[32] The *Fancy*'s second rounding of the Cape was as routine as its first. Every avoided the Dutch Cape and Britain's St Helena Island, common re-victualling points on the East Indiamen's return voyage, even though this was to be the longest leg of their cruise, over 5,200 miles. The *Fancy*'s next stop was Ascension Island, midway between the African and South American landmasses. Ascension was uninhabited and largely barren, but the pirates filled their hold with fifty of the sea turtles that come ashore to lay their eggs from January to April. They departed in March 1696, leaving behind about seventeen men, the last of those who rejected Every's leadership or feared returning to the British king's dominions.[33]

Every kept to his strategy of avoiding land on the 4,800 mile voyage from Ascension to the Bahamas. Consequently, with 113 men and 90 slaves aboard, the *Fancy* was down to a two-day supply of food when it arrived late in April at Royal Island off Eleuthera, fifty miles from New Providence (modern Nassau). Knowing the Bahamas' reputation for conniving with pirates, Every sent one of his quartermasters, Henry Adams, to Governor Nicholas Trott with a proposal that the ship berth unmolested in New Providence Harbour in return for a large bribe. Trott accepted and a collection was quickly made 'afore the Mast', whereby 100 men contributed:

20 pieces of eight (£4) a man and the Captain 40, to present the Governor with, besides Elephants Teeth and some other things to the value of about £1000'.[34]

With this deal in hand, Every took the *Fancy* into New Providence and gave her to Major Perient Trott. Governor Trott later defended himself before the Board of Trade against bribery charges by claiming his decision to welcome the *Fancy* was just and prudent. According to Trott, Every had disguised his identity by using the alias 'Henry Bridgeman' and assuring the governor that they 'had done nothing but what they were ready to answer and were willing to surrender themselves to Government'. Moreover, with 'not above 60 Men at Providence in all', the *Fancy* was too strong to oppose and urgently needed to defend against a French invasion.[35] Trott maintained that when he received the Lords Justices' proclamation against Every (dated 17 July 1696), he immediately moved to arrest 'as many as possible of the men... in the hope that evidence might be found before the Assizes'. Indeed, a few of Every's crewmen were tried in 1697 but probably to clear their names when sufficient evidence was lacking, an old trick of colonial courts friendly towards the pirates.[36]

Even with the governor's protection, most of the pirates moved on as quickly as possible. The majority took passage for Bermuda, the Carolinas, Pennsylvania, New Jersey, New England and Virginia, where they often found the officials pliable. The first ship to sail directly for Great Britain was the *Isaac*, which had carried sixteen or seventeen pirates in June 1696 to Achill, Westport and Galway. The story of Every's escape in the other ship illustrates more fully the arch-pirate's craftiness. Still calling himself Henry Bridgeman, Every set out with nineteen others for remote northern Ireland in the sloop *Seaflower* commanded by Captain Faro and landed at Dunfanaghy, County Donegal. Here they divided in two, one group heading for Dublin, the other – Every, Dann, the wife of Henry Adams, five men and two boys – taking the road towards Letterkenny.[37] The second group had gone only six miles from Dunfanaghy when Every and Mrs Adams left to pursue their own route to safety.

By the middle of July 1696 the details of Every's astonishing crimes were thrilling the capital and mortifying the East India Company, whose trade with Mughal India was embargoed and station at Surat cut off by imperial troops. In addition to shocks abroad, attacks on the Company at home by interlopers who resented its monopoly in the Far East came to a head in the late 1690s. The company understood that its very life depended upon convincing Aurangzeb that it had not collaborated with Every. The Company's strategy was first to have the pirates proclaimed and pardons and rewards offered to cooperative suspects and then to take command of the investigation and spend whatever it took to get convictions. By mid-August it had formed a sub-committee of its directors (including Isaac Houblon, younger brother of Sir James) to oversee the search for those named in the proclamation of 17 July. The hunt was worldwide, but the most productive areas were America, the West Indies and Great Britain itself. When suspects began to surface in Ireland and England, the company sent out agents, or 'messengers', to bring them to Dublin, Exeter, Chester or London, where they were first interrogated and then handed over to the government. Meanwhile, the Company's Committee of Law Suits was assembling a record of the evidence in preparation for trial.[38]

Every's escape route after Esquire Rays is unknown. We have only rumours, some perhaps started by him to throw off his hunters. Our source for the most credible is John Dann who, on 28 July, was passing through St Albans when he met Mrs Adams about to board a coach. She said that she had been with 'Captaine Bridgman' at Donaghadee, County Down, and was going to him now, but she refrained from telling where he was. It is plausible that Every would have sought anonymity in London, but Dann doubted her story since Every had told him that 'he would goe to Exeter when he came into England'. With the hounds on Every's trail and a £500 reward on his head, looks of suspicion and fear no doubt passed between these two on the road before the coach stand.[39]

On 30 July John Dann stopped at an inn on the way to his home in Rochester. The next morning, while he was out of his room, the maid noticed that his waistcoat had a rather large sag. She examined it more closely and was astonished to find many coins in its pockets and lining. Before long Dann was under arrest, his coat in the Mayor of Rochester's custody, and his horde counted – more than 2,260

sequins, worth today about £93,300![40] Faced with hanging or informing, Dann chose on 3 August to cooperate with the authorities in
London. A few days later, Phillip Middleton and William Phillips surrendered to the pardon and, together with Dann, gave the government
what appeared to be an ironclad case against their captain and mates.

Despite the Company's energy, organisation and funding, and the
government's sustained efforts, a pitifully small number of the roughly
260 men who sailed into battle against the *Ganj-i-sawai* were ever
brought to justice. There were about thirty-six of Every's men in
Ireland and England when the dragnet began to tighten in August
1696, but only fifteen were brought to trial and six convicted between
October 1696 and December 1699. The situation in the colonies was
much worse. About seventy-five sought refuge there, but only seven
were tried (1697–1705) and all of these acquitted. This embarrassing
record is explained by the venality of colonial officials, the perennial
hunger of the colonies for specie and cheap pirate goods, and the
requirement before 1700 that pirates be tried in England. Colonial
protection of the pirates was especially flagrant in Philadelphia, where
Every's men freely walked the streets and boasted of their deeds 'publicly over their cups'. Acting governor William Markham was on social
terms with them, his daughter had married one, and he had thoroughly compromised the judiciary: 'when Avery's men were here in
1697', an American pamphleteer wrote in 1703, 'the Quaking justices
were for letting them live quietly, or else they were bailed easily'.[41]

Making do with what they had, the authorities decided to give the
Grand Mughal and the world a potent symbol of British justice. It was
for this reason, I believe, that the government disallowed the Company's
request to mount a private prosecution. A state trial and execution would
undergird the tottering East India Company and have a like bracing effect
on foreign relations. (See Illustration 38, 39) The government had every
reason to be confident; its evidence was strong and it could present the
trial in broad international as well as self-interested terms: 'this piracy', the
King's advocate would declare, 'was begun in Europe, carried on through
Africa, and ended in the remotest Indies… all the world is concerned in
this trial'. Moreover, as Lemuel Gulliver states in his critique of British
justice, 'State-Tryals… ever… terminate as the Judges thought fit to direct'.[42]

The first trial began on 19 October 1696 at the Old Bailey before a court duly commissioned to hear piracy cases under Henry VIII's statute. Symbols of admiralty jurisdiction were prominently displayed in the courtroom, a short silver oar in front of the judges and 'three Anchors... on a cloath above the Kings Arms, over the Bench'.[43] At the head of the court twenty powerful men of law, commerce, government and the military were on show. The presiding judge, Sir Charles Hedges, Lieutenant of the High Court of Admiralty, was flanked by Sir John Holt, Chief Justice of the King's Bench, Sir George Treby, Chief Justice of the Common Pleas, and six other prominent judges. Also in attendance were the First Lord of the Admiralty Sir Edward Russell, Admiral Sir George Rook, and the secretaries of the navy. (See Illustration 40) The new alliance between Commerce and Government was represented by the most illustrious of James Houblon's brothers, Sir John Houblon, recently made a Lord of the Admiralty and the first president of the Bank of England. This brilliantly costumed group did not constitute a jury, but rather a dramatic tableau of might and right in the kingdom. They had come in force to celebrate a great national victory over evil and restraint of trade.

In stark contrast were the defendants, six shabby men smelling of their cells in Newgate a few yards away: Joseph Dawson, 39, from Yarmouth, Edward Forseith, 45, Newcastle on Tyne, and William May, 48, London, were professional seamen nearing the end of their working lives; William Bishop, 20, Devon, James Lewis, 25, London, and John Sparkes, 19, London, were young men recruited by Houblon from the trades or repatriated prisoners of war. Dawson had been an officer on the *Fancy*, a quartermaster, but 'old May', Capt. Gibson's former steward, was a favourite whom Every had called one of the 'true cocks of the game, and old sportsmen'.[44] They were charged with taking the *Ganj-i-sawai*, the crime that mattered above all to Aurangzeb. After the grand jury voted the indictment, only Joseph Dawson pleaded guilty and the other five went to trial. Dr Thomas Newton, judge advocate of the Admiralty, warned the petty jury in his opening that the defendants' actions threatened no less than 'the total loss of the Indian trade, and thereby the impoverishment of this kingdom'. A word to the wise, he thought, would be sufficient.

The 'wise', however, did not listen. Despite the strong evidence of Dann and Middleton, the jury acquitted the defendants. Very little information about this trial has survived because the government moved quickly to prevent an independent newspaper from printing it: 'We had prepared a more ample account of the Tryal of the Pyrates', revealed the *Post Man* (no.226, 17–20 October 1696),

> but in compliance with the prohibition of Authority have omitted it, there being a large account to be printed by their order.

Such an account was never published. (We do know from the court's official Latin record that to counter the prosecution's evidence, the accused called as character witnesses five officers of the Spanish Expedition Shipping, including William Dampier.) The verdict was an instance of *jury nullification* in the age-old struggle between the English jury and the bench, a struggle that grew especially heated in the seventeenth century as crown and Commonwealth alike used the courts to punish their enemies and required the bench to fine and imprison jurors who refused to convict. The Court of Common Pleas' ruling in favor of jurors who acquitted William Penn for illegal public worship (*Bushel's Case*) ended jury harassment in 1671, but, as we shall see, late-Stuart and Georgian judges found other effective means of controlling juries.

The men on the dais were apoplectic with rage at 'the dishonourable proceedings' of the jury, accusing it of irrational bias. Indeed, the jury's composition gives support to their claim, for the defendants made sure at *voir dire* that no supporters of the company were seated, but they accepted at least one juror who had been prosecuted for interloping by the East India Company along with another who was his relative. The charge of bias cuts both ways, however. Sir James Houblon's interests were represented on the grand jury by a major investor in the Spanish Expedition Shipping and by the relative of another investor.[45] The court thus came to reflect the current bitter conflict between the company and those who wished to break its legal monopoly of the lucrative India trade. The company was better provided than its enemies, however. Among its friends were Sir Charles Hedges, cousin of the former chief of the company's operations in

Bengal, and Sir John Holt, a very successful former counsel to the company. The charge of judicial conflict of interest was never raised by the accused, and after the verdict of 19 October, the only relevant legal question became one of double jeopardy.

To the government, the verdict was an intolerable national scandal. Twelve days later, the prosecution won a new indictment that the six had conspired to take the *Charles II* with piratical intent. This was a less controversial charge but potentially troublesome, for it relied on the notion that the accused wilfully engaged in mutiny to further the commission of a crime of which they had already on one count been found not guilty. There were, of course, other, less culpable incentives for supporting the mutiny: the sailors' hardships at Coruña, their fear of being betrayed to the Spanish and French, the impoverishment of their families and their need to find lawful employment with a likelihood of gain.

The aim of Judge Hedges's long opening charge to the grand jury was to condemn the former petty jury and rouse the one before him to vote with 'a true English spirit'. He instructed the jury that 'especially in the cases of great and public offences, you are to use your utmost endeavours that justice, the support of government, be not obstructed by any partial proceedings'. If, on the other hand, they emulate the offending jury, 'the barbarous nations will reproach us as being a harbour, receptacle, and a nest of pirates; and our friends will wonder to hear that the enemies of merchants and of mankind, should find a sanctuary in this ancient place of trade'. Wary that his words might be taken as partisan, Hedges shrewdly deflected that criticism upon the former jury.

> I hope what hath been said upon this unexpected occasion, will not be looked upon as intended to influence any jury; I am sure it is far from being so designed... the judge, as well as the juryman then best discharges his duty, when he proceeds without favour or affection, hatred or ill will, or any partial respect whatsoever.

He ended by encouraging the jury to 'support... the navigation, trade, wealth, strength, reputation, and glory of this nation'.[46]

Hedges may appear, by our lights, deceitful when he denies trying to influence the jury. But his words were intended less to cloak his quite obvious opinion about the defendants' guilt as to project the image of a reformed judge, one who has repudiated the autocratic practices of the Tudor and early-Stuart bench. Chief Justice Holt was much less temperate and tactful. When, at the very beginning of the trial, he learnt that some of the earlier jurors were still on the panel, he publicly berated the court clerk: 'If you have returned any of the former jury, you have not done well; for that verdict was a dishonour to the justice of the nation'. This remark was echoed almost immediately by Dr Thomas Littleton, Advocate General of the Admiralty, in his address to the new petty jury:

> We shall therefore proceed to call our witnesses, not doubting but that you will act like honest men, for the honour and welfare of your country without having any respect to the dishonourable proceedings of the former jury.[47]

How could three intelligent and learned men claim impartiality while at the same time engaging in a concerted effort to damn the accused before any witnesses could be heard? The answer lies partly in the irrationality of the first jury's finding: Hedges, Holt and Littleton believed that the verdict was based not on the facts but on 'partiality' towards a political faction. On the other hand, they looked upon themselves as impartially affording the accused all the rights and protections of British law, even including the 'right' of jury nullification, the practice of bringing in a verdict contrary to fact or law. If they conveyed their opinions from the bench, it was to give the jury the benefit of their cumulative trial experience. Moreover, their kind of court did not require judicial neutrality. In the early modern period the felony trial was not considered an adversarial exercise in which the judge stands as umpire between two opposing sides, but rather a mutual search for the truth in which the judge plays an active role in eliciting and evaluating evidence. The judge's expression of opinion was a form of jury guidance and control felt necessary to protect the community as a whole from 'dangerous verdicts', especially in light of the double jeopardy rule and the absence of a consistent appeals process. Finally, strong guidance from the bench was seen as preferable to the form of jury control prior to *Bushel's Case*.

In keeping with the non-adversarial nature of the court, defence lawyers were rare in felony trials, limited to technical matters, and not allowed to introduce or sum up their cases. There was no government counsel either, except in state trials where they could question witnesses and make opening and, sometimes, closing statements. It fell to prisoners to defend themselves, to raise questions of law and procedure, cross-examine prosecution witnesses, call and examine their own. Of course, most defendants were either too ignorant or too much in awe of the court to mount even a mediocre defence so that they were supposed to be assisted, at least on technical matters, by the 'impartial' judges. This feature of criminal trials is illustrated when one of the defendants tried to stop the state from calling a witness who was, at the time, under indictment for treason: 'I do not understand law; I hope your lordship will advise us'. Justice Holt replied, 'I will do you all right', and allowed the witness because he had not yet become a convicted felon.[48] Setting aside Holt's unintended ambiguity, this exchange reflects the relationship supposed to exist between judge and defendant. Defence lawyers were not needed if the judge would do them right.

The objection to a prosecution witness shows something else about the current defendants; although they pretended – like Henry Morgan – not to understand the law, they knew enough to obstruct, if not to halt, the government's onslaught. Every's men were more astute than most defendants.

Courts acknowledged that mere presence on a pirate ship did not prove one guilty of piracy. 'Forced' men (typically doctors, musicians and craftsmen) or those without the power to act freely, such as boys, slaves and indentured apprentices, were innocent at law if they acted at their masters' command. The accused claimed to have been either forced or uninvolved in the taking of the *Charles II*: one was asleep during the mutiny, one was below decks, three were ordered to board the *Charles* to subdue the conspirators and were then coerced into joining them. In only one case was there direct testimony that a defendant had refused an order to resist the mutiny. There was, however, a good deal of circumstantial evidence of the defendants' willingness to join in piracy after the mutiny. Anticipating this evidence, Hedges expanded on the fundamental concept of criminal intent:

If the mariners of any ship shall violently dispossess the master, and afterwards carry away the ship itself, or any of the goods, or tackle, apparel or furniture, with a felonious intention, in any place where the lord Admiral hath, or pretends to have jurisdiction, this is also robbery and piracy.

Moreover, proof of 'felonious intention' lies in subsequent action:

The intention will, in these cases, appear by considering the end for which the fact was committed; and the end will be known, if the evidence shall shew you what hath been done.[50]

A reasonable mode of proof if the defendants had not already been acquitted of piracy against the *Ganj-i-sawai*. To bring the facts of the former trial – if not the verdict – into evidence, the prosecutors asked John Dann and Phillip Middleton to narrate the *Fancy*'s entire course from Coruña to New Providence.

At the very beginning of the trial, William Bishop signalled that the defendants had anticipated and intended to resist this move. He asked to have the first indictment read before he pleaded to the second in order to recall precisely what they had been acquitted of and to remind the jury of the acquittal. When, a few minutes later, Dann started to describe events at the Isle of May, several prisoners rose to challenge the admissibility of that testimony, implying that it dealt with crimes allegedly committed after the mutiny and not laid in the indictment. Both challenges were disallowed, but they had made their point with the jury. Henceforth the jury seems to have looked sharply for direct evidence of what the defendants knew and when they knew it. For example, one juryman rose to ask Middleton if any of the accused could have heard Every '[give] leave to any to go ashore that were not willing to go with them'.[51] And just before announcing the verdict, the foreman asked to hear again 'any evidence to prove that John Sparkes consented to the running away of the ship'. Holt responded peevishly that

he was with them at the carrying off the ship, and at the taking of the several prizes, and had his share afterwards. What is consent? Can men otherwise demonstrate their consent, than by their actions?

Juryman. But we understand, my lord, that he was tried upon his consenting to carry away the ship.

In the absence of direct evidence that Sparkes consented to seize the
Charles II, the judge would substitute later bad acts unspecified in the
indictment and, in one case, covered by an acquittal.

L.C.J. *Holt.* What do you mean by consenting? If a ship be carried away
with force from the captain, divers piracies are committed with her, one
continues aboard and receives a share of the profit of the several piracies;
is not that an evidence of consent to the piratical design?
.... When a ship is run away with, and people are aboard that ship so run
away with, that proves their consent, unless they can produce evidence to
the contrary.[51]

The prosecutors' first indicting on the taking of the *Ganj-i-sawai* placed
them on 31 October in the awkward position of relying on evidence of
consent to piracy that the jury had rejected on 19 October. Equally dubious, from a twenty-first-century perspective, is Holt's assumption that the
accused has the legal burden of proving himself innocent if found aboard
'a ship... run away with'. But judges were not required until the nineteenth century to advise juries that the accused is innocent until proven
guilty and were reluctant to disallow irrelevant and prejudicial evidence.

The most puzzling aspect of the trial, however, is the prisoners'
refusal to make their sufferings at Coruña the heart of their defence. In
their final statements, one of them mentioned the wage dispute and
another the belief of several mutineers that they were to return home,
but only in passing.[52] Instead, they insisted throughout either that they
had been inactive or forced to participate in the mutiny. Although their
legitimate grievances undermined the charge of 'felonious intent' and
had been documented before the Privy Council in 1694, the men
apparently had no hope that they would be taken seriously.[53]
Consequently, the jury never heard a coherent narrative that would
have distinguished their original intent, to free themselves from involuntary, unpaid service and bad living conditions in the Spanish
Expedition, from their subsequent attacks on Muslim shipping.

It was the rule that because the accused had introduced new information during their defence, the prosecution was allowed to speak last.[54] Accordingly, no less a figure than King William's Solicitor General, Sir John Hawles, rose to emphasise that piracy was a crime 'against the law of nations' and that once taken, the *Charles II* was put by the defendants 'to very bad purposes'.

> We do not produce this to prove them guilty, but to shew that they made use of this ship to this very purpose.[55]

Given the conventional understanding of 'felonious intent', this was a distinction without a difference. At last, it was the chief justice's duty to sum up the evidence. Justice Holt did a masterful job of retelling the story of the mutiny so as to heighten the evidence against the accused and second the Solicitor General: 'you have heard what was done in the whole progress of this wicked design; every one of these men had their share'.[56] Holt concluded by calling for a reasonable weighing of the evidence and a verdict according to the conscience of each juror.

> If you are not *satisfied in your consciences* that the evidence is sufficient to find these men guilty, in God's name acquit them. But if you are *satisfied in the sufficiency of the evidence* to convict them, you must find them guilty.[57]

This standard of the satisfied conscience of the jury was becoming the norm in capital trials at common law, in part because of the growing belief among contemporary Enlightenment philosophers that human reason was capable of coming not to absolute truth, but to a 'moral certainty' regarding natural and social phenomena. Several decades later, the legal community would formalise this faith in the modern standard of proof in criminal trials, 'guilty beyond a reasonable doubt'.[58]

Despite the flaws that jurymen had discovered in the government's case, all of the accused were found guilty in 'a very little time'. The day of their conviction, the six were indicted on new counts of piracy against the *Fath Mahmamadi* and the two Danish privateers. Six days later, they were tried and convicted and all were sentenced to be hanged, but Dawson – the only one to confess and throw himself on the mercy of the court – was soon granted a reprieve.

At Execution Dock on 25 November, the Ordinary of Newgate Paul Lorrain and the assembled crowd were satisfied with the final scene in the drama of justice; each of the five behaved with admirable contrition, lamenting his part in 'those crying and bloody Cruelties, in the *East-Indies*'. Old Edward Forseith, for example, provided the audience with the kind of emblematic moral wisdom they longed to hear from the gallows:

> [he] truly own'd that besides the Guilt of his Offences, and the present capital Punishment, his Wicked Life, attended with many Hardships and Hazards he had undergone in his Robberies, was little less than a Punishment; for wickedness (let it prosper never so much) brings great many troubles and afflictions along with it.

The least commonplace and most personal confession came from the youngest, John Sparkes:

> [he] exprest a due sense of his wicked Life, in particular to the most horrid Barbarities that he had committed, which though upon the Persons of Heathens and Infidels, such as the foremention'd poor *Indians*, so inhumanly rifled and treated so unmercifully; declaring, that his Eyes were now open to his Crimes, and that he justly suffer'd Death for such Inhumanity, much more then his Injustice and Robbery, in Stealing and Running away with one of his Majesties Ships, which was of the two his lesser concern.[59]

The 'dying speeches' of the five appeared in print immediately after their death. In the last weeks of 1696, the Ludgate Street bookseller John Everingham, probably under close government supervision, issued a lengthy report of the court proceedings, which, although it lacked details of the first trial, contained a full account of the second. We can be reasonably sure that several copies of this pamphlet were put on the next company ship to India to moderate the rage of the Grand Mughal. (See Illustration 41)

In the years to come only a few more were punished for crimes in the *Fancy*. Dann, Middleton, Dawson and some others were pardoned and kept in reserve to testify against new suspects as they were found. In 1706, after Phillip Middleton had finished a ten-year stint as an informant and had been educated at the expense of the East India Company, he was appointed purser on the ship *Halifax* bound for Madras and Bengal.[60] One imagines him frequently looking up from the ledger to recall his great adventures aboard the *Fancy*.

The fate of Henry Every remains a mystery to this day. He disappeared completely from the public record, but, because there were from time to time unconfirmed 'sightings', he was routinely disqualified from subsequent offers of pardon. The evidence suggests that Every had, indeed, retired from piracy and found a hideout in England. London was the place in which to attract the least attention, but in the summer of 1988 when I began to follow his paper trail, I had a conversation in a Dartmouth pub that made me incline towards Devon. I told the barman of my research and of Every's comment about taking refuge in Exeter. 'Oh, ay', he replied at once, 'we would have heard the redcoats coming'.

The man himself vanished, but stories about him did not. They were to be heard in popular songs, seen on the London stage, and read in chapbooks, histories and novels. Two broadside ballads were published by 1696, one a conventional warning that death is the doom of villainy– '*let Pyrates then take care*'[61]; the other a lively, heretical celebration of 'Bold Captain Avery', a modern Robin Hood at sea who repudiates his 'false-hearted Nation' and takes what he needs on his own moral authority.

> My Commission is large, and I made it my self,
> And the Capston shall stretch it full larger by half...

The song ends with a black mass that seals the bond among the pirates and bids the bourgeois shudder in fear:

No Quarters to give, no Quarters to take,
We save nothing living, alas 'tis too late;
For we are now sworn by the Bread and the Wine,
More serious we are than any Divine.

To this volatile blend of independence and terror, the ballad owed its survival in various forms until the early twentieth century.[62]

The mythic Avery introduced by the ballad was elaborated in a chapbook of 1709, *The Life and Adventures of Capt. John Avery*. Its hero takes a great prize in which he finds and marries an Indian princess and rules a pirate community on Madagascar that evolves into a just and powerful state. (See Illustration 42) In 1712 this story was brought to the stage in *The Successful Pyrate* by the professional playwright Charles Johnson. He saw in 'Arviragus' a rude but noble leader who derives his power from his own heroic will, not 'from a long Line of lazy Ancestors'.[63] The historian Captain Charles Johnson was so attracted to the burgeoning myth that he devoted a long chapter in the *General History* (II, ch. 1) to it, a political fantasy in which an idealistic Captain Misson rules over *Libertalia*, the new name for Madagascar, a Lockean utopia that guarantees freedom for all, democratic government, and property rights. (See Illustration 43)

A less inflated version of Every found his way into realistic fiction in Daniel Defoe's *King of the Pyrates* (1719), an exciting novella that distorts the historical facts in order to emphasise the hero's self-control and wit in the midst of constant danger. Defoe's 'Avery' captures a truth about the real pirate, who, as we have seen, was a shrewd pragmatist ever ready to take on a new shape as circumstances required – veteran mariner at London; artful conspirator at Coruña; bold man of fortune at Johanna; Mr Henry Bridgeman, slaver at New Providence; at Dunfanaghy a passenger of Captain Faro; finally at Donaghadee and London, only a man travelling with his wife. (See Illustration 44)

William Kidd:

'Because I Would Not Turn Pirate, You Rogues, You Would Make Me One'

Where Every was bold but elusive, William Kidd was a large and combative man who would break before he would bend. Kidd was the last of the famous pirates who clung to the falsehood that his actions were sanctioned by a lawful privateering commission. Sent out in 1695 to intercept and capture Captains Tew, Mayes, Wake and Ireland, known to be on the prowl in the Indian Ocean, he ended up himself a pirate but without the success of the principal villains he hunted. His story would have attracted only moderate attention if his cruise had not been financed by prominent Whig politicians. After the revelation of his crimes, Tories jeeringly nicknamed the Whig ministry the 'Corporation of Pirates'.[1] His notoriety undermined the ministers, but its lasting effect was to fuel efforts to devise keener tools to fight piracy in the new age of colonial expansion.

Little is known about Kidd's origins. Tradition has it that he was born about 1645 in Greenock, Scotland, but it is well documented that by the summer of 1695, when he sailed to London on a trading voyage, he had earned the reputation of a brave commander and responsible burgher of New York City. He had distinguished himself as a privateer in the West Indies during the war with France (1689–97) and fought to suppress Jacob Leisler's rebellion against crown authority in New York (1689–91), for which services he had been honoured by the provincial assemblies of New York and Antigua.

Kidd's purpose in London went beyond the disposal of his cargo, for he aimed to secure a new privateering commission against the French. Soon after arriving, he joined forces with Robert Livingston of Albany, a fellow Scot and influential member of the New York assembly whose connections and skill at political intrigue he needed; it would not be easy to overcome the Admiralty's reluctance to create new privateers during the scarcity of able seamen. Livingston, on his part, wanting to reduce the hazards to his investment in the East India trade, crafted a plan for a privateering cruise not only against the French, but also against the Indian Ocean pirates. The moment was ripe for such a venture: in a few months the capital would be gripped by fears of losing its most profitable trade upon news that the Grand Mughal held the East India Company liable for Every's piracies.

It was not long before Livingston won the support of Richard Coote, Earl of Bellomont, who brought Edward Russell and three more of William III's cabinet onboard. When Livingston recommended that Kidd command the privateer, the captain resisted, probably because of the harm it would do several New York acquaintances engaged in supplying the Madagascar pirates. But the lords were not to be denied; in a letter to Russell (now Earl of Orford), Kidd describes being treated to a hard sell at Bellomont's house in Dover Street:

> The Lord Bellomont told me he was to be Governor of New York, as well as of New England, and would protect me from any charge or accusation to be brought against me; and that he had powerful friends in the Government, who would not let me suffer any damage or prejudice either in England, or elsewhere.

I, notwithstanding, pressed to be excused, and to pursue my voyage to New York; whereupon the Lord Bellomont added threats to his wheedles, and told me I should not carry my own ship out of the river of Thames, unless I would accept the command of the ship to be fitted out.[2]

Fearful that 'Lord Bellomont might oppress me at New York if I disobliged him here', Kidd complied, but sensing his reluctance, Livingston took him on a tour of the noble houses belonging to Lords Somers, Romney, Russell and the Duke of Shrewsbury, principal secretary of state, 'for my satisfaction that those great men were concerned in the expedition, where he discoursed them, but would not suffer me to see or speak with any of them'. In the following weeks, the great men continued to reassure Kidd of their support and his impunity from criminal prosecution. Bellomont told him

that the noble lords... should stifle all complaints that should be made in England, and he himself would prevent all clamours in those parts where he was Governor by condemning all the goods and treasure I should bring in, and disposing of them privately, and satisfying the owners for such part as should be due to them.

Lords Orford and Romney twice 'promised to stand by me in all my undertakings'.[3]

There was yet another party interested in the project: King William had initially considered investing, but later declined; instead, he was promised ten per cent of the profits. (There is no documentary evidence that Kidd was told of the King's involvement, but it is easy to imagine Livingston's using it to put the captain's last doubts to rest.) How could a seaman from the fringes of empire not be overwhelmed by the London grandeur and power of his new friends? If Kidd is truthful about the promises he received from the mighty – and there is good reason to think he is – much of his later reckless behaviour loses its mystery: henceforth, the man would be guided by self-pride and a sense of invulnerability.[4]

At the end of the day, Bellomont, Livingston, Kidd and two wealthy merchants, Sir Edmund Harrison and Sir Richard Blackham, were joined in the partnership by four members of the Junto (as the Whig ministry was called) – Russell, Somers, Shrewsbury and Romney – their total investment coming to about £50,000.[5] The remaining difficulties were finessed by two skilful evasions of the law. A privateering commission against the French was granted on 11 December 1695, a few days after the *Adventure Galley* was launched at Castle's Yard in Deptford, but the Admiralty withheld a licence to take pirates pending the approval of a judge. To avoid dangerous delays, the partners applied directly to the crown and received a licence on 26 January 1696 from one of their own, Lord Keeper of the Great Seal Sir John Somers. An even more serious departure from practice was successfully negotiated by Lord Shrewsbury: on 27 May 1697 a royal grant was issued giving the partners exclusive ownership of all the pirate goods Kidd might seize.[6] This action encouraged the partners to go forwards by waving the Admiralty's share of prize money (fifteen per cent) and, more importantly, by preventing the rightful owners from reclaiming their goods. Of course, infringement of property rights for the public good – in this case, the protection of the East India trade – was an accepted practice, then as it is now, but it was highly suspect as a means of enriching the king and a few select politicians. The history of privateering and piracy is laced with such instances of conflict of interest.

It was agreed that the expedition's profits would be shared as follows: if the privateer's officers and men took the maximum allowed to them (twenty-five per cent) and the King his ten per cent, the nine partners would share sixty-five per cent, with Kidd and Livingston each receiving ten per cent, but Kidd was further encouraged by the proviso that if the profits should exceed £100,000, he would be given the ship outright. All the mariners – including Kidd – served on the same terms as ordinary privateersmen, 'no purchase, no pay'. (See Illustration 45)

Captain Kidd sailed for home in the *Adventure Galley* on 23 April, taking on the way a French fishing ship off Newfoundland, which, in accordance with his privateering instructions, he had condemned in a court of vice-admiralty at New York. He also used the time at home to get his affairs in order and increase his crew to 152. The outgoing Governor Benjamin Fletcher took a dim view of the company he assembled, informing the Board of Trade that they were:

men of desperate fortunes and necessities in expectation of getting vast treasure... that if he missed therof the design intended for which he has commission, 'twill not be in Kidd's power to govern such a horde of men under no pay'.[7]

It was not long before the euphoria of his privileged status began to wear off and Kidd started to appreciate the wisdom of Fletcher's prediction. After departing from New York early in September 1696, he provisioned only at the Madeira and Cape Verde Islands so that by 27 January 1697, when the ship anchored near Augustin Bay, Madagascar, its men were desperate for fresh food. Unlike Every, who brought nearly all of his men back in good condition, Kidd lost thirty to disease at Mohilla in the Comoro Islands, leaving a crew of 122. The replacements he found in the Comoros, like the men he hired in New York, were of dubious reputation and no doubt included some castaway French pirates. One historian has speculated that Kidd decided to become a pirate himself at this time, largely out of fear of not turning a quick profit for his partners and losing control of his crew.[8] Moreover, he must by now have seen the danger of engaging battle-hardened pirates near their Madagascar base and begun to think of taking weak Muslim traders as Tew and Every had done so brilliantly. Pursuant to his original instructions, he would carry his takings to New York, where Bellomont would protect him, as other governors had protected successful pirates since Morgan's day. (See Illustration 46)

With his plans changed, Kidd sailed for the mouth of the Red Sea, where he arrived early in August 1697. The tactics he used to ambush the Mocha fleet were the same as Every's two years earlier; he sent spies into Mocha, set lookouts on the heights of Barim Island in the Strait of Bab al Mandab, and positioned his ship off the island. Kidd, too, was embarrassed to find that the Mocha fleet had slipped by in the night, but he quickly caught up with it on 15 August, identified a suitable target, and prepared for battle by running up French colours at the stern and at the topmast 'a red broad pennant... without any cross on it'.[9]

French colours were intended to lure the merchant captain into the trap of shifting identities, a trick of privateers and sometimes of warships. If the captain thought the *Adventure* a French privateer, he might send up a French flag or produce a French pass for inspection. (Commanders put in a stock of various flags and passes for this purpose, the former giving rise to the expression, 'to travel under false colours'. In the navy it was acceptable to sail but not to attack under false colours.) Kidd could then seize him by virtue of his commission against the French.[10] But the Mughal ship did not fall for the trick, even when the pirate opened fire. Instead, it fired back, surprising Kidd. The reason for its fearlessness was that riding nearly abreast of the *Adventure* was the *Sceptre*, an East Indiaman of thirty guns commanded by Edward Barlow and assigned to protect the fleet by an agreement reached between the company and the Grand Mughal after Every's outrages in 1695. Kidd believed the *Sceptre* a harmless merchantman until Barlow put up his English flag, commenced to fire, and made for the pirate. Kidd prudently sought to withdraw rather than fight, but there was little wind and Barlow was slowly closing on him. Fortunately, the *Adventure* was a galley fitted with oars, which enabled it to pull away from its adversary.

After he was clear, Kidd formed a second plan, to lie in wait for the fleet's scattered vanguard near its homeport. He therefore set a course for waters off the highlands of St John, where Every had caught up with the *Ganj-i-sawai*. By September, he was near Goa when he met a small Arab merchantman with an English captain, one Parker. The *Adventure* was by now divided by quarrels and weakened by a shortage of fresh food. During the long, dispiriting voyage across the Arabian Sea, full-scale mutiny had been avoided only by the captain's reign of terror. Kidd was not the boldest of pirate chiefs, but he was loud and violent, 'fighting with his men on any little occasion, often calling for his pistols and threatening any one that durst speak of anything contrary to his mind to knock out their brains, causing them to dread him'. Seeing the Arab ship as a means of venting the crew's frustration, Kidd ordered them to hoist two captives up 'by the Arms and... [drub them] with a naked Cutlace' to reveal their riches.[11] They found little of value, yet the episode is important as their first successful act of piracy.

About this time, Kidd heard that a rich Surat merchantman was expected to return soon from Bengal, intelligence that caused him to change plans once more. With Captain Parker as his guide, he would cruise along the Malabar coast (south-west India) to intercept this ship. But a pirate alert had been sent down the coast so that the next ships he sighted were two Portuguese men-of-war from Goa looking for a fight. Kidd's strategy was simple but effective: by making a feint to escape, he lured the faster, smaller ship into pursuing him out of the range of its consort, then turned to batter it with his cannon. The larger warship could do little but help its wounded consort back to port, leaving Kidd to crow over his victory. '...The said fight was sharp', he reported,

> and the said Portuguese left the said Galley with such Satisfaction, that the Narrator believes no Portuguese will ever attack the King's Colours again, in that Part of the World especially.[12]

Full of his power and cunning, Kidd put in at Calicut for supplies early in October and then steered west for the Laccadive Islands, where the ship was careened. His crew's brutal treatment of the natives, however, led to the murder of the *Adventure*'s cooper and the massacre of a village by way of retaliation.

Back at sea again, the *Adventure Galley* wandered further south without purchase, and Kidd's hold on the men began to slip. Finally, in mid-October near Cape Cormorin, they came upon an East Indiaman, the *Loyal Captain*, which most of his men wanted to take, but Kidd was convinced that if he did not steal from the English, his crimes against Muslims would be overlooked. He was outnumbered but not out-talked in this debate. At last, he told them that

> if they attempted any such thing, they should never come on board the Galley again, nor have the Boat, or small Arms... and that he would attack them with the Galley, and drive them into Bombay.[13]

The men succumbed to his threat, but two or three weeks later, Kidd overheard the gunner William Moore, a participant in the earlier rebellion, talking about seizing a nearby Dutch ship. Kidd's ensuing rage was to be disastrous for both men. In the words of a crew member,

Captain Kidd came and walked on the Deck, and walks by this Moore; and when
he came to him, says, Which way could you have put me in a way to take this
Ship, and been clear; Sir, says William Moore, I never spoke such a Word, nor ever
thought such a Thing. Upon which Captain Kidd called him a Lousie Dog. And
says William Moore, If I am a Lousie Dog, you have made me so; you have
brought me to Ruin, and many more. Upon his saying this, says Captain Kidd,
Have I ruin'd you, you Dog?

He now broke off and, nurturing his wrath, 'walked two or three
Times backward and forward upon the Deck', then 'took a Bucket
bound with Iron Hoops, and struck him on the right Side of the
Head, of which he died the next Day [i.e. 31 October]'. One crewman reported that Moore's head 'was bruised a considerable Breadth;
and in one Place I could feel the Skull give way'. According to another,
Kidd believed himself immune to punishment for this deed, but was
afraid of being charged with piracy:

Some Time after this, about two Months, by the Coast of *Malabar*, Captain
Kidd said, *I do not care so much for the Death of my Gunner, as for other Passages*
of my Voyage; for I have good Friends in England, that will bring me off for that.[14]

Kidd was probably saved from a second, more decisive mutiny in
November off Calicut when the Dutch trader *Rupparell* fell for the
flag-and-pass trick, whereupon he exclaimed in joy and relief, '*By*
God, Have I catch'd you? You are free Prize to England'.[15] At Caliquilon
(now Quilon) on the Malabar coast, he found a safe harbour and willing market for the *Rupparell's* cargo. With his men content for now
with their shares and more hopeful that their leader would do right
by them, Kidd dropped the mask of legitimacy, and simply took what
he needed from small Muslim and Portuguese traders.

The large ship that was to 'make his voyage' was sighted just north-
west of Cape Cormorin on 30 January 1698. It was the *Quedah Merchant*
laden with cloth from a successful voyage; its owner was Abdul Ghafur,
the principal merchant of Surat, whose ship the *Fath Mahmamadi* Every
had seized in 1695. His misfortunes at the hands of English pirates made
him a dogged enemy of the East India Company at the court of

Aurangzeb so that the Englishman who molested Ghafur's enterprises could expect no mercy from the company and its friends. Ignorant of Ghafur and indifferent to Mughal politics, Kidd raised the French flag and ordered his prey to heave to. The *Quedah's* English commander John Wright fell easily into the trap and, after showing the 'appropriate' flag and pass, was quickly informed of the *Adventure's* real identity. Kidd put away Wright's French pass along with one from the *Rupparell* should Bellomont and his friends in England falter. (See Illustration 47)

His third plan seemed to have worked so well that he spurned a ransom offer of 20,000 rupees for the *Quedah's* cargo, said to be worth at least ten times as much. Instead, he sold much of it at a huge discount in Caliquilon and out of the profits, probably £7,000–8,000, paid each of the crew 200 rupees (£25).[16] With the promise of more when the rest of the goods were sold in New York, the men willingly hauled for home. *En route* to Madagascar for provisions and repairs, Kidd dismissed his remaining qualms about piracy; the *Adventure* and its two consorts, the *Rupparell* and *Quedah Merchant*, took several small traders and even threatened an English East Indiaman, which only the *Adventure's* poor sailing prevented them from capturing.

Kidd's flagship was now in an advanced state of decay; its pumps were kept going around the clock, and he had 'to woold her round with Cables to keep her together'. On 1 April 1698 he brought it into its last port, St Marie's Island (currently, Nosy Boraha), the main pirate base on Madagascar. His reception was cool, word having come to the residents that he was a pirate hunter, but according to the ship's surgeon, he swiftly relieved them of their fears: 'Capt. *Kidd* swore he would be true to them, and that he would do them no harm'.[17] He stayed at St Marie's for seven months in company with Robert Culliford, captain of the *Resolution,* and Dampier's old friend Captain Edward Davis. The *Resolution,* formerly known as the *Mocha,* was one of the East Indiamen that had chased Every's *Fancy* from Johanna in 1695; it became a pirate after a mutiny in which its oppressive Captain Edgecomb was murdered by crewman James Kelley.

The bad effect of leisure was that it made Kidd's men quarrelsome and rebellious until they forced him to divide the remaining booty. After he paid them off in goods, retaining only forty per cent for himself and the owners, ninety-four deserted to continue pirating with Culliford in the Indian Ocean. Kidd later maintained that before they left, they stole the journal that he was legally required to keep and that would have exonerated him.[18] Gone, too, was his dream of delivering hundreds of thousands to his friends in England. Now he must look to his legal defence. But would the government accept the story that what he had done was under the duress of rebels and pirates? In November 1698, Kidd burnt the decrepit *Adventure Galley* and ordered the *Quedah Merchant* to sea. Among the crew were Edward Davis and a deserter from the *Resolution,* James Kelley, not the best companions with whom to enter the reach of the High Court of Admiralty.

As the *Quedah Merchant* was driven along by the north-easterly Agulhas current, a storm was brewing that would drive several of its passengers to destruction, its epicentre Leadenhall Street in London where the old East India Company had its headquarters. (There was now a new company created by Parliament in 1698 at the demand of the interlopers.) Its directors would use the experience gained in operations against Every to mount an even more complex war against Kidd. First it would heighten and publicise tales of Kidd's atrocities and the pirates' strength at St Marie's Island.

The few rude shacks on the island were transformed into a fort bristling with forty to fifty cannon defended by fifteen hundred hardened rene-gades and seventeen ships.[19]

Then the company would go after the merchants in British America who supplied the pirates and the colonial governments that protected them when they returned from the east. The long-range goals of the campaign were the permanent destruction of the Madagascar base, the pacification of the Indian Ocean, and the rejuvenation of the Old Company. (See Illustration 48)

A wave of reform had already engulfed Governor Benjamin Fletcher of New York who, along with merchants in the Jersies and Connecticut, had profited scandalously from trade with the Madagascar pirates. By 1699 the actions of his successor Lord Bellomont against pirates and their accessories had polarised the colony. But Bellomont, still hopeful that Kidd's booty was great and that it was taken lawfully, was reserving judgement despite Whitehall's instructions to arrest him if he came home. Meanwhile, Kidd had learnt in the Leeward Islands 'that he and his People were proclaimed Pirates, which put them into... Consternation'.[20] From now on they must seek out-of-the-way places to harbour and approach Lord Bellomont with circumspection. On the coast of Hispaniola he clandestinely sold a portion of his cargo to New York merchants based at Curaçao, left the ship at Hispaniola still laden with about 150 bales to be sold for him by Henry Bolton, a merchant of Antigua, and sailed in the sloop *Saint Antonio* to the mid-Atlantic colonies. At Hore-kills (currently Lewes) in Delaware Bay, he sold more of the cargo and then stood north-north-east for the safety of Gardiner's Island, well known to smugglers and freebooters. From this base and at Tarpaulin Cove, Massachusetts, he continued to sell parcels or tranship them to New York.

Kidd depended on a network of Scots friends to negotiate for his return home. He wrote first to Robert Livingston in Albany of his predicament, who, in turn, informed James Emott, an agent for New York merchants trading to Madagascar. When Kidd took the sloop to Oyster Bay to be with his family, he found Emott in their party, and the two friends discussed how to proceed. Emott then went to Boston where, on 13 June, he put Kidd's case before the Governor, who was receptive but insisted on evidence of the captain's truthfulness. To collect such evidence, Emott contacted New York City's postmaster, Duncan Campbell, and sailed with him to meet Kidd off Block Island. The three decided that while Emott returned to the Governor with documents, Campbell would disburse presents of gold and jewels to Lady Bellomont and others 'that he expected to do him Kindnesses'.[21] Accordingly, on 19 June, Emott delivered into Bellomont's hands not only Kidd's brief account of the voyage, formally witnessed by Campbell, but the two French passes. In his statement, Kidd claimed that he had faithfully adhered to his commission and that the *Rupparell* and *Quedah Merchant* were lawful prizes, but that his rebellious crew had forced him into 'irregularities'. If he and his men were allowed to come into port without fear of imprisonment, he would surrender to Bellomont the plunder he had on board and immediately sail for the

West Indies to retrieve the rest. The governor received the documents, accepted Kidd's terms, and vowed 'on my word and honour' to work for his pardon should the evidence support his story. Bellomont admitted afterwards that his letters to Kidd were baited with honey to draw the suspect into his custody.[22]

Kidd came with his family into Boston on 1 July 1699, trusting in Bellomont but also calculating that, although far smaller than they had anticipated, his partners' share of his winnings would protect him from prosecution. (The value of what he brought home has never been determined. Bellomont found and sent to England gold, silver, jewels and cloth worth about £14,000 (today, £1,321,000); Kidd wildly exaggerated what he had left in the West Indies, at one time claiming it worth £30,000, at another £90,000.[23]) He was not aware that, under great pressure to arrest Kidd and to advance his own self-interest, Bellomont was wavering. As vice-admiral, the governor's share of captured pirates' goods might be greater than his share of the *Adventure*'s profits, especially when they were continually being reduced by the captain's illicit trading.[24] When after three delays Kidd failed to submit a complete narrative of his cruise, he was arrested on 6 July at the door of the Massachusetts council chamber. He managed to wrench himself away from the constable and rush in, calling for Bellomont, but was finally subdued and, still shouting, dragged to gaol.

The man who could shout down a pack of mutinous English tars would presently know the great and solemn terror of the state.

From April 1700, when Kidd arrived in England in chains, various parties began to jockey for advantage in the conflict that would culminate in his trial. The Whig ministry, playing defence, manoeuvred to be the first to interview him, but they were countered by Tories in the Admiralty who kept him incommunicado. The Old East India Company, angered by Whig support for interlopers and the recent loss of its monopoly, allied itself with the Tories, spread rumours about the identity of Kidd's partners, and called for the dismissal of the ministry. Using newly discovered documents, the Tories in Parliament argued that the Junto should be impeached on the grounds that Kidd's commission granted him the property of Tew, Mayes, Wake and Ireland before they had been tried and convicted, and before their victims might claim their property. (Ordinarily, pirate booty reverted to the King, from whom its owners might claim it one year after conviction.) The commission struck, therefore, at 'due process', the very root of liberty and property in England. It is a case, fulminated an admiralty official,

> of the highest immorality that ever was attempted in this nation by any one, much less by such as hath had the ministry of the most important affairs thereof; and for which there is hardly any punishment or censure universal enough to reach unto the proportion and extent of so national a villainy and a mischief so universal to all corners in the world.[25]

Unfortunately for him, Kidd did not understand how to turn the political situation to his own advantage. Preoccupied by the miseries of imprisonment and naïvely trusting for salvation to his Whig partners, he botched two chances to strike a deal. On 27 March and again on 31 March 1701, he appeared before a committee of the Commons, but offered nothing useful to the Tories, leading one MP to conclude, 'The fellow is a fool as well as a rogue, and I will never credit what he shall say hereafter'.[26]

Despite the Tories' strong arguments, the government prevailed in votes on 6 December 1699 and 27 March 1701, and the Junto was spared impeachment. The outlook for Kidd was not so hopeful. His state of body and mind had already greatly deteriorated; by the end of 1699 he had lost hope for an acquittal, and in April 1700, having endured nine months of imprisonment – first in New York and then in the Marshalsea, the Admiralty's gaol in London – he begged for a knife to commit suicide.[27] He survived this period of despair only to be sent for another year to Newgate, the foul and disease-ridden gaol adjacent to the Old Bailey, while the great tried to use him to their advantage. When his 'friends in England' concluded that getting him hanged might preclude more deadly attacks against themselves, he was thrown into court. (See Illustration 49, 50)

Because Kidd was arrested in a colony with no independent piracy law and before the 1700 reform act had gone into effect, he became the last of the legendary pirates to be sent to London for trial under Henry VIII's law.

34 *Right:* 1694 broadside that began the myth of 'Captain John Avery'.

35 *Below:* Map of Arabia including the Red Sea and the dangerous Strait of Bab el Mandab. Thomas Astley, *New General Collection of Voyages* (London, 1745).

A
COPY of VERSES,

COMPOSED BY

Captain Henry Every,

LATELY

Gone to SEA to seek his FORTUNE.

To the Tune of, *The two English Travellers.*

Licens'd according to Order.

COme all you brave Boys, whose Courage is bold,
Will you venture with me, I'll glut you with *Gold?*
Make haste unto *Corona,* a Ship you will find,
That's called the *Fancy,* will pleasure your mind.

Captain *Every* is in her, and calls her his own;
He will box her about, Boys, before he has done:
French, Spaniard and *Portuguese,* the *Heathen* likewise,
He has made a War with them until that he dies.

Her Model's like Wax, and she sails like the Wind,
She is rigg'd and fitted and curiously trimm'd,
And all things-convenient has for his design;
God bless his poor *Fancy,* she's bound for the *Mine.*

Farewel, fair *Plimouth,* and *Cat-down* be damn'd,
I once was Part-owner of most of that Land;
But as I am disown'd, so I'll abdicate
My Person from *England* to attend on my Fate.

Then away from this Climate and temperate Zone,
To one that's more torrid, you'll hear I am gone,
With an hundred and fifty brave Sparks of this Age,
Who are folly resolved their Foes to engage.

Those Northern Parts are not thrifty for me,
I'll visit the *Anterhilie,* that some Men shall see
I am not afraid to let the World know,
That to the *South-Seas* and to *Persia* I'll go.

Our Names shall be blazed and spread in the Sky,
And many brave Places I hope to descry,
Where never a *French man* der yet has been,
Nor any proud *Dutch man* can say he has seen.

My Commission is large, and I made it my self,
And the Capston shall stretch it full larger by half;
It was dated in *Corona,* believe it, my Friend,
From the Year Ninety three, unto the World's end.

I Honour St. *George,* and his Colours I wear,
Good Quarters I give, but no Nation I spare,
The World must assist me with what I do want,
I'll give them my Bill, when my Money is scant.

Now this I do say and solemnly swear,
He that strikes to St. *George* the better shall fare;
But he that refuses, shall suddenly spy
Strange Colours abroad of my *Fancy* to fly.

Four Chivileers of Gold in a bloody Field,
Environ'd with green, now this is my Shield;
Yet call out for Quarter, before you do see
A bloody Flag out, which is our Decree,

No Quarters to give, no Quarters to take,
We save nothing living, alas 'tis too late;
For we are now sworn by the Bread and the Wine,
More serious we are than any Divine.

Now this is the Course I intend for to steer;
My false-hearted Nation, to you I declare,
I have done thee no wrong, thou must me forgive,
The Sword shall maintain me as long as I live.

London: Printed for *Theophilus Lewis.*

384

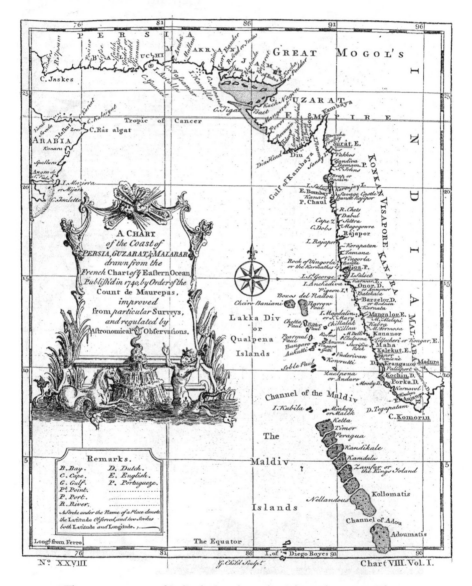

36 The western coast of India during the early eighteenth century. Thomas Astley, *A New General Collection of Voyages and Travels* (London, 1745).

37 Captain Every and the battle between the *Fancy* and the *Gang-i-sawai*.
Alexander Smith, *General History of the Highwaymen and Pirates* (London, 1734).

Willm Overley Joyner at the Sign of the East India House in Leaden-hall Street LONDON. Makes all sorts of Sea Chests in Deal or Wainscot, Ruff or Smooth, Packing Chests or Cases, and Cases of Bottles, & Boxes of all sizes, Presses in Deal or Wainscot, & Bedsteds, Tables, Desks, Book Cases, Bureous & Writing Desks, Letter-holes, & Drawrs for Shops Allso Counters and all sorts of Joyners worke done — at Reasonable Rates —

38 Headquarters of the East India Company in London, early eighteenth century. George Birdwood, ed., *Report on the Old Records of the India Office* (London, 1891).

39 The Grand Mughal Aurangzeb rides to battle.

40 Portrait of Sir John Holt, Chief Justice of the King's Bench. R. Van
Bleeck, c. 1700.

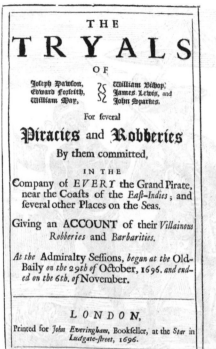

THE
TRYALS

OF

Joseph Dawson, } { William Bishop,
Edward Forseith, } 25 { James Lewis, and
William May, } 52 { John Sparkes.

For several

Piracies and Robberies

By them committed,

IN THE

Company of *EVERY* the Grand Pirate,
near the Coasts of the *East-Indies*; and
several other Places on the Seas.

Giving an **ACCOUNT** of their *Villainous*
Robberies and *Barbarities.*

At the Admiralty Seffions, *begun at the* Old-
Baily *on the* 29th *of* October, 1696. *and end-*
ed on the 6th. *of* November.

L O N D O N,

Printed for *John Everingham,* Bookseller, at the *Star* in
Ludgate-street, 1696.

41 The government-sanctioned
report of the trials of Every's
men.

42 Captain Avery's encounter
with the Emperor's
granddaughter, a twentieth-
century rendering. G.H.
Maynadier, ed., *The Works of
Daniel Defoe* (New York: Jenson
Society, 1905).

43 'John Avery', King of Madagascar. Captain Charles Johnson, *General History of the Pirates* (London: Midwinter, 1725).

J 2277

Avery the Pirate

On his return from India either landed or was shipwrecked near the Lizard where he buried three chests or boxes full of treasure in the sands of the Sea shore

"environ trois milles à l'Est du Liz. près trois pierres grises ou rochers, dans une ___ *cove?* au Sud ouest des trois pierres

Mr K: says "ces trois pierres sont converted with grass. *now nearly overgrown with furze & grass.*

It is near where the corner of a high promontory juts out into the sea. He said, the spring tides now come over the place.

1 Chest. Haslarwood 2 feet long & 1 f wide. In it were precious stones & bracelets. large rubies saphirs emeralds topazes & diamonds

2 Chest almost the same size & make as the first 120 ingots of gold. 40 thick flat pieces of gold as large as a round tobacco box, with various characters on some of them. 25 bars of gold, some of which were 4 or 5 inches long

3 Chest has 3.000. pieces of 8. besides Bullion not weighed but crammed in with pieces of brocades.

44 Avery's buried treasure, a nineteenth-century hoax.

45 The *Charles Galley*, a ship that resembles Kidd's *Adventure*. Willem van der Velde (1676).

46 Kidd buries his bible and joins the Devil's party. Charles Ellms, *The Pirates' Own Book* (Portland, Maine, 1837).

47 Kidd's French pass from the *Quedah Merchant.*

48 Arms of the New East India Company established by Parliament in 1698. George Birdwood, ed., *Report on the Old Records of the India Office* (London, 1891).

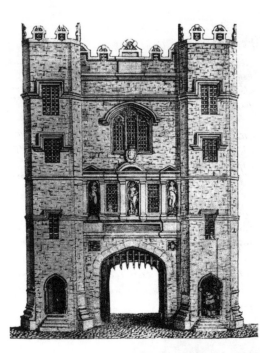

49 Entrance to
Newgate Prison in
1672. Charles Gordon,
*The Old Bailey and
Newgate* (London,
1902).

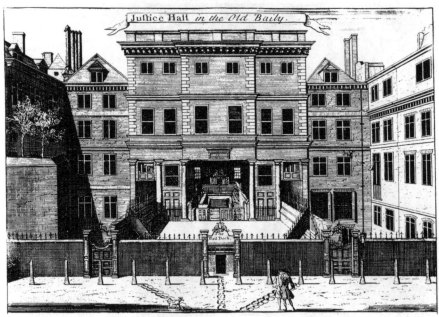

50 The Old Bailey, where Every's men and Kidd were tried.

51 Kidd explains his refusal to plead in a letter to a lord, c.1701.

52 The taking of testimony in the Old Bailey. Charles Gordon, *The Old Bailey and Newgate* (London, 1902).

53 Hanging of a pirate at Execution Dock, Wapping, after 1747.

54 The Thames near
Execution Dock in
1746. John Roque,
*A Plan of the Cities
of London and
Westminster*
(London, 1747).

55 The execution of the idle apprentice. William Hogarth, 'Industry and
Idleness' (1747) in *The Works of William Hogarth* (London, 1806).

56 The bodies of hanged pirates placed between high water and low, a woodcut in use since 1639. *Villany Rewarded*, or, the *Pirates Last Farewel* (London, 1696).

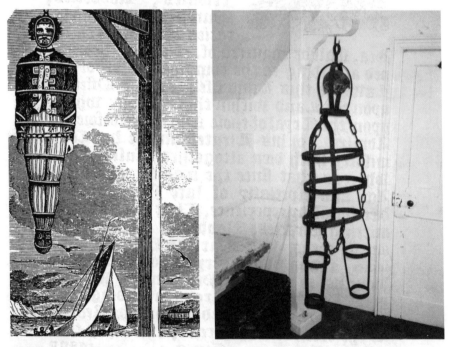

57 *Left:* Captain Kidd hanging in chains at Tilbury Point, a nineteenth-century depiction. Charles Ellms, *The Pirates' Own Book* (Portland, Maine, 1837).

58 *Right:* Set of giblet chains with skull.

Gulielmi III. Regis.

An ACT for the more effectual Suppreſſion of Piracy.

Hereas by an Act of Parliament made in the Twenty-eighth Year of the Reign of King Henry the Eighth, it is Enacted, That Treaſons, Felonies, Robberies, Murthers and Confederacies committed on the Sea, ſhall be enquired of, tried, and determined according to the common Courſe of the Laws of this Land uſed for ſuch Offences upon the Land within this Realm; whereupon the Tryal of thoſe Offenders before the Admiral, or his Lieutenant, or his Commiſſary hath been altogether difuſed: And Whereas that ſince the making of the ſaid Act, and eſpecially of late Years, it hath been found by experience, That Perſons committing Piracies, Robberies and Felonies on the Seas, in or near the Eaſt and Weſt Indies, and in Places very remote, cannot be brought to Condign Puniſhment without great Trouble and Charges in ſending them into England to be Tryed within the Realm, as the ſaid Statute directs, inſomuch that

G α α 2   many

59 The piracy act of 1700, 11–12 William III, c.7.

60 *Above:* Instructions to colonial governors for the trying of pirates under 11–12 William iii, c.7.

61 *Right:* Copy of the trials of John Augur and his crew (1718) sent from the Bahamas to the High Court of Admiralty.

Felony trials in early eighteenth-century England were usually over in an hour and verdicts brought on the same day. The prosecution of Kidd and nine others at the Old Bailey lasted two days, because Kidd won a brief delay and because it was divided into four separate and contentious trials. In the first, Kidd was accused of murdering William Moore; the others for piracy involved all ten defendants. The proceedings began on Thursday 8 May 1701, under the control of the clerk of arraigns and the recorder of London. After some preliminaries, one of the nation's distinguished legal scholars, Dr George Oxenden – Regius Professor of Civil Law at Cambridge, Whig MP, and nephew of the East India Company's late Governor of Bombay – rose to charge the grand jury. The charge typically explained 'the Nature of the Commission, and the Crimes inquirable by vertue of it by the Grand Jury', but Oxenden may, as Hedges in the trial of Every's men, have used it to convey the state's fears for the loss of the India trade.[28]

The charge given, the state's witnesses stood up and were sworn, and the grand jury retired to examine them. A short while later, the jury returned with six indictments for murder and piracy, and proclamation was made summoning potential witnesses to 'draw near and give your attendance'. Up to this point the proceedings had moved along nicely, the forms of law all respected. The Recorder of London and the clerk of arraigns knew exactly what to expect: the prisoners at the bar would mount a token defence and then become passive, overcome by the machinery, if not the majesty, of the court. But Kidd refused to lie down. Evidently, his spirit was renewed by the challenge of the trial, a final chance to take command of his life. The court's managers were thus surprised when Captain Kidd rudely stopped the wheels of justice.

Rather than plead to the indictments, he asked that his counsel, Dr William Oldys and Mr Lemmon, speak to a matter of law, a move that put the clerks off their game. But when he explained that they would ask the court for time to collect exculpatory evidence, they dismissed his motion as dealing with matters of fact, not law. (In most felony trials defence counsel might only address the court on points of law and procedure, a limitation in effect until late in the eighteenth century.)

Mr. Recorder. There is no Issue joined, and therefore there can be no
Council assigned. *Mr. Kidd*, you must plead.
Kidd. I cannot plead till I have those Papers that I insisted upon.

At this point, Mr Lemmon sprang excitedly to his feet:

He ought to have his Papers delivered to him, because they are very
material to his Defence. He has endeavoured to have them, but could not
get them.

Unimpressed by his eloquence, the court told Lemmon to sit down:

Mr. *Coniers.* You are not to appear for any one till he pleads, and that the
Court assigns you for his Council. [29]

A hubbub arose among the onlookers as the trial veered off the rails.
'Make Silence', ordered the crier. The officials tried to go to the other
defendants, but emboldened by their captain – or instructed by their
own counsel – three refused to plead, claiming immunity under the
terms of a pardon issued in December 1698.

Assuming that Kidd's ignorance was fuelling the disorder, the clerk
and recorder explained the 'Course of Courts' to him, that after he
pleaded, the judges would enter and matters of fact be considered.
They underestimated him. In a letter written before the trial, Kidd
revealed to an unknown lord the rationale behind his refusal to plead:

I shall not Contribute to my own destruction by pleading to this
Indictment till my passes are restored to me, It is not my fault that I have
them not here, but It will be my fault if I admit my selfe a pyrate as I must
doe if I plead without having those [French] passes to produce.

Let me have my passes, I will plead presently, but without them I will
not plead. I am not afraid to dye, but will not be my own Murderer, and
if an English Court of Judicature will take away my life for not pleading
under my Circumstances, I think my death will tend very little to the
Credit of their Justice. [30] (See Illustration 51)

These lines suggest that Kidd and Oldys forced an opportunity to shame the court into giving the defence what it needed.

But this tactic was also, perhaps, something more radical, a plea for qualified representation throughout the trial. By declaring that 'If I plead, I shall be accessary to my own Death, till I have Persons to plead for me', Kidd was challenging the ancient custom of requiring the felony defendant to conduct his own defence.[31] Since nothing in his background prepared him for this degree of legal sophistication, it was probably his counsel's idea. Oldys had been hired by Kidd for his expertise in admiralty law but also, perhaps, for his independent streak; when advocate for the Admiralty in 1693, he refused to prosecute mariners captured aboard privateers commissioned by the exiled James II, arguing that they were lawful combatants and no pirates. King William was not amused and fired him. The learned maverick may have wished to argue for defence counsel in all aspects of the felony trial, as was already permitted in civil proceedings and trials for treason.[32]

It took some wrangling before the Recorder reminded Kidd that the penalty for 'standing mute' was death, that 'You are accessary to your own Death, if you do not plead', whereupon he and the others relented and declared themselves not guilty. 'How wilt thou be tried', intoned the clerk of arraigns, to which Kidd and his men replied with the ritual 'By God and my country'. 'God send thee a good Deliverance', replied the clerk.[33] The most colourful part of trial ceremony now followed, the entrance of the judges. Because this was a state trial, six judges walked towards the dais, preceded by the silver oar of the Admiralty. When they were seated, the full indictment was read publicly and the prisoners once more required to plead. Shortly afterwards Kidd renewed his request for counsel, to which Justice Powell acceded.

William Oldys now rose to request that Captain Edward Davis be allowed as a defence witness and that Kidd be given time to locate other evidence. The court granted the first but denied him a delay for the present, reasoning that on the count of murder, 'there was no pretence of want of Witnesses or Papers'. The trial now moved to the *voir dire*; before the petty jury was sworn, the clerk of arraigns informed

Kidd that 'if you have any Cause of Exception, you may speak to them as they come to the Book'. 'I shall challenge none', he replied, 'I know nothing to the contrary but they are honest Men'.[34]

Such obliging language from the usually pugnacious defendant bears scrutiny. *Voir dire* was then and continues to be a powerful resource for the defence as shown when Every's men made sure East India Company supporters were not on their first jury. It stands to reason that Kidd, in a very similar situation, would also use it, but he made no challenges because the panel presented were 'honest men'. Did he have reason to believe that the panel were likely to be impartial or even to favour his cause? While reading the minds of jurymen who sat three centuries ago is generally impossible, in this case we have particular evidence of their biases: six of its members had also served on the jury that acquitted Edward Forseith *et al.* in 1696 for taking the *Ganj-i-sawai,* and a seventh was kin to another member of that jury, a fact that has to date eluded historians.[35] That acquittal was motivated by the opposition of many London merchants to the East India Company, a driving force behind the prosecution of both Every and Kidd. How jurors who rendered a highly controversial verdict four and a half years ago were placed on Kidd's jury remains a mystery, but coincidence seems unlikely.[36] I believe that Kidd's strategy was less to ingratiate himself than to disguise a plot to pack the jury on his behalf.

The first trial began in earnest with the calling of Joseph Palmer, a mariner Kidd had hired in New York. (See Illustration 52) This eyewitness and the next, ship's surgeon Robert Bradinham, described the killing of William Moore and supported the charge that it was no accident. They told of the gap in time between the crew's outright mutiny and Moore's death and of Kidd's walking 'two or three Times backward and forward upon the Deck, before he struck the Blow'. The state used their words to prove that the killing of William Moore was intentional, murder not manslaughter:

> The Law implies Malice [prepense], when one Man, without any reasonable Cause or Provocation, kills another... What Mutiny or Discourse might be a Fortnight or Month before, will not be any Reason or Cause for so long continuance of a Passion.[37]

Kidd, on the other hand, expressed remorse for his intemperate actions but got a defence witness to say that there was talk of another mutiny and that Moore had been active in the first. He also sought to destroy Bradinham's credibility by showing that he himself was mutinous. Given the nearly tyrannical power allowed a captain at sea during this period, Kidd's explanation of his rage should have carried the day.

The judges worked to undermine his defence even to the point of denying the relevance of Bradinham's disloyalty and of dismissing a juryman's request for information about what Kidd did to save Moore's life: '[Justice] *Ward*. Will you put him to produce more Evidence than he can?'.[38] Such judicial behaviour was the norm at a time when judges were not expected to stifle their personal opinions. But the most striking disability suffered by Kidd – or anyone else accused of a felony in this period – was that the prosecutors and judges had nearly total control of the narrative received by the jury. At the outset the state's story was framed in the indictment then amplified in the prosecutor's and judge's opening speech, while the defendant was not permitted an opening. Having established the plot of its narrative, the state now called its witnesses. The defendant might cross-examine these witnesses, but any editorialising he offered was cut short:

> *Ward*. You may ask him any Questions you have a Mind to, but you must reserve what you have to say for your self till you come to make your Defence. [39]

Furthermore, because felony trials were supposed to be communal searches for the truth, Kidd's cross-examination and questioning of his own witnesses were frequently interrupted by questions from prosecutors, judges and jurors. Under these conditions, no one but a quick-witted and forceful advocate could manage to convey the defendant's story as a whole. The state's final advantage was that it could rebut the defence or sum up with no interruptions if defence witnesses had introduced new, substantive evidence. (This procedure is preserved today in the United States, where the prosecution usually speaks last because the state bears the heavy burden of proving the charges beyond a reasonable doubt, a standard not fully articulated until the nineteenth century). Even when denied the last word, the prosecutor could often count on the presiding judge to favour the state in his concluding speech.

In addition to these built-in disabilities, Kidd made major errors typical of a defendant acting as his own lawyer: he forgot to call character witnesses at the right time and two of his own witnesses did him more damage than good. He asked them the right questions, but he had not completely discovered ahead of time what they were going to say. Abel Owen, for example, testified that Kidd did not throw the lethal bucket but gripped it purposefully by the strap and that there was no active mutiny at the time. Worse yet, Kidd did not understand the value of a full and detailed rendition of his narrative. Four of the prosecutors, along with Justices Powell and Ward, tore into the defence witnesses, which so demoralised Kidd that he had little more to say. Indeed, when he asserted that 'I had no Design to kill him, I had no Malice or Spleen against him', Ward countered, 'This must be left for the Jury to consider the Evidence that has been given; you make out no such matter'.[40]

Although Ward would seem to deprive Kidd of the basic right to affirm his innocence, the judge is technically correct. At this time the accused was not allowed to be sworn in as a witness at his own trial, a restriction not lifted until 1898; since only witnesses could give evidence – another term for witness was, in fact, 'evidence' – Kidd's mere assertions 'make out no such matter'. Nevertheless, Ward made a great flourish of giving Kidd

> the Liberty to produce what Evidence he can for himself... If he has any more to say, it will be in his Interest to say what he can, the Court is willing to hear him as long as he hath any thing to offer for himself

In other words, as long as he argued his innocence from the testimony of witnesses. In response to this invitation, Kidd delivered his closing: 'It was not designedly done, but in my Passions, for which I am heartily sorry'. His defence had gone so badly that the prosecution waved its prerogative of summing up; defence counsel would not be permitted to close until 1836.[41]

Lord Chief Baron of the Exchequer Sir Edward Ward was an eloquent speaker and somewhat more verbose than the defendant. He
would send the jury off with a detailed story of murder prepense
wherein all the evidence against Kidd appeared sound and the pieces in
his favour irrelevant or tainted. The supposedly impartial speech was
also a charge to the jury that carefully distinguished between murder
and manslaughter. Unlike much modern practice, Ward's charge was in
plain English without legal jargon, but he omitted what today is considered essential, an explanation of the burden of proof. (It took until
the early nineteenth century before such an explanation was expected
from judges.) Instead, early eighteenth-century jurors were exhorted to
satisfy their conscience that a certain verdict is correct. Today, it would
be hard to construe Kidd's murderous rage as premeditated under the
highest burden, guilty beyond a reasonable doubt.[42] In fact, we can
detect in the jury's questions towards the end of the trial a desire to find
exculpatory evidence, a desire sternly rebuked by Justice Ward.[43]

Ward and his brethren would have been shocked to hear that their
procedure might appear unfair to later generations. They might have
acknowledged the advantage it gave to the state, but defended that
advantage as a prudent check upon crime. If criminals had skilled and
eloquent counsel and a chance to create a specious counter-narrative,
they might have argued, the simple truth of the evidence would often
be overborne. Ward's legal culture did not gladly entertain the notion
that the medium is the message, that evidence *per se* is seldom trans-
parent unless skill and eloquence make it appear so – whether for or
against the accused.

As soon as the jury went out to deliberate, the second trial for
piracy aboard the *Quedah Merchant* began before a second jury. The
same principles of procedure that shaped the first trial affected the
second to an even greater degree. The major difference was that Kidd
seems to have lost his focus. He should at the start have renewed his
request for the French passes and for more time to prepare, but he let
the opportunity go by. Defendants Howe, Churchill, and Mullins, on
the other hand, repeated their claims of immunity. Ward ruled that
they were excluded from the royal pardon of 1698 because they
had not surrendered to the right officials.[44] Then, in the middle of

prosecutor Dr Newton's opening, the first jury returned to announce Kidd guilty of murder.[45] The impact of this verdict on the piracy jury is hard to gauge, but this kind of highly prejudicial intrusion was common practice.

Dr Newton's lengthy account of Kidd's cruise from England to Madagascar was the story of a man who abandoned the noble task entrusted to him by the king and fell to pillaging ships of all nations: 'He had taken Moors before, but *Moors* and *Christians* are all alike to Pirates, they distinguish not Nations and Religions'. Instead of destroying pirates, this man lived at Madagascar in amity with Robert Culliford, one of the worst of them. Moreover, Kidd along with Every has brought disgrace upon the English for the 'growing Trouble' of piracy, 'the Scandal and Reproach of the European Nations, and the Christian Name'. Newton therefore beseeched the jury to

> do justice to the injured World, the English Nation, (our Common Country) whose interest and Welfare so much depend on the Encrease and Security of Trade.[46]

The prosecutors' strategy was to imply that Kidd was a pirate from the moment he left New York for Madagascar. If there was a pre-existent conspiracy to turn pirate, the state could argue felonious intent even though the *Quedah Merchant* carried a French pass and was flying French colours. As evidence of this they elicited from Joseph Palmer that the articles recruits were made to sign at New York included the no-purchase-no-pay rule. To a layman, this rule smacked of piracy, but it was, in fact, no more than the 'Jamaica discipline' in force aboard all British privateers, a fact surely known to Dr Newton, Judge Advocate of the Admiralty. Kidd's strongest defence, of course, lay in the French pass he had taken from the *Quedah*'s captain. Its suppression was probably the doing of Secretary of State Sir James Vernon at the behest of the Junto, but the chief prosecutor had implied that he would reconsider Kidd's motion to produce it when it became relevant. Kidd apparently forgot to remind the court of this until moments before the summation when Justice Ward, ignoring the defendant's earlier claim of disability, ruled it too late.[47]

More bits and pieces of a defence – mostly unsubstantiated or con-
tradicted – emerge in the trial report: Kidd could not arrest Culliford
because many of his men were on shore; he didn't condemn most of
his prizes because his men prevented him; Palmer and Bradinham lied
about his chumminess with Culliford; he was absent when the crew
shared the *Quedah*'s booty. But when Ward offered him a final chance
to tell his story, Kidd said nothing. This is all the more surprising
because he had already prepared a brief but comprehensive account
for Bellomont in 1699. It was not the whole truth but it was well
written, and it made a plausible case for his being forced into crimes
by a mutinous crew. But even if Kidd had attempted a full summation, his speech might have been interrupted by questions and comments from prosecutors, judges and even hostile witnesses.

Failure to demand the French pass early in the trial and to deliver
a coherent summation were not the only errors Kidd made in defending himself. He should have justified his failure to have his prizes
legally condemned by noting that 'the special grant given to the
investors exempted them from prize courts'.[48] Furthermore, Kidd
complained that he was being convicted on hearsay, but he failed to
stress the insufficiency of the evidence. He made little of the fact that
Palmer was not on board when the *Adventure* seized the *Quedah
Merchant* and never asked Bradinham for his whereabouts. They could
testify to the consequences but not necessarily to the actual taking. In
a modern Anglo-American court, such errors might support a challenge to the conviction on the grounds of incompetent counsel!

Ward's summation and jury charge was, as before, long, eloquent and
tendentious. Like Justice Hedges in the trial of Every's men, he argued
from the doctrine of 'implied intent': 'no Man knows the Mind and
Intention of another, but as it may be discovered by his Actions'.
Consequently, he focused on the articles signed in New York, the
abortive attack on the Mocha fleet, the killing of natives in the Laccadive
Islands, and Kidd's relations with Culliford to establish the defendants'
piratical mind set. (His powerful use of such circumstantial evidence is
precisely what was intended by the shift in 1536 from civil to common
law procedure in piracy trials.) Ward delivered the *coup de grâce* by slight-
ing the captain's best defence, the existence of French passes:

there is nothing of that appears by any Proof, and for ought I can see, none saw them but himself, if there were ever any.[49]

It took the jury only half an hour to return a verdict. The three indentured servants were cleared of the charges while Kidd and the other six were found guilty.

The remaining two counts of piracy aboard Muslim and Portuguese ships were addressed in two trials held on the next day. Lacking rebuttal evidence, Kidd had little choice but to attack the credibility of the two witnesses with charges of theft, mutiny and perjury. At the very least, Kidd proved that the supposed eyewitnesses were often purveyors of hearsay. Unhappily for him, however, early eighteenth-century judges 'showed scant disposition to filter evidence from the jury' and often admitted second-hand testimony now excluded under Anglo-American rules of evidence.[50]

When Kidd's complaints were ignored or deflected by the judges, he grew increasingly frustrated and intemperate.

'This Fellow [i.e. Bradinham] used to sleep 5 or 6 Months together in the Hold'.

'I am sure you never heard me say such a word to such a Logger-head as you'.

'Because I would not turn Pirate, you Rogues, you would make me one'.

Kidd found Bradinham particularly repulsive. After one heated exchange between the two, the clerk of arraigns asked Kidd to resume his cross-examination. 'No, no, so long as he swears it, our Words or Oaths cannot be taken'.[51] Once more Kidd objects explicitly to a basic rule in the 'course of courts', that the accused cannot be placed under oath (a protection from being forced to testify against oneself under penalty of perjury). Even witnesses for the defence, allowed at felony trials since Queen Mary's reign, were not given the oath until one year after Kidd's trial. When Kidd speaks of 'our words or oaths' he probably refers to both defendants and defence witnesses.[52]

The judges were quite patient during these outbursts, but when Kidd accused the surgeon of lying to save his skin, they struck back.

William Kidd. Mr. *Bradinham,* are not you promised your Life, to take away
  mine?
Mr. Justice *Turton.* He is not bound to answer that Question. He is very
  fit to be made an Evidence for the King, perhaps there can be no other
  in this Case, than such who are in his Circumstances.[53]

By today's standards, Turton was wrong to forbid the question, and the
jury should have been warned about accomplices turned state's witnesses. But judges were not yet required to give such a warning.[54] It is
easy to understand why they were reluctant to do so in piracy cases:
since victims were often dead or at sea, the guilty might not be punished without the help of accomplices. In addition, it was highly desirable, though not required in common law procedure, to have two
eyewitnesses against suspected pirates, which explains why the judges
bristled every time Kidd questioned either of the star witnesses' honour.

When the last two trials ended with the same results as the second,
the convicted were asked if they had anything to say about why they
should not be sentenced to death.

Kidd. I have nothing to say, but that I have been sworn against by perjured
  and wicked People.

After all ten had spoken, 'The Proclamation for Silence was made,
while Sentence was pronouncing'.

*You shall be taken from the Place where you are, and be carried to the Place from
whence you came, and from thence to the Place of Execution, and there be severally
hanged by your Necks until you be dead. And the Lord have Mercy on your Souls.*

Dismayed and bitter, Kidd blurted out a last protest:

My Lord it is a very hard Sentence. For my Part, I am the innocentest
Person of them all, only I have been sworn by Perjured Persons.[55]

In this breach of decorum, Kidd scored a tiny victory over the machine
dead set on killing him with dignity.

I have examined the 'flaws' in Kidd's trials not to argue that he was blameless or that the court was corrupt, but rather to convey the differences between early eighteenth-century conceptions of justice and our own and to underline the place of procedure in those differences. It should be said to its credit that the court was scrupulous in affording Kidd the protections against juridical tyranny that the English had won over the ages and that were incorporated in Henry VIII's anti-piracy law. Among these protections I include the public trial, the grand jury, the written indictment, the *voir dire*, the twelve-man petty jury of one's peers, the unanimous verdict, the defendant's right to call his own witnesses and cross-examine those of the state, and the right to speak in his own defence. It had even provided some money (£50) – although little time – for him to find witnesses. As will be seen in the next chapter, these protections could not be taken for granted. In 1700 Parliament radically altered piracy trial procedure, stripping most defendants of ancient rights and protections.

At the end of the day, the trials did not live up to their potential as political theatre. The judges sugarcoated the Junto's motives in setting forth the *Adventure Galley* by calling the enterprise 'a very honest Design', and Kidd, having thrown away his chance to implicate his friends before the trials, said nothing about them, except for accusing Bellomont of keeping the French passes from him.[56] He probably still believed that the others would save him from the gallows. This was not an irrational hope, since mitigation of the death penalty was a common feature of English justice in the seventeenth and eighteenth centuries. Indeed, five of the nine convicted of piracy with Kidd were spared hanging. By the letter of the law, all convicted felons were to be executed, but in the cause of mercy juries would acquit lesser offenders, convict them of misdemeanours, or petition the bench for leniency. Judges tended to accept these forms of mitigation except in cases of treason or other attacks upon the state. (During the eighteenth century transportation and incarceration were increasingly substituted for the gallows.)[57]

Kidd's hanging was scheduled for Friday 23 May 1701, so that the minister of Newgate, Reverend Paul Lorrain, had two weeks to bring him to a satisfactory repentance. While he acknowledged to the priest his sins in general, he refused to admit to murder and piracy.

'Tis true he spake some words expressing his confidence in God's mercy thro' Christ, and likewise declared that he died in charity with the world, but still I suspected his sincerity, because he was more reflective upon others than upon himself, and still would endeavour to lay his faults upon his crew and others, going about to excuse and justify himself, much about the same manner as he did when upon his trial.[58]

Until Kidd was brought to Execution Dock, the priest would find his efforts frustrated by what he called his charge's 'Heroick Temper'.[59]

Public hangings are usually rendered palatable and 'instructive' rather than realistic in pictures from the eighteenth century. For example, one famous print of a pirate about to be hanged captures the fear of the condemned before being 'turned off' and accurately depicts the siting of Execution Dock about two and a half miles from Newgate in the parish of St John Wapping (close to where King Henry's Stairs and Captain Kidd's Pub now stand). (See Illustration 53, 54) But it greatly misrepresents the mood of a typical hanging. The artist gives us an orderly, middle-class society coming together to participate in a ritual they believed to combine compassion with justice. The pomp and grandeur of the law is but faintly present in the silver oar carried by the horseman at the left. Everything – even the mild sky – is domestic and human in dimension. The condemned stands on the stage of the gallows surrounded by those who would assist him in his passage to the next world; the onlookers huddle towards the gallows as if to support him. In the crowding of bodies and things, the terrible drop is erased. Through the arch of the short, unadorned gallows, we see warehouses on the opposite shore, symbols of the maritime folk against whom the condemned man has sinned, but who now extend him their version of 'tough love'. The narrow arch frames six human figures and part of the village church whose spire and cross barely overtop the mast of a merchant ship. The image of the church echoes the black-clad minister, who prays with the condemned. Surprisingly, then, the gallows conveys a sense of inclusiveness, not alienation or outlawry. True, the apex of the pyramid in the foreground coincides ominously with the fatal cord, but the picture's

movement is from the lower left – the rod of admiralty law – through
the priest and condemned man, towards the church steeple and the
dramatic dark clouds above it, a movement from law through faith
and death towards divine judgement and the hope of salvation.

Hangings were, in reality, a wild farrago of ceremony, tumult, piety,
hucksterism and horror. Hogarth captures this discord at Tyburn in his
Industry and Idleness sequence, where Tom Idle approaches the gallows
minutes before hanging for theft and murder, (See Illustration 56) but
Tom's figure is sidelined by the drunks, pickpockets, pedlars, lechers,
whores, Methodists, burghers, adulterers, sadists, surgeons, innocents
and termagants who jostle before him. Here the movement is also
from left to right, but it is decidedly horizontal, through an undulat-
ing sea of bodies towards the distant gallows but no further. The brutality that marked Tom's short life is echoed by the diverse folk in the
foreground. Their evident disinterest in his agony – the bell does not
yet toll for them – is in sharp contrast to the pirate's reception at
Execution Dock. Anger and cruelty rule this scene where pikes, staffs,
clubs and crutches abound. Hogarth, too, intends to please and instruct,
but like Brueghel, he means to do it in a biting satire of human folly.

Kidd's execution was closer in spirit to Tom Idle's. He too was
drawn towards Wapping in a cart with other condemned felons, Darby
Mullins of his own crew and two of Culliford's men. The crowd that
formed on 23 May 1701 to see them die was as least as large as that
depicted by Hogarth, since Kidd was a notorious villain. Because his
execution did not take place in the city but in a distant suburb, the
procession must have grown prodigiously by the time it reached the
gallows. As the two carts came by preceded by the silver oar, people
along the way alternately cheered and scorned the condemned, who
reeked with the foulness of Newgate. Many offered them drinks so
that they were soon woefully unprepared to die well. When they
arrived at Execution Dock, where pirates had been hanged for their
crimes since the reign of Henry VI, the pedlars and pickpockets moved
in – as did the hack writers eager to turn a penny by selling the 'dying
speeches' of the condemned.

Those whose duty was to maintain the seriousness of the ritual were
hard put. Reverend Lorrain struggled one more time to bring Kidd to

a full repentance but drink, bitterness and lingering hopes of a pardon hardened Kidd's heart. At the place of death, however, he confessed to piracy and abuse of his commission, but still maintained that his killing of Moore was 'without any premeditated Malice' and that his conviction had been tainted by hearsay and treacherous friends.[60] With an unquiet mind, Kidd ascended the hangman's ladder, the noose was affixed, his body was turned off, and he fell to the ground gasping for breath. Lorrain saw this as a miraculous second chance for him to make a heartfelt confession; he rushed up to the gallows, urged him to 'embrace (before it was too late) the mercy of God', and listened intently to the half-strangled man. The hangman quickly moved the rope from the broken crossbeam of the gallows to a rung on his ladder, carried him to the noose, and on the second try, Kidd died. Lorrain reported that the fierce pirate had, indeed, 'repented with all his heart, and died in Christian love and charity with all the world'.[61]

If tradition were honoured, his body would have been left 'within the Flood-marks', i.e. between the high and low water marks, for three tides before burial.[62] But Kidd, like most notorious pirates, was made a special example for the maritime people. His corpse was dipped in pitch and displayed about twenty-five miles down river at Tilbury Point in Essex wrapped in a set of iron chains that kept it in human form. (See Illustration 58) The famous 'Lamentable Ballad of Captain Kidd', a broadside that appeared on the streets shortly after his death, poignantly expresses what the authorities hoped to teach by this grisly sight.

You captains, brave and bold, hear our cries, hear our cries,
You captains, brave and bold, hear our cries.
You captains, brave and bold, though you seem uncontroul'd,
Don't for the sake of gold lose your souls, lose your souls,
Don't for the sake of gold lose your souls.

You cannot then withstand, when you die, when you die;
You cannot then withstand, when you die;
You cannot then withstand, the judgments of God's hand,
But bound in iron bands, you must die. [63] (See Illustration 57)

Perhaps the only unalloyed good to come from Kidd's affair was that his estate was forfeited by law and used to build Greenwich Hospital for sailors.

My re-examination of Kidd's life indicates that, although guilty of serious crimes, he attempted to live and profit, like Morgan and Dampier, in the grey zone between the legal and the abominable. But unlike the other two, Kidd had assurances from the nation's most powerful men that he might plunder 'uncontroul'd' in the Indian Ocean. A master mariner, he was unqualified to read the direction in which the political winds were blowing. He became confused and therefore bitter, interpreting as personal betrayal what could only be understood as the 'collateral damage' of profound political and legal changes, the movement towards state monopoly over the use of violence and a new system of crime control suited to the government of an empire. Figuratively speaking, Kidd died in the iron bands of a new social order and was strangled twice for good measure – once for his crimes and once for relying on the 'Dispositions of great Princes and Ministers'.[64]

Chapter 6

Blackbeard and the
Pirates of the Bahamas:
'They Shall Plant No Colony in
Our Dominions'

The subjects of this chapter – Captain Edward Thatch and his allies –
were at times based at New Providence and engaged in making that
place what Port Royal, Jamaica, and St Marie's Island, Madagascar, had
once been. After the death of Kidd, Madagascar declined as a pirate
base, chiefly because the East India Company was committed to con-
voying the Mocha fleet, yet there was a resurgence of piracy after the
Treaty of Utrecht ended Queen Anne's War in 1713 and threw thousands of colonial seamen out of work. A second cause of renewed
piracy was the sinking of the Spanish plate fleet in July 1715. News
that a mountain of silver had been recovered off the Bahamas tempted
English freebooters to attack the Spanish salvaging operation. In 1716,
more than 300 men from several British colonies plundered a ware-
house containing a small part of what the Spanish had retrieved (about

350,000 pieces of eight or £87,500). This outrage restarted the old cycle of conflict – reprisals by Spanish warships and *guarda del costa*,[1] the commissioning of English privateers, and the decay of privateering into piracy. To make matters worse, rugged logwood cutters were expelled by the Spanish from Campeche and the Bay of Honduras and once again rallied under the black flag.

As the number of British pirates operating in the Caribbean began to rise dramatically, they again sought bases in the West Indies. But the old hospitable retreats like Tortuga and Jamaica were barred to them by their governors. The Bahamas' weak government, proximity to the grave of the galleons and access to Atlantic trade routes made it a favourite choice of refuge. The pirates who came here, however, were different from the privateers of the late seventeenth century. They might take a commission from time to time, but had fewer scruples about robbing promiscuously than men like Morgan, Dampier, Every and Kidd. They were more aptly described by the popular quasi-legal phrase of the day, 'enemies of all mankind'. At first, England was slow to respond to this new threat, but by the start of 1718 a combination of naval force and legal process had begun to take a toll on the pirates. The many convictions and hangings this year were due to the law passed in 1700 but never before used with such deadly effect. It will be valuable, then, to take a close look at the new law before revisiting the story of Blackbeard.

A critical weakness of the old law was the requirement that pirates be sent to England for trial, clearly an obstruction to justice in an age of global commerce and colonial expansion. It comes as no surprise, then, that the force driving the piracy law's reform was the merchant interest and, above all, the East India Company. The novel notion that what is good for the merchants is good for the nation was expressed succinctly in 1697 by the economist Charles Davenant: 'In a trading nation, the bent of all the laws should tend to the encouragement of commerce, and all measures should be there taken, with a due regard to its interest and advancement'. As today in the United States where business lobbyists draft many of the bills voted on by Congress, a select group of the Company's directors worked with Sir Charles Hedges to write 11–12 William III, c.7, a measure that brought coherence to the prosecution of pirates in the colonies.[2] (See Illustration 59)

For nearly a century, colonial courts had contributed very little to the fight against piracy; civil law courts of vice-admiralty were rare and common law courts that sometimes tried pirates might be reversed for violating proper procedure and overstepping their jurisdiction.[3] Under Hedges's reform piracy would again be tried 'according to the Civil Law, and the Methods and Rules of the Admiralty', but its real genius was to allow for courts 'in Places very remote' – in 'Islands, Plantations... Dominions, Forts or Factories' as well as chartered colonies – while establishing a structure by which they could be made permanent and dependable instruments of imperial policy. The law greatly expanded the number of royal piracy commissions set up in 1536, but required conformity to the centre by placing the high piracy commission in London in charge of nominating their members and monitoring their decisions. Each colonial commission was empowered to investigate and arrest suspects, preside over courts of vice-admiralty, and serve as triers of fact.

This collapsing of the investigators', judges' and jurors' functions was, of course, a great help to the prosecution, but there were many other measures in the law to assure that zealous pirate haters would dominate the commissions. Those qualified to sit on them included

> Admirals, Vice-Admirals, Rear-Admirals, Judges of Vice-Admiralties, or Commanders of any of his Majesty's Ships of War... the President or Chief of some *English* Factory, or the Governor, Lieutenant Governor, or Member of his Majesty's Councils.

We can gauge the depth of distrust felt even towards some of these by the oath required of commissioner/jurors before each trial:

> I... do swear in the Presence of Almighty God, That I... have no Interest, directly or indirectly, in any Ship or Goods, for the Piratically taking of which any Person stands accused, and is now to be tried: So help me God.[4]

Bolder yet, King William's law regularised and radically changed procedure in piracy trials. It rescinded the venerable right of a jury trial by twelve 'good and lawful Inhabitants in the Shire' by substituting a

panel of no fewer than seven commissioners with or without permanent local habitation. The fewer and more detached the commissioners were from the local community, the easier it would be to convict,
and as the law allowed a verdict reached by a plurality; as few as three
votes might secure conviction. Should the commissioners number less
than seven, only persons selected from among

> Merchants, Factors, or Planters, or such as are Captains, Lieutenants, or
> Warrant Officers in any of his Majesty's Ships of war, or Captains, Masters,
> or Mates of some *English* Ship

would be eligible to make up the difference.[5] Panels thus composed
resemble the military tribunals established in 2002 by the United
States to try another kind of stateless terrorist in that both compromise the principle that accused felons be tried by a jury of their peers.

The court's anti-pirate bias would be further assured by two more
extreme departures from common law tradition: the requirement of a
grand jury, believed at the time to protect defendants from frivolous
charges, was dropped for piracy, and there would be no *voir dire*. In
place of independent jurors, defendants would have to accept all the
members of the military-dominated commission that had investigated
and indicted them. Such new rules went far towards allaying fears that
defendants would be acquitted because pirates were popular with the
locals. The law was ambiguous as to its purview. It seemed to control
all piracy trials in the colonies, but it contained language that might
be taken to allow colonial prosecutions under the old law. Legislation
of 1717 (4 George I, c.11) was required to make clear that the 1536
and 1700 laws were, in fact, alternatives. In practice, however, defendants tried in the homeland continued to enjoy common law rights
and protections while those in the colonies almost always came under
the new, harsher law. After its passage there was a sharp and permanent decline in piracy trials in Great Britain.

Sections XIV and XV threatened American colonies, crown and
proprietary, with loss of charter for failure to comply. At the least, governors who refused to do their duty under the new law invited official
inquiries and recall. In practice the reformers fell especially hard upon

the proprietary colonies, before and after 1700. Whitehall's agents risked life and limb in America and were often brutally frank in denouncing recalcitrance in the proprietaries. For example, the indomitable Edward Randolph, surveyor general of customs for North America, reported in 1698 that

> so long as the Bahamas, Carolina, Pennsylvania, the two Jerseys, Connecticut and Rhode Island, remained separate governments and independent of the Crown, it was impossible to suppress piracy.[6]

Randolph and other agents were the shock troops in the movement to bring all the colonies under direct crown rule, a common goal at the time among European colonial powers. Their goal came into reach when in 1701, at the height of the pirate menace, the Board of Trade introduced a Reunification bill that came very close to being enacted.

To ensure uniformity and prevent errors made out of ignorance or malice, all colonial governors were sent detailed instructions on the proper form of a piracy trial and required to send a copy of every trial to the High Court of Admiralty in London. (See Illustration 60) (Today, this document is often the only surviving record of a trial and a boon to historians.) But in addition to critical procedural changes, the law dealt broadly with the substance of piracy. The crime was expanded to include '[making], or [endeavouring] to make a Revolt in the Ship', a provision that, even when not rigorously enforced, had the pleasant, incidental benefit of giving shipmasters more leverage in the frequent labour disputes with their men. Another section made it piracy for 'any of his Majesty's natural-born Subjects, or Denizens of this Kingdom' to take British ships 'under Colour of any Commission from any foreign Prince or State, or Pretence of Authority from any Person whatsoever', a provision meant to disable the common ploy of the West Indian buccaneers and also to overturn the claim to legitimacy of Jacobite privateers.[7] A third innovation subjected those who harboured or traded with pirates to the death penalty although they were to be tried under Henry VIII's law. A concerted attack on their support system – corrupt governors and judges, providers of naval stores, and receivers of stolen goods – might do just as much to discourage the pirates as physical force or threat of prosecution.

The 1700 law attempted to broaden the means of suppressing the pirates by offering more effective rewards and punishments. It promised merchant crews who defended their ships up to two per cent of the freight's value, and seamen who revealed a plot to mutiny, £10 or £15 apiece. Conversely, deserters – frequently recruited by the pirates – would forfeit all their wages, and masters who abandoned their men on foreign shores to reduce their payroll would be imprisoned for three months. Most severe of all, it made the death penalty mandatory throughout the empire for those convicted of piracy, a penalty that theoretically could be imposed by three commissioners instead of the twelve jurors hitherto required. The law encroached dangerously upon civil rights, but there is evidence in its 'sunset' provision – it would expire after seven years – that it was conceived as emergency legislation. We will see, however, that any qualms legislators may have had about it were put aside as chained and rotting bodies of the hanged began to grace waterfronts from Barbados to Boston.

Tradition holds that Edward Thatch or Teach – best known as Blackbeard – was born in Bristol about 1680 and fought courageously in privateers during Queen Anne's War. On the authority of Captain Charles Johnson, he is supposed to have received his first pirate command from Benjamin Hornigold in 1716 and to have moved next year from Jamaica to New Providence where Hornigold became 'governor' of the island's pirates.[8] Also in 1717 he joined in Hornigold's last cruise as a freebooter, but some months before they were to sail, he encountered an odd figure of a pirate who would help to make his name a terror along the American coast.

Major Stede Bonnet was born in 1688 in St Michael's parish, Barbados, scion of a thriving plantation family. This studious gentleman, respectable sugar planter, and officer in the colonial militia had experienced a mid-life crisis that ended in the notion of turning pirate, a career move for which he was unqualified by experience or temperament. Out of his own pocket, he purchased a sloop of ten guns, called it the *Revenge*, and hired a crew of seventy. Bonnet revealed himself a fool from day one by paying his men wages rather than going 'no purchase, no pay'. Surprisingly, the *Revenge* did well on its maiden voyage; from Chesapeake Bay to Long Island it took five ships before putting in at Gardiner's Island, Kidd's old hideout. On its return south two more traders were taken near Charleston, South Carolina, but as the *Revenge* made for the Bahamas, it was mauled by a Spanish man-of-war, Bonnet seriously wounded, and half the crew killed. In September 1717 the badly damaged sloop limped into New Providence where, in return for provisions, repairs and reinforcements, Bonnet agreed to let Thatch command the *Revenge* on a cruise along the northern colonies.

Under Thatch the *Revenge* became a scourge to commerce off Virginia and Delaware; during October, it took more than eleven ships and maliciously destroyed whatever the pirates did not want. The account of one of its captives gives us a glimpse of Bonnet's role in the cruise:

> On board the Pirate Sloop is Major [Bonnet], but has no Command, he walks about in his Morning Gown, and then to his Books, of which he has a good Library on Board.[9]

The *Revenge* sailed back to New Providence late in October but did not stay long; by November it was once more at sea as consort to Hornigold's *Ranger*, their destination the Lesser Antilles. This chain of islands, with its six passages between the Atlantic and the Caribbean, gave the pirates choke points ripe with merchant navigation.

At the Martinique passage the pirates took the large French trader *Concorde*, in which they found African goods including gold and jewels. 'Now', a biographer writes, 'Blackbeard could dine in grand style, savoring French cuisine served on silver plate, accompanied by music'. (Pirates – and seamen in general – considered music one of the necessities of life; from the *Concorde* Thatch accepted four volunteers but also took by force 'a pilot, three surgeons, two carpenters, a cook, a gunsmith, and a black trumpeter'.[10]) After sharing out, Hornigold gave the ship to Thatch, who returned the smaller *Revenge* to its original captain. The fleet was soon reduced when Hornigold left for New Providence with the intention of taking the royal pardon issued 5 September 1717, but Thatch and Bonnet continued to range along the Leewards. At Barbados, the thirty-gun HMS *Scarborough* got word of their approach and, in keeping with the Admiralty's new, aggressive policy, came out to hunt for them. It was fortunate that the *Scarborough* did not find the *Concorde*, which now carried 250 men, thirty-six cannon, and the provocative name *Queen Anne's Revenge*, an affront to George I, Britain's first Hanoverian monarch.

In March 1718, Thatch arrived at the Turneffe Islands near Bélize and waited for the *Revenge*. While *en route*, Bonnet had attacked a large merchantman from Boston, but realised too late that, in the language of the time, he had 'caught a Tartar'; at 400 tons and carrying twenty-six guns, the *Protestant Caesar* forced the sloop to withdraw after a three-hour battle. When Bonnet rendezvoused with Thatch in April, his disappointed crew clamoured for a new leader. Thatch defused their mutiny by welcoming Bonnet onto his own, more comfortable ship and nominating his man Richards for captain of the *Revenge*.

Thatch now set out to hunt in the Bay of Honduras. The first victim, taken while loading logwood, was the same ship that had humiliated Bonnet, the *Protestant Caesar*. When its crew realised that the *Revenge* was among the squadron bearing down on them with 'Black Flags and Deaths Heads', they ran terrified into the Honduran forest. Thatch ransacked and then burnt the *Protestant Caesar,* vowing henceforth to destroy all the New England ships he took in retaliation for the hanging of six pirates at Boston in October 1717.[11] The fleet appeared next off Charleston, South Carolina, in May 1718, where it looted five traders of goods valued at about £1,500 and took several hostages. Before leaving Charleston, Thatch demanded a chest of medicines, but the town baulked even though it was cut off and the ransom insignificant. As the days passed, Thatch's hostages became more and more afraid; from his sudden outbursts of rage, they thought themselves goners.

Thatch is the most charismatic pirate chief we have met since Morgan. He could be a beguiling companion and inspiring leader, but he had also mastered the simulation of maniacal aggression for effect; his manner, gestures, and even appearance were intended to panic those he could not charm into immediate compliance. Here is Charles Johnson's sensational description of him.

our Heroe, Captain *Teach*, assumed the Cognomen of *Black-beard*, from
that large Quantity of Hair, which, like a frightful Meteor, covered his
whole Face, and frightened *America* more than any Comet that has
appeared there a long Time...

This Beard was black, which he suffered to grow of an extravagant Length;
as to Breadth, it came up to his Eyes; he was accustomed to twist it with
Ribbons, in small Tails... and turn them about his Ears: In Time of Action,
he wore a Sling over his Shoulders, with three Braces of Pistols, hanging in
Holsters like Bandoliers; and stuck lighted Matches under his Hat, which
appearing on each Side of his Face, his Eyes naturally looking fierce and
wild, made him altogether such a Figure, that Imagination cannot form an
Idea of a Fury, from Hell, to look more frightful. (See Illustration 62)

Thatch's fierceness was intended as much to terrify his crew as his
prey; Johnson cites the following incident to show how he employed
unpredictable violence as a means of control.

One Night drinking in his Cabin with *Hands*, the Pilot, and another Man;
Black-beard, without any Provocation, privately draws out a small Pair of
Pistols, and cocks them under the Table... When the Pistols were ready, he
blew out the Candle, and crossing his Hands, discharged them at his
Company; *Hands*, the Master, was shot thro' the Knee, and lam'd for Life....
Being asked the meaning of this, he only answered, by damning them, that
if he did not now and then kill one of them, they would forget who he was.

The source of Thatch's power was the imagery and rituals of the
demonic: 'some of his Frolicks of Wickedness, were so extravagant, as
if he aimed at making his Men believe he was a Devil incarnate'.
Perhaps the most bizarre of his 'frolics' was the staging of a contest
among his Men to reveal the True Satan among them.

Come, says he, *let us make a Hell of [our] own, and try how long we can
bear it*; accordingly he, with two or three others, went down into the
Hold, and closing up all the Hatches, filled several Pots full of Brimstone,
and other combustible Matter, and set it on Fire, and so continued till
they were almost suffocated, when some of the Men cry'd out for Air; at

length he opened the Hatches, not a little pleased that he held out the longest.[12]

It is not difficult to understand how as 'Blackbeard', this small-time operator – in comparison with Morgan, Every, or even Kidd – became what has been called a 'global icon of piracy'.[13]

Before the bar at Charleston, Thatch called a general consultation that voted to punish the town. His fleet – now grown to eight – thereupon moved across the bar into the harbour, their guns primed to raze one of the most prosperous ports in British America. Just before the command to fire, the pirates spied a boat rowing out to them with the precious chest of medicines. Charleston had complied in full with Thatch's ultimatum, giving evidence of how vulnerable even an established colonial port of the early 1700s could be to a modest naval assault. The shock of this near disaster was felt from Savannah to Chesapeake Bay and spurred the authorities in several colonies to consider a joint defence.

Thatch would never again command so many men and ships; his fortunes were swiftly reversed in June 1718 when he attempted to come through North Carolina's Outer Bank. Two of his large ships ran aground at Beaufort (then called Topsail) Inlet leaving the fleet dangerously vulnerable to attack. After most of the seamen escaped into the neighbouring countryside or the northern colonies, he was obliged to once more give the *Revenge* back to Bonnet. Now, for the first time in their relationship, Bonnet led the way: he left the *Revenge* in Beaufort harbour and went directly to Bath, North Carolina, to 'surrender' to the royal pardon of 1717. In return for swearing to abandon piracy, he was absolved of all his robberies and murders at sea before 5 January 1718 and allowed to keep his plunder, absent claims at law by its previous owners. Full of benign intentions, he returned to his sloop only to find it stripped of food and treasure and Thatch gone to Ocracoke Inlet on the Outer Bank. Bonnet pursued with a vengeance but for the second time arrived too late.

The traitors had also gone to Bath for a pardon from Governor Charles Eden, which was granted a few days after Bonnet had left town. Thatch found Bath very much to his liking; it was well situated to discourage a naval surprise and give his sloops quick access to shallows where most warships could not go. Although the colony's capital, Bath was a small community eager to buy his goods on the cheap and so weakened by hardships that it lacked the will to oppose him. He was not only tolerated at Bath, but like many alluring, rich scoundrels before and after, he 'overnight became a sensation – the center of a society feasting on the swirl of notoriety and wealth that surrounded him'.[14] For students of the intersection of law and piracy, this is an interesting, if short, period in his career.

Thatch fraternised with Governor Eden and his ally Tobias Knight, chief justice of the colony, as well as with the planters, and when he married one of their young daughters, the governor officiated. The first practical result of his rapid social climb was that he received permission to go to St Thomas for a Danish commission against the Spanish. (England and Denmark were at war with Spain from 1718 to 1720.) Subsequently, Eden's admiralty court condemned a Spanish sloop Thatch had taken near Cuba and later gave him rights to a French ship full of sugar which he claimed to have found adrift during the summer of 1718. In reality, the ship was among several, English and French, he had taken by force while cruising under Danish colours. Thatch was not only a danger at sea again, he was also a pest on land. Immune from prosecution, his men sailed the area's waterways bullying the populace and robbing at will. When the colony's leading merchants could stand it no more, they plotted behind the governor's back to get outside help. Messages were sent to Alexander Spotswood, governor of Virginia, and plans were laid to use the warships in his jurisdiction to enter North Carolina and hunt Thatch down.

In the meantime, Bonnet had rebuilt his crew with men Thatch had marooned near Beaufort Inlet and celebrated the rebirth of his command by renaming his sloop the *Royal James*, explicitly associating himself, as had Thatch and other pirate chiefs, with the Old Pretender and the departed Stuarts. Wishing to honour the terms of his pardon, he traded for supplies with the ships he stopped, but late in July fell into old ways, taking numerous small vessels off Virginia, Delaware and New Jersey. Among them were the *Fortune* (Captain Peter Mainwaring) and *Francis* (Captain Thomas Read), two sloops loaded with great quantities of food and drink. Thus richly provided, Bonnet sailed to the North Carolina coast to refit and shelter from the late summer hurricanes. When the pirates arrived at Cape Fear early in August, they threw a gargantuan party that ended in Bonnet's flogging two of them for insulting their 'superiors'. Ordinarily, pirate crews would over-throw captains who applied the lash, a hated memory of their former subjection. But on this occasion, there was too much rum to mind – 1,800 gallons! The mood of good and plenty was a boon for their hostages; the *Fortune*'s captain Mainwaring reported that during his long detention among them, the pirates were 'civil to me, very civil'. [15]

Cape Fear is within easy reach of Charleston, which at this time was suffering from yet another blockade by a Bahamas pirate, the tur-bulent Captain Charles Vane. (See Illustration 63) Vowing never again to be humiliated by such rogues, Charleston sent on the offensive 130 volunteers in two armed sloops. Vane presently moved off, but when Bonnet's crew was spotted at the cape, the sloops changed course to confront them. The squadron's commander was Colonel William Rhett, an aggressive and proven naval officer. Rhett's ships, the *Henry* (eight guns, seventy men) and *Nymph* (eight guns, sixty men), came into the Cape Fear River late on the afternoon of 26 September hoping to surprise Bonnet next morning. (See Illustration 64)

When dawn broke, it was Rhett's turn to be surprised. As the *Henry* and *Nymph* got underway, there was the *Royal James* with its ten guns, forty-five men, and red flag coming towards them. What happened next would be comical if it had not opened both parties to lethal fire: all three sloops ran aground – Rhett and Bonnet separated by the range of a pistol.

Rhett's position was worse than Bonnet's. The *Royal James* was tilted away from the *Henry*, rendering its big guns useless, but the *Henry* was tilted towards the pirate, exposing its deck to intense small-arms fire. The *Henry*'s men took whatever cover they could, but their casualties soon began to mount. Sensing a victory, the pirates 'made a Wiff of their bloody flag', that is, formed it into a long roll and raised it up at the stern, a mocking signal for its enemies to come aboard.

The battle raged for five hours before the tide released the *Henry*, which, after a few repairs and the priming of cannon, made for the

Royal James. At this point the pirates had killed twelve and wounded eighteen of the enemy, losing only nine. Yet, seeing that he was out-numbered and immobilised, Bonnet ordered the ship blown up, but when his men protested and Rhett promised to recommend them to the court's mercy, he surrendered.

On 3 October Rhett turned thirty-six prisoners over to Charleston's provost-marshal. Four days before their trial, however, two escaped – the *Royal James*'s sailing master, David Herriot, and captain, Stede Bonnet. They fled to densely overgrown Sullivan's Island, where they were protected by a small marooned community of Indians and run-away slaves. A huge reward of £700 was immediately posted, but it took Rhett two weeks to corner them on the island. In the ensuing gunfight Herriot was killed and Bonnet recaptured.

From 28 October to 5 November 1718, thirty-three men were indicted and tried in Judge Nicholas Trott's court at Charleston for piratically seizing the sloops *Francis* and *Fortune*; Bonnet's trial came on 10 November. The proceedings were unusual for piracy trials in the colonies since, according to the 1717 statute, South Carolina chose to proceed under Henry VIII's, not William III's piracy law. To be sure, the state ran the risk of jurors friendly to the accused, no small problem in light of the angry demonstrations in Charleston after Bonnet was cap-tured. On the other hand, anti-pirate sentiment was at its height in the wake of Thatch's outrages, and in Nicholas Trott the colony had an aggressive scourge of such 'beasts of prey'. (See Illustration 65) Trott's duty as the colony's chief justice was to uphold the law, especially in light of the home government's anti-piracy campaign. But I suspect that his zeal during the trials reflects a more personal motive, the wish to restore his family's honour. It will be recalled that Governor Nicholas Trott and Major Perient Trott had protected Captain Every and his crew in 1696. Nicholas, cousin to the South Carolina judge, payed dearly for it: he had been replaced and summoned to London in 1697, and the Board of Trade had rejected his petition for reinstatement. Judge Trott was going to show the world that he detested piracy and, perhaps, to vindicate proprietary government along the way.

In his charge to the grand jury, he chose to rehearse many of the precedents for British admiralty jurisdiction over piracy. This part of his speech must have brought the jurors to a stupor, but no matter, its real audience was sitting in London. Having established his credentials for learning and orthodoxy, he went on to reveal the fire of his passion for justice and revenge. 'This very *Company*, which will now be charged before you with the Crime of Piracy', he reminded the Charleston audience, 'were belonging to that *Crew*, which first insulted us'. Trott's rhetoric soared as he remembered those who fought to save the city's honour and trade.

> in this *Attack* made upon those *Enemies of Mankind*, many of our People lost their Lives in the discharge of their Duty to their King and Country, and who fell by the hands of those inhuman and murdering *Criminals* which will now be brought before you. And the Blood of those murdered Persons will cry for Vengeance and Justice against these Offenders.

Trott had shifted skilfully from the rationality of the law to the raw emotions of a frontier society, a shift, to the modern observer, more in keeping with the role of prosecutor. If there were any doubt about the judge's opinions, it was swept away in his final paragraph:

> as to those *Indictments* that will now be brought before you, I am very well assur'd the *Proofs* will be so clear and full, that you'll have no reason to doubt of the Truth of the Facts charged therein: and then I shall not question your faithful Discharge of that great Duty and Trust the Law hath reposed in you, in bringing such Criminals to Justice.[16]

Trott's bias is less disguised than that of his august London brethren Holt, Hedges and Ward, but to much the same effect. The speech asserted a control over the juries in his court that prevailed throughout both sets of trials.

The several indictments dutifully handed down by the grand jury stated, as required by law, the dates, places and victims of the alleged crimes – the seizure of the *Fortune* and *Francis* – and the types and value of the goods stolen. But for both sloops, the indictments gave the wrong dates, off by a few days in one case and a month in the other, errors that could have invalidated the proceedings. The common law was then characterised by great preoccupation with formal accuracy and resistance to reductions in the leverage defendants had when errors in indictments could be proven.[17] Without counsel, however, the defendants at Charleston could hardly benefit from this aspect of the law. After the first indictment was read, Attorney General Richard Allein and Mr Thomas Hepworth opened the case to the jury of twelve. Their speeches and Trott's show that for the government these were 'state trials' analogous to those of Kidd and Every's crew. In fact, they covered the same topics that Justice Hedges addressed in 1696: the critical condition of the state, 'the discipline of the seas', the evil of jury bias, and the necessity of protecting English trade with 'a true English spirit'. And like Hedges, Hepworth spoke without the least intent to 'influence any of the jury'.[18]

The evidentiary phase of the trials is interesting largely for the relentless efforts of the judge to ridicule the accused and their meagre attempts at a defence. Trott's sharpest weapon was the sarcastic rhetorical question. For example, in response to a prisoner's asserting that they took ships for food, he remarked, 'So you took it where you could find it, because you had it not of your own: but pray what did you with so much Molosses?' He later scored against Bonnet with the same jibe, 'What need had you of so much Molosses?' A master of dry wit, Trott lunged at one defendant who said he planned to run away from the pirates in one of their sloops: 'So, I find you wanted a Vessel of your own'. He dismissed another man's excuse that the *Royal James* was headed to St Thomas to receive a lawful privateering commission by inquiring, 'But was that your manner of going for a Commission, to take *thirteen* Vessels by the way?' Trott was thoroughly bewildered when Bonnet denied responsibility for the theft of the molasses: 'You gave Orders for it to be done, and yet it was contrary to your Inclinations'. Turning from Bonnet's only defence witness towards the accused, he dropped the mask to state, 'If this be all the Evidence you have, I do not see this will be of much use to you'.[19]

In a modern American court, Trott's utterances might be grounds for a mistrial. But for the Charleston juries, his opinions were an accepted guide to the proper reading of the evidence in the pursuit of truth. Nor would they have winced at his invariable manner of sending them off to deliberate with this sentiment: 'tho I think the Evidence is very plain and clear, yet I shall not pretend to direct your Judgments'.[20]

While all the defendants claimed to have been forced, not all of their claims were rejected. The judge and jury found convincing evidence to acquit four; the rest, including Bonnet, were sentenced to hang until they be 'dead, dead, dead'. But before passing sentence, Trott did an unusual and entirely admirable thing for his day. He stepped, as it were, off the bench and took considerable time to instruct the condemned as a Christian, urging them first to 'acknowledge that you have all of you had a fair and indifferent Tryal' and then to repent their sins.[21] Unfortunately, for twenty-two there was not much time for soul-searching. On Saturday 8 November, only three days after sentencing, they were executed at White Point near Charleston. Through the intervention of his friends, Bonnet survived his trial by four weeks, but was hanged on 10 December. Judging from a bizarre letter he wrote to Governor Johnson, he had not reconciled himself to his fate; in a fever of anxiety, he begged the governor to commute his sentence, offering in return to '[separate] all my Limbs from my Body, only reserving the Use of my Tongue, to call continually on, and pray to the Lord, my God'.[22] (See Illustration 66)

Except for the factual errors in the indictments, the Charleston trials were legally correct and fair, given the standards of the time. But Trott's behaviour might appear excessive even to contemporaries. We do not know if Charles Johnson's burlesque of a piracy trial published six years later alludes to Trott or any actual proceedings, but it certainly captures his prosecutorial exuberance. The setting is an unnamed island off the south-west coast of Cuba, the event a play put on by the crew of Captain Anstis, a former consort of Bartholomew Roberts.

> The Court and Criminal being both appointed, as also Council to plead, the Judge got up in a Tree, and had a dirty Tarpaulin hung over his Shoulders; this was done by Way of Robe, with a Thrum Cap on his Head, and a large Pair of Spectacles upon his Nose: Thus equipp'd, he settled himself in his Place, and abundance of Officers attending him below, with Crows, Handspikes, &c. instead of Wands, Tipstaves, and such like. –

The Criminals were brought out, making a thousand sour Faces; and one who acted as Attorney-General opened the Charge against them; their Speeches were very laconick, and their whole Proceedings concise. We shall give it by Way of Dialogue.

Attorn. Gen. An't please your Lordship, and you Gentlemen of the Jury, here is a Fellow before you that is a sad Dog, a sad sad Dog; and I humbly hope your Lordship will order him to be hang'd out of the Way immediately. – He has committed Pyracy upon the High Seas, and we shall prove, an't please your Lordship, that this Fellow, this sad Dog before you, has escap'd a thousand Storms, nay, has got safe ashore when the Ship has been cast away, which was a certain Sign he was not born to be drown'd; yet not having the Fear of hanging before his Eyes, he went on robbing and ravishing Man, Woman and Child, plundering Ships' Cargoes fore and aft, burning and sinking Ship, Bark and Boat, as if the Devil had been in him, But this is not all, my Lord, he has committed worse Villainies than all these, for we shall prove, that he has been guilty of drinking Small-Beer, and your Lordship knows, there never was a sober Fellow but what was a Rogue. – My Lord, I should have spoke much finer than I do now, but that, as your Lordship knows our Rum is all out, and how should a Man speak good Law that has not drank a Dram. – However, I hope, your Lordship will order the Fellow to be hang'd.

Judge. – Hearkee me, Sirrah, – you lousy, pittiful, ill-look'd Dog; what have you to say why you should not be tuck'd up immediately, and set a Sun-drying like a Scare-crow? – Are you guilty, or not guilty?

Pris. Not guilty, an't please your Worship.

Judge. Not guilty! say so again, Sirrah, and I'll have you hang'd without any Tryal.

Pris. An't please your Worship's Honour, my Lord, I am as honest a poor Fellow as ever went between Stem and Stern of a Ship, and can hand, reef, steer, and clap two Ends of a Rope together, as well as e'er a He that ever cross'd salt Water; but I was taken by one George Bradley [the Name of him that sat as Judge] a notorious Pyrate, a sad Rogue as ever was unhang'd, and he forc'd me, an't please your Honour.

Judge. Answer me, Sirrah, – How will you be try'd?

Pris. By G- and my Country.

Judge. *The Devil you will. – Why then, Gentlemen of the Jury, I think we have*
  nothing to do but to proceed to Judgment.
Attor. Gen. *Right, my Lord; for if the Fellow should be suffer'd to speak, he may*
  clear himself, and that's an Affront to the Court.
Pris. *Pray, my Lord, I hope your Lordship will consider –*
Judge. *Consider! – How dare you talk of considering? – Sirrah, Sirrah, I never*
  consider'd in all my Life. – I'll make it Treason to consider.
Pris. *But, I hope, your Lordship will hear some Reason.*
Judge. *D'ye hear how the Scoundrel prates? – What have we to do with Reason?*
  – I'd have you to know, Raskal, we don't sit here to hear Reason; – we go
  according to Law. – Is our Dinner ready?
Actor. Gen. *Yes, my Lord.*
Judge. *Then heark'ee, you Raskal at the Bar; hear me, Sirrah, hear me. – You*
  must suffer for three Reasons: First, because it is not fit I should sit here as Judge,
  and no Body be hang'd. – Secondly, you must be hang'd, because you have a
  damn'd hanging Look. – And thirdly, you must be hang'd, because I am hungry;
  for know, Sirrah, that 'tis a Custom, that whenever the Judge's Dinner is ready
  before the Tryal is over, the Prisoner is to be hang'd of Course. – There's Law for
  you, ye Dog. – So take him away Gaoler.[23]

This amusing playlet was the creation not of rough-and-tumble pirates
but of an educated London author, yet it probably captures accurately
enough the pirates' contempt for the official forms of justice and for
the abusive hanging judges they were encountering with more and
more frequency.

We left Thatch settling comfortably into the social life of the Bath
gentry and terrorising the waterways, unaware of Governor
Spotswood's plans to invade North Carolina and destroy him. In
addition to his town accommodations, Thatch had set up a base about
fifty-five miles to the south at Ocracoke Inlet where he could store
plunder and supplies in secret and have immediate access to the
ocean. The base worried Spotswood who was convinced that Thatch
wanted to fortify and draw pirates to it, a common fear nourished by
the rise of the Bahamas base and lingering memories of the one on
St Marie's Island off Madagascar. To eliminate the danger at Ocracoke,

Thatch must not be allowed to escape; consequently the governor devised a synchronised descent by soldiers on Bath and by naval sloops on the Inlet. Captain Ellis Brand of HMS *Lyme* would be commander-in-chief and lead the land contingent from Virginia across the Dismal Swamp into Carolina. Robert Maynard, first lieutenant of HMS *Pearl*, would take fifty-four men in two sloops, the *Jane* and the *Ranger*, and secure the Inlet. Governor Eden would not be informed lest he or his council members warn the pirates. Despite the sophisticated legal system brought over from England, Spotswood was about to supersede his jurisdiction and violate the explicit instructions to the contrary given to him by the crown.[24] The upcoming battle, one of the most famous in the annals of piracy, was probably illegal.

Thatch was at Ocracoke on the morning of 22 November 1718, when he saw two sloops approaching slowly through the shallows, probably traders on their way to Bath, Beaufort or Southport. Thinking to bid them welcome, he slipped anchor and the *Adventure* moved leisurely towards them. The quiet of the scene was disturbed by the splash of oars from the *Jane's* boat as it took soundings, then the sharp crack of a pirate's musket warning the boat to come no closer. Thatch's eye caught shadows in the water between him and the strangers. If he changed course slightly, they might follow him towards the shore, run aground on the sandbar and become easy prey. It worked, the *Jane* stuck – and then the *Ranger*. In the *General History's* imaginative rendering, Thatch and Rhett now spoke to each other across the gap.

> *Damn you for Villains, who are you? And, from whence came you?* The Lieutenant made him Answer, *You may see by our Colours we are no Pyrates....* *Black-beard* took a Glass of Liquor, and drank to him with these Words: *Damnation seize my Soul if I give you Quarters, or take any from you.*[25]

Thatch's fighting spirit rose with these words. He gave the order to fire a broadside. His guns were loaded with small shot that ravaged the enemy and killed the *Ranger's* captain, but in the smoke that obscured the area, he too ran onto the bar. Meanwhile, the *Jane* had refloated and was bearing down on the *Adventure*. The ships collided with a groaning of timbers and the shouts of the pirates. When no one appeared to stir on the deck of the *Jane*, Thatch called on his men – now reduced to eighteen – to bomb the enemy with grenades and board. No sooner had they done so than the *Jane*'s survivors counter-charged from out the hold. The pirates were stunned and outnumbered while Maynard's men fought fiercely for justice, a cut of the pirates' treasure, and a bounty voted by Virginia's legislature. Johnson's rendering of the battle's climax is in the melodramatic style of 1930s Hollywood.

> *Black-beard* and the Lieutenant fired the first Shots at each other, by which the Pyrate received a Wound, and then engaged with Swords, till the Lieutenant's unluckily broke, and [Maynard] stepping back to cock a Pistol, *Black-beard*, with his Cutlash, was striking at that Instant, that one of *Maynard*'s Men gave him a terrible Wound in the Neck and Throat, by which the Lieutenant came off with only a small Cut over his Fingers.
>
> They were now closely and warmly engaged, the Lieutenant and twelve Men against *Black-beard* and fourteen, till the Sea was tinctur'd with Blood round the Vessel; *Black-beard* received a Shot into his Body from the Pistol that Lieutenant *Maynard* discharg'd, yet he stood his Ground, and fought with great Fury, till he received five and twenty Wounds, and five of them by Shot. At length, as he was cocking another Pistol, having fired several before, he fell down dead; by which Time eight more out of the fourteen dropp'd, and all the rest, much wounded, jump'd over-board, and call'd for Quarters, which was granted.... Here was an End of that courageous Brute, who might have pass'd in the World for a Heroe, had be been employ'd in a good Cause.[26] (See Illustration 68)

Thatch had wanted the *Adventure* blown up rather than surrendered, but, like Bonnet's, his apocalypse was cancelled when Caesar, a black pirate entrusted to light the fuse, was overcome by one of the captive passengers.

The nine surviving prisoners and a few taken at Bath were shipped to Williamsburg, colonial capital of Virginia, where they were tried in March and all but one hanged. Spotswood's right to hold this trial and control the recovered pirate booty was hotly denied by Governor

Eden but to no avail. Blackbeard's hoard of £2,238 was shared among the victorious, but the most notable memento of the action was his head. To prove his company's claim for the £100 bounty, Maynard cut it off and hung it from his bowsprit. A biographer reports that 'the rest of Blackbeard's corpse was thrown overboard. According to legend, when the headless body hit the cold water, it defiantly 'swam around the sloop several times before it sank'. The head was later displayed for years on the banks of Hampton Roads harbour (Virginia) to deter would-be pirates. Some say it was afterwards made 'into the base of a large punch bowl... long used as a drinking vessel at the Raleigh Tavern in Williamsburg'.[27] (See Illustration 69)

Bonnet and Thatch's operations for the most part fit the pirates' routine of moving north in the summer and south in the winter. Situated roughly in the middle of this course, the Bahamas were a convenient resting place, but by the middle of 1718, its days as a pirate haven were numbered. Several of Thatch's New Providence comrades, led by his mentor Benjamin Hornigold, had declared their intention to reform. The power vacuum thus created before the coming of the Bahamas' first royal governor was filled by Charles Vane. Thatch's bark was worse than his bite, but according to mariners taken by Vane, he was cruel indeed. The crew of the *Diamond* was needlessly beaten and one man hanged; when this failed to kill him, he was viciously hacked with a cutlass. To learn where a man from the *Edward and Mary* had hidden his money, Vane had him lashed to the bowsprit and terrorised by fire played about his eyes.[28]

Vane tried to rouse New Providence to resist the governor's coming, Johnson reports, by swearing 'while he was in the Harbour, he would suffer no other Governor than himself'. He may be the model for the 'pirate sailor' in Defoe's *The Farther Adventures of Robinson Crusoe* (1719) who threatens to destroy the community Crusoe has fostered on his island: 'they shall plant no colony in our dominions'.[29] But despite Vane's defiant rhetoric, he did nothing to weaken the forces of reform. The governor was Woodes Rogers, the courageous and steadfast commander of Dampier's last cruise; Rogers would suffer many hardships and setbacks in the coming years, yet Vane's departure signalled the beginning of the end for the Bahamas pirates and the renewal of lawful government.

In the midst of establishing that government and preparing to repel a threatened Spanish attack, Rogers pushed for the prosecution of the unreformed and of those who had, as the preachers would say quoting Scripture, returned like a dog to its vomit. The first test of the government's ability to bring pirates to justice in their own stronghold was the trial on 9–10 December 1718 of John Augur and nine other recently pardoned pirates. Augur, captain of the merchant sloop Mary, had joined with mutineers from two other English ships at Green Key, a small island south of New Providence, to plunder commerce in the area. One evening, this flotilla attacked three innocent-looking Spanish sloops which proved to be privateers; after the battle, in which several pirates were killed, Augur and other survivors were gathered up by Rogers's henchman, the repentant and retooled pirate-hunter Benjamin Hornigold, and returned to New Providence for prosecution.

The issue was less the accused's guilt or innocence than the new government's ability to hold a piracy trial at all. The Bahamas had been in a state of lawlessness for so long that Rogers's plans for a salutary conviction and mass hanging were seriously in doubt. He had landed with a regiment of loyal troops, but his most powerful weapon was the reformed piracy act. Because it allowed him to dispense with the grand jury, limit the number of commissioners to seven, and hand-pick those from among his officers, it would give him a court willing to convict despite overwhelming sympathy for the accused throughout the colony.

There was one serious obstacle, however. Rogers had not been empowered by the crown to organise a piracy commission for the Bahamas so that a trial under 11–12 William 3, c.7, might be thrown out as a matter of law. But with his government and his own life on the line, he would not be hamstrung by technicalities. He gambled that there would be no proper challenge before the bodies swung and the issue was moot. Rogers secretly informed his council on 28 November 1718 that he had 'no direct Commission for Tryal of Pyrates' but argued that his powers as Captain-General and Vice-Admiral 'shew the Intention of his Majesty, for such Authority here'. Although everyone knew that the right course was to send the accused to London, the council unanimously concluded that:

his Majesty will approve of the Necessity for the Governor's judicial
Proceeding with these Pyrates, by a Tryal in the best Manner we can
according to Law; and do verily believe the speediest Execution for those
who shall be found guilty, will conduce most to the Welfare of this
Government.[30]

The 'best Manner we can according to Law' was to name a piracy
commission dominated by an admiralty judge and three naval officers
and to proceed, in the words of the trial report, 'according to the
Intent and Meaning of a late Act of Parliament'.[31]

Perhaps because of its dubious authority and the crisis atmosphere
in which it sat, the court was extraordinarily fair and deliberate. It
gave the accused ample opportunity to make their case and even
acquitted one defendant as a forced man. The executions of Augur
and eight others were scheduled for two days after the trial, causing
the condemned to ask for more time to prepare their souls. This delay
the ailing Governor denied them in a speech expressing the great
pressure he was under to save the colony from dissolution:

> the Governour told them [that]... he was obliged to employ all his People
> to assist in mounting the Great Guns, & in finishing the present works,
> with all possible dispatch, because of the expected War with Spain, &
> there being many more pyrates amongst these Islands, and this place left
> destitute of all Relief, from any man of War, or Station'd Ship much
> wanted which with other Reasons, he knew too long to enumerate in
> the Court, [He] thought himselfe indispensably obliged for the wellfare
> of the Settlement to give them no longer time.

If the governor presented himself as a generous but harried leader
forced by circumstances to take harsh measures, the condemned
Dennis McCarty ascended the gallows with a gaiety that scorned
both his oppressors and the coward audience who would not rise up
to save him from the rope.

> He put on a clean shift of Cloaths, adorn'd at Neck, Wrists, knees, &
> Capp with long blew Ribbons when on the Rampart lookt Cheerfully

arround him, Saying he knew the time [when] there was many brave fellows on the Island that would not suffer him to dye like [a] dog, at the
same time pull'd off his Shoes kicking them over the Parapet of the [Fort]
saying he had promised not to dye with his Shoes on, & he descended
the Fort Wall, & ascended the Stage with as much agility, and in a dress
as if he was [going] to fight a prize, when Mounted He exhorted the
People who were at the foot [of] the Walls to have Compassion on him
but they saw too much power over their heads to practice any thing.[32]

We do not need Captain Johnson's help to see in the governor and
the pirate on the ramparts of Nassau's partially restored fort a tableau
symbolic of two worlds in collision. (See Illustration 70)

The last major event in the campaign against the Bahamas pirates was
the destruction of Vane's old crew now commanded by his former
quartermaster, John Rackam. After a brief cruise in the western
Caribbean, Rackam came into the Atlantic early in 1719 and sailed to
one of the outlying Bahamas to refit. He liked this base too much, for
Rogers finally learnt where he was and sent out an armed sloop.
Rackam abandoned his prizes, barely eluded the sloop, and hid out
on the south shore of Cuba for many months until he was flushed out
by another enemy. (See Illustration 71) Towards the end of the year, a
formidable *guarda del costa* happened to bring a captured English sloop
into Rackam's bay. When discovered, the pirate had to duck behind a
small island to avoid the enemy's broadsides, but as the light was fading,
the Spanish decided to block the river channel, and wait until morning to finish him off. Rackam had another idea. In the quiet of the
night, he got all his men into a boat and silently rowed alongside the
captured sloop. On the signal, they sprung aboard, surprised the
Spanish sentries, and frightened them into compliance. Vane then
piloted his new ship out to sea while the '*Spanish* Man of War was so
intent on their expected Prize, that they minded nothing else'.[33]

His sloop next appeared in August 1720 off the north-west coast of
Jamaica, the area most vulnerable to pirate forays. Here he pillaged
many small vessels and took on a group of French volunteers. Once
again, however, Rackam played it too close to the wind, for early in

November, Jamaica's governor sent out a sloop under Captain Barnet to take him. The pirates were then at North Negril Point celebrating their newest prize and drinking with nine turtle fishermen whom they had invited aboard to recruit. These hapless guests 'had no sooner laid down their Arms, and taken up their Pipes, but *Barnet*'s Sloop... came in Sight'.[34] The pirates had time to get underway, but the nimble sloop caught up and fired across their bow. Rackam tried to resist but the enemy's superior force obliged him to surrender. Both veteran marauders and turtle fishers mouldered in Spanish Town prison for two weeks before their trials began on 16 November 1720. (See Illustration 72)

Like the proceedings at New Providence in 1718, those at Spanish Town were governed by King William's piracy act, but they depended upon bad procedure and evidence that would not support an indictment in a London court. For example, there were 'articles' for which there was no evidence at trial and others for which there was only one eyewitness, in violation of explicit directions to all colonial governors.[35] In one trial of four defendants, there were no witnesses against one of them, in another the only crimes cited in the indictment were committed before the defendants entered Rackam's ship. Even more serious was the prosecutors' failure to produce evidence of criminal acts for individual defendants, such as signing pirate articles, participating actively in battle and sharing in the plunder. Usually, their mere presence on a pirate ship was offered to prove felonious intent. The malice or sloppiness of the court, especially in the drawing up of indictments, is in stark contrast to the professionalism we have seen in other trials and amply demonstrates the evil of merging the grand jury with the triers of fact.

The results were highly unjust. While two prisoners were acquitted 'for want of full Evidence only', twenty-three were sentenced to be hanged.[36] Among them were the most unfairly treated of all, the nine turtle fishermen. Most of these could be accused of nothing worse than entering the pirate ship with their pistols and cutlasses; a few were seen to help row the pirate's ship away from Capt. Barnet, but neither of the two witnesses could tell which! The court ignored the most exculpatory testimony, that when Barnet attacked, 'the Prisoners at the Bar went down under Deck' and that 'when Captain

came up with them, they all readily and willingly surrendered themselves'. One does not need a modern sensibility to be shocked at the
court's verdict; Charles Johnson, too, was surprised that they were
sentenced to die, 'which', he comments, 'every Body must allow
proved somewhat unlucky to the poor Fellows'.37 Poor fellows of all
sorts would have to wait until the next century before judges routinely instructed juries that the accused were presumed innocent
until proven guilty and that the prosecution must prove their guilt
beyond a reasonable doubt.

If the fishermen were unjustly consumed by Jamaica's fury against
pirates, two other defendants profited from the legal system's mercy.
Mary Read and Ann Bonny were arrested with Rackam and tried on
28 November for the same crimes. Four witnesses provided strong
evidence that the women were enthusiastic supporters, not passive
victims of the pirates. Dorothy Thomas, taken by Rackam while fishing in a canoe off Harbour Island, Bahamas, testified that they

> wore Mens Jackets, and long Trouzers, and Handkerchiefs tied about their
> Heads; and that each of them had a Machet and Pistol in their Hands,
> and cursed and swore at the Men, to murther the Deponent; and that
> they should kill her, to prevent her coming against them...

John Besneck and Peter Cornelian recalled seeing them

> very active on Board, and willing to do any Thing; That *Ann Bonny*...
> handed Gun-powder to the Men, That when they saw any Vessel, gave
> Chase, or Attacked, they wore Men's Cloaths; and, at other times, they
> wore Women's Cloaths; That they did not seem to be kept, or detain'd by
> Force, but of their own Free-Will and Consent.

Finally, Thomas Dillon told that when he was captured by Rackam,

> Ann Bonny... had a Gun in her Hand, That they were both very profli-
> gate, cursing and swearing much, and very ready and willing to do any
> Thing on Board.38

Faced with evidence of their adherence to the pirates, the defendants had nothing to say and the court had no choice but to sentence them to death. But the women knew that they would not die with the others. 'After Judgment was pronounced... both the Prisoners inform'd the Court, that they were both quick with Child, and prayed that Execution of the Sentence might be stayed'.[39] Their prayers were granted under a legal exception dating from Anglo-Saxon times. The law permitted a stay of execution if a woman could 'plead her belly' and prove herself pregnant; the stay could be lifted after the child was born, but it was more common for the new mother to be pardoned or transported. (The law permitting execution of a woman after giving birth survived until 1931, but was last used in 1873.[40]) There is nothing documented about Bonny and Read beyond the trial report, which did not prevent Charles Johnson and many others from recounting their youth and continuing their lives after their pregnancies.

They are less interesting as prisoners at the bar than as avatars of an eternally fascinating type, the woman who passes for a man in a patriarchal society. There is extensive evidence that many such daring women existed in fact and that the female cross-dresser was a popular figure of early modern folklore.[41] Especially engaging were ballads about the pretty, genteel, young woman with a mind for rambling who dresses as a sailor, joins the merchant marine, reveals her identity to her mess mate or an officer, and becomes his lover. Read and Bonny, however, were as polar opposites to the plucky but romantic maidens of the songs. No exercise of the male imagination created or controlled them. They wore men's clothing in battle to enable fighting and prevent identification. They joined in the work of piracy with a right good will, would curse as sharply as any man, and hack any potential witness to death to avoid the hangman's rope.

If in this period male pirates were considered monsters and an affront to 'humane nature', how could one comprehend female pirates? Read and Bonny were handled in eighteenth-century publications by being placed in the familiar category of alluring but destructive temptress, as shown in the salacious illustrations from the *General History of the Pirates*. (See Illustration 73, 74) In our own day, they have been rediscovered as models of women's rebelliousness, courage and hard-won freedom,

sisters in spirit with nineteenth- and twentieth-century fictional hero-
ines surviving on the fringes of society. Their creators almost never have
them emulate or even think about pirates – conventional figures of
male fantasy and aggression – but there is one notable modern work in
which the image of the female pirate reveals disturbing truths about
gender, desire and violence.

At her wedding to Mac the Knife in Berthold Brecht's *Three Penny
Opera* (1928), Polly sings a song she learnt from Jenny, a lowly bar-
maid, who, longing to take revenge on her oppressors, imagines herself a pirate in command of 'a ship with eight sails and/All its fifty
guns loaded'. In her daydreams those fifty guns level the town.

> And a hundred men will land in the bright midday sun
> Each stepping where the shadows fall.
> They'll look inside each doorway and grab anyone they see
> And put him in irons and then bring him to me
> And they'll ask: which of these should we kill?
> In the noonday heat there'll be a hush round the harbour
> As they ask which has got to die.
> And you'll hear me as I softly answer: the lot!
>
> And as the first head rolls I'll say: hoppla!
> And that ship with eight sails and
> All fifty guns loaded
> Will vanish with me.[42]

Brecht's use of the pirate as symbolic liberator of underclass women
and expression of their hidden rage may help to explain the figure's
appeal even in the world of Bonny and Read, where most struggled
hopelessly against the chains of poverty, sexism and the rich man's law
masquerading as justice.

In the next chapter we will encounter a pirate chief and crew who,
in contrast to their violence towards their prey, created a code of law
to secure themselves from their own anarchic impulses as well as from
the power of the state.

62 Thatch of the terrible
eyes. Alexander Smith,
*General History of the
Highwaymen and Pirates*
(London, 1734).

63 Captain Charles Vane.
Captain Charles Johnson,
*History and Lives of the
Pyrates* (London:
Midwinter, 1725).

64 'The crews of Blackbeard's and Vane's vessels carousing on coast of Carolina'. Charles Ellms, *The Pirates' Own Book* (Portland, Maine, 1837).

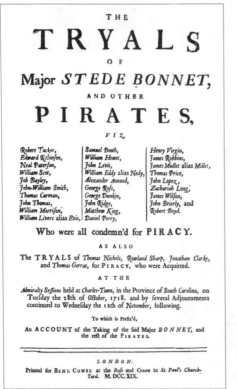

THE

TRYALS

OF

Major *STEDE BONNET*,

AND OTHER

PIRATES,

VIZ,

Robert Tucker,	Samuel Booth,	Henry Virgin,
Edward Robinson,	William Hewet,	James Robbins,
Neal Paterson,	John Levit,	James Mullet alias Millet,
William Scot,	William Eddy alias Nedy,	Thomas Price,
Job Bayley,	Alexander Annand,	John Lopez,
John-William Smith,	George Ross,	Zachariah Long,
Thomas Carman,	George Dunkin,	James Wilson,
John Thomas,	John Ridge,	John Brierly, and
William Morrison,	Matthew King,	Robert Boyd.
William Livers alias Evis,	Daniel Perry,	

Who were all condemn'd for PIRACY.

AS ALSO

The TRYALS of *Thomas Nichols, Rowland Sharp, Jonathan Clarke,* and *Thomas Gerrat,* for PIRACY, who were Acquitted.

AT THE

Admiralty Sessions held at *Charles-Town,* in the Province of *South Carolina,* on Tuesday the 28th of *October,* 1718. and by several Adjournments continued to Wednesday the 12th of *November,* following.

To which is Prefix'd,

An ACCOUNT of the Taking of the said Major *BONNET,* and the rest of the PIRATES.

LONDON:

Printed for BENJ. COWSE at the *Rose* and *Crown* in *St. Paul's Church-Yard.* M.DCC.XIX.

65 The report of the trials of Captain Bonnet and crew in Nicholas Trott's court.

66 Execution of Stede Bonnet at Charleston. A.O. Exquemelin, *Der Engelsche Zee Roovers* (Amsterdam, 1725).

67 Anstis's crew holds a mock piracy trial. A.O. Exquemelin, *Der Engelsche Zee Roovers* (Amsterdam, 1725).

68 Blackbeard surprised by Lieutenant Maynard's ruse. Charles Ellms, *The Pirates' Own Book* (Portland, Maine, 1837).

69 'Black Beard's Head on the end of the Bowsprit'. Charles Ellms, *The Pirates' Own Book* (Portland, Maine, 1837).

70 *Above: Woodes Rogers and his Family.* William Hogarth, 1729.

71 *Right:* Captain John Rackam. Captain Charles Johnson, *History and Lives of the Pyrates* (London: Midwinter, 1725).

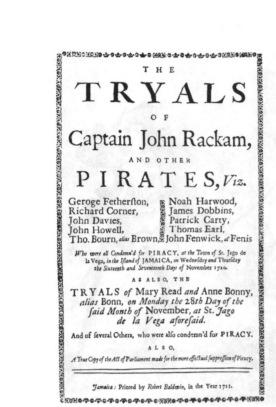

THE

TRYALS

OF

Captain John Rackam,

AND OTHER

PIRATES, *Viz.*

Geroge Fetherſton,   Noah Harwood,
Richard Corner,   James Dobbins,
John Davies,   Patrick Carty,
John Howell,   Thomas Earl,
Tho. Bourn, *alias* Brown, John Fenwick, *at* Fenis

Who were all Condemn'd for PIRACY, *at the Town of* St. Jago de
la Vega, *in the Iſland of* JAMAICA, *on Wedneſday and Thurſday
the Sixteenth and Seventeenth Days of* November 1720.

AS ALSO, THE

TRYALS *of* Mary Read *and* Anne Bonny,
alias Bonn, *on Monday the* 28th *Day of the
ſaid Month of* November, *at St. Jago
de la Vega aforeſaid.*

And of ſeveral Others, who were alſo condemn'd for PIRACY.

ALSO,

A True Copy of the Act of Parliament made for the more effectual ſuppreſſion of Piracy.

Jamaica : Printed by *Robert Baldwin,* in the Year 1721.

72 *Left:* Report of the trials of
Rackam and crew, *Tryals of
Captain John Rackam, and other
Pirates* (Jamaica, 1721).

73 Pirate Anne Bonny. A.O.
Exquemelin, *Der Engelsche
Zee Roovers* (Amsterdam,
1725).

74 Pirate Mary Read. A.O. Exquemelin, *Der Engelsche Zee Roovers* (Amsterdam, 1725).

Bartholomew Roberts doodgebleeven.

75 Captain Roberts dressed as a man of fashion. A.O. Exquemelin, *Der Engelsche Zee Roovers* (Amsterdam, 1725).

76 Captain Roberts before fort at Bonthe Island. Alexander Smith,
General History of the Highwayman and Pirates (London, 1734).

77 'Captain Roberts' Crew carousing at Old Calabar River'. Charles Ellms, *The Pirates' Own Book* (Portland, Maine, 1837).

78 *Above:* Roberts's two versions of the Jolly Roger on display before the slaving port of Whydah. Captain Charles Johnson, *General History of the Pyrates* (London: Warner, 1725).

79 *Left:* Admiral Sir Chaloner Ogle in the early 1740s. Engraving by J.M.B.

80 'A View of Cabo Corso Castle'. Jean Barbot, *A Description of the Coasts of North and South Guinea* (London, 1746).

81 The Gold Coast in 1723. George Peacock, *The Guinea or Gold Coast of Africa* (Exeter, 1880).

82 Report of the trials at Cape Coast.

ames Skyrme, John Walden, Israel Hinde, James
Greenaim, Peter Scudmore, Agge Jacobson, Michael Maur
James Clements, John Parker, Marcus Johnson, William Petty,
Robert Crow, Robert Haws, John Phelps, William Vernon,
Daniel Harding, John Duigdon, Joseph More, and
Abraham Harper

You and each of you are Sentenced
and adjudged to return to the Place from whence
Yu Came, from thence to the Place of Execution
and there within the Flood Marks to be hanged
by the Neck 'till ye are Dead, Dead, Dead,

And the Lord have mercy on your Souls

After this You James Skyrme, John Walden,
Israel Hinde, Peter Scudmore, Agge Jacobson
Jn° Phelps and William Vernon shall be
taken down and yr bodies hung in Chaines

Dated at Cabo Corso
this 9th of April 1722

James Phipps
Henry Dodson
Boye
Jn° Barnsley
Cho: Fanshawe
Robt Menzies

83 Death warrant for Roberts's men, 9 April 1722.

Bartholomew Roberts:
'No, a Merry Life and a Short One Shall be my Motto'

Bartholomew Roberts has a claim to be the greatest of the pirates. He cruised without ever depending on the protection of a commission or accepting a pardon, captured more vessels, and was active longer than any other prominent captain of the golden age. He was also the only notable British pirate not to have a base in either the West Indies or the Indian Ocean, but he ranged freely throughout the Atlantic – from the Antilles to Brazil, Newfoundland and the coast of Africa. Even though his 'take' was considerably less than that of Morgan, Tew or Every, his company was the most destructive to trade in the Atlantic, seizing about 400 vessels in four years. For Roberts, piracy was not a temporary respite from work in the maritime services or on land, as it was for many under the black flag. Insofar as it was a profession for him, he fits the stereotype most of us have of eighteenth-century pirates: rolling stones with contempt for the law and those enslaved by it, men whose motto was 'a merry life and a short one!'.

Roberts has two more claims to historical importance: according to Captain Charles Johnson he was the most fashionably attired of the pirate chiefs. In several editions of the *General History*, he is shown sporting necklaces, brocades and plumed hats to the point of dandyism, and he left a standing order that, should he die at sea, his finery was to be thrown overboard with his body. Pirates sometimes used flamboyant dress as a gesture of independence from conventional society: 'They delighted in such brilliant costumes because in Europe the use of luxury fabrics was confined by law to the upper classes'.[1] But Roberts took this practice one step further, for by dressing like a gaudy aristocrat he not only asserted his power aboard the pirate ship, but expressed the whole company's derision for their 'betters', petty men who were generally soft and cowardly. (See Illustration 75) More importantly, the villains under his command came to operate under the most detailed 'constitution' that any crew of pirates had adopted, according to their ways, by democratic vote.

Roberts was born about 1682 in the village of Casnewydd Bach, Pembrokeshire, and was baptised as John Roberts. When and why he assumed the name 'Bartholomew' is unknown, but his nickname 'Black Bart' derived from his dark complexion. About his early career we know only that he had become a skilled mariner by 1718 when he was appointed mate of a Barbados trader. In June 1719 he was mate of the Royal African Company *Princess* when it was taken by the pirate Howel Davis off Anoumabo, south-east Ivory Coast. Johnson reports that at first he declined Davis's invitation to join the company, but 'the gay, carefree life... and how easy it was to accumulate wealth as a gentleman of fortune' at last persuaded him to sign on.[2] A few weeks later Davis was ambushed and killed by the Portuguese at Principe Island in the Gulf of Guinea. Although still a pirate-in-training, Roberts had so impressed the company with his seacraft and courage that they elected him to replace Davis.

What happened in the first three months of his command amply justified their choice. By late July 1719 the *Rover* had taken two ships, a Dutch merchant and the Royal African Company's slaver *Experiment*, from which the pirates got supplies and a host of volunteers. Roberts now set a course for Brazil where he was to demonstrate determination and boldness against impossible odds. In September the *Rover* encountered off Bahia, Brazil, a convoy of forty-two Portuguese merchantmen protected by two ships-of-the-line. Roberts was vastly outgunned but, instead of retreating prudently, as Kidd had done at the Babs, he sent his crew below and quietly penetrated the fleet. When he found a vulnerable ship, he slipped alongside before the Portuguese realised what he was. The pirates then rushed on deck with their swords flashing to second their ccaptain's demand to know which was the richest of the merchantmen. Their terrified prey complied immediately, and Roberts had without a shot the intelligence he wanted and the Portuguese captain to act as decoy.

The *Salgrada Familia* was a formidable opponent protected by forty cannon and a crew of 150. Roberts manoeuvred his ship next to it without incident, but when the decoy invited the *Salgrada Familia*'s captain aboard, the enemy smelt a rat. It was not easy for a homebound merchant ship to become battle-ready after a successful voyage. Cargo and supplies clutter the deck, cannon and ammunition need to be hauled up, unpractised gun crews to be assembled. The pirates saw these preparations, got off a broadside, and boarded. Their sharp, fierce attack – a signature tactic of pirates the world over – subdued the defenders, but informed the whole fleet of Roberts's presence. As the prize was sailed out to sea, the *Rover* took up the rearguard in anticipation of the warships' counter-attack, but none came.

At Devil's and Cayenne Islands (French Guiana) the pirates discovered the full extent of the riches they had taken – 90,000 gold moidores [£121,500] and a diamond-studded cross made for the King of Portugal – and enjoyed the pleasures it enabled them to buy.[3] But shortly after leaving Guiana, Roberts learnt a nearly fatal lesson about overconfidence; when what looked like an easy mark sailed by, he and forty others went after it in a sloop, but contrary winds drove them back to the Guiana coast, and he had to send to the *Rover* for help. His boat returned with the appalling news that his lieutenant Walter Kennedy had gone off with both the *Rover* and its prize! Roberts's party were now in a pickle; low on supplies, few in number, poorly armed, and in a leaky ship, they were vulnerable to attack and facing starvation.

Charles Johnson speculates that Roberts's painful experience caused him to draw up the following set of 'articles' or ship's rules for the better preservation of the company.

I. Every Man has a Vote in Affairs of Moment; has equal Title to the fresh Provisions, or strong Liquors, at any Time seized, and may use them at Pleasure, unless a Scarcity... make it necessary, for the Good of all, to vote a Retrenchment.

II. Every Man to be called fairly in Turn, by List, on board of Prizes, because (over and above their proper Share) they were on these Occasions allowed a Shift of Cloaths: But if they defrauded the Company to the Value of a Dollar, in Plate, Jewels, or Money, MAROONING was their Punishment.

III. No Person to Game at Cards or Dice for Money.

IV. The Lights and Candles to be put out at eight a-Clock at Night: If any of the Crew, after that Hour, still remained inclined for Drinking, they were to do it on the open Deck.

V. To keep their Piece, Pistols, and Cutlash clean, and fit for Service.

VI. No Boy or Woman to be allowed amongst them. If any Man were found seducing any of the latter Sex, and carry'd her to Sea, disguised, he was to suffer Death.

VII. To Desert the Ship, or their Quarters in Battle, was punished with Death or Marooning.

VIII. No striking one another on board, but every Man's Quarrels to be ended on Shore, at Sword and Pistol...

IX. No Man to talk of breaking up their Way of Living, till each had shared a 1000. If in order to this, any Man should lose a Limb, or become a Cripple in their Service, he was to have 800 Dollars, out of the pub-lick Stock, and for lesser Hurts, proportionably.

X. The Captain and Quarter-Master to receive two Shares of a Prize; the Master, Boatswain, and Gunner, one Share and a half; and other Officers one and a Quarter.

XI. The Musicians to have Rest on the Sabbath Day, but the other six Days and Nights, none without special Favour.[4]

Pirate articles like these were modelled on regulations aboard naval ships and privateers. A comparison of this set with others collected by Johnson reveals that Roberts's are the most extensive and specific and that they place more restrictions on shipboard drinking, sex and gambling. Roberts himself was a teetotaller who preached that self-control was necessary to the preservation of the company; he is imagined by Johnson to have thought it 'every one's Interest to observe [the articles] if they were minded to keep up so abominable a Combination'.[5]

Pirate articles cover such topics as preservation and governance of the company, rights of the individual and shipboard punishments and rewards. There were also unwritten rules covering the hierarchy of command at sea and relations between captain and crew, rules that radically broke with maritime tradition. In all fighting ships of the time, the captain had absolute power in battle, but afterwards the pirate captain lost his supremacy and had to obey the will of the 'people' – the ordinary seamen. In 'affairs of moment' that will was expressed in open discussion and by vote – one man, one vote – but in daily affairs, the people's welfare was protected by the quartermaster, who was a kind of shipboard ombudsman. Responsible for mediating conflicts between individuals and doling out punishments determined by the company, the quartermaster was on a par with the captain except during battle. David Simpson, Roberts's quartermaster, spoke true when he boasted that 'he was as good a Man as *Roberts*'.[6]

Pirates were understandably very reluctant to execute one of their own; only two capital offences are given in the sets of articles printed by Johnson: desertion during battle and seducing a virtuous woman.[7] The banning of women and sometimes boys from pirate ships was probably not intended to impose a code of morality but rather to prevent shipboard sexual jealousies from breaking up the company. On occasion, the pirates held trials to deal with serious infractions of their articles; we have already looked at Charles Johnson's comic rendering of such a trial and shall shortly see his account of another aboard Roberts's ship. (The reader must be aware, however, that these 'trial reports' have not been corroborated by other sources.)

The principal elected officers of a pirate ship were the captain and the quartermaster, but other positions including sailing master, bosun

and bosun's mate, carpenter and chief surgeon were also elective.
When an officer lost the people's confidence, he could be removed
immediately, as happened to Simpson for his abuse of power. To affirm
their scorn for elitism the people denied captain and officers their
usual perquisites – sole enjoyment of special food, drink and luxury
items. They allowed the captain his cabin aft but kept the right to use
it at will; 'any body might come and eat and drink with [Roberts]'.[8]
In fact, as we have already seen, the upper work on a pirate ship was
sometimes removed, cabin and all, primarily to improve its agility but
also to eliminate class differences among its crew.

Chroniclers of the pirates beginning in the 1670s frequently marvelled at the resemblance of their 'articles' to the laws of the state. We
learn from Exquemelin's *Bucaniers of America* that even among the
bloodthirsty West Indian pirates,

> honesty in sharing booty, the safety of property and person, swift arbitra-
> tion of disputes, and democracy in the making of decisions were guaran-
> teed on the pirate islands of Tortuga and Hispaniola. Buccaneer 'articles'
> also made it clear that members of the commonwealth were expected to
> be civil to one another, to aid their fellows in time of want, to make pro-
> vision for the wounded, and to preserve the booty of dead pirates for
> their 'nearest relations' or their 'lawful heirs'.[9]

Indeed, interest in stories of the pirates was fuelled not only by their
atrocities, courage and treasure, but also by the discovery that pirate
communities recapitulated the evolution of law in 'legitimate' soci-
eties. Readers of Plato, Hobbes and Locke were alerted to the philosophical value of pirate biography in prefaces and reviews of the two
primary compilations. The preface of the 1699 London edition of the
Bucaniers found it

> very remarkable, that in such a lawless body as these buccaneers seem to
> be, in respect to all other, that yet there should be such an economy (if I
> may say so) kept, and regularity practised amongst themselves, so that
> everyone seemed to have his property as much secured to himself, as if
> he had been a member of the most civilized community in the world.[10]

And Johnson promoted his *General History of the Pyrates* with the sub-title, 'Their *Policies, Discipline,* and *Government, From their first Rise and Settlement in the Island of Providence, in 1717, to the present Year 1724'*. Johnson's first reviewer was enlightened by the remarkable system of laws in force among pirates, 'as excellent for Policy as any Thing in *Plato's* Commonwealth'. The reviewer found in the pirates' lives ample confirmation of his belief that all government is the prod-uct of a covenant to curb 'particular Appetites... for the Benefits of Society.'[11] Those human 'sea monsters' and 'beasts of prey' – Cotton Mather's favorite epithets for pirates – turn out to be not so com-pletely outlandish. While some genteel readers might have been appalled to discover a kinship with pirates, the more philosophical would have welcomed new proof of Locke's thesis 'that man is by necessity a law-making and law-obeying animal'.[12]

Making the most of his bad luck, Roberts renamed his sloop *Fortune* and in the winter of 1719 left the coast of Guiana for the Windward Islands in desperate need of food. At first he found 'good purchase', rifling four small ships off Guadeloupe before releasing them, but his luck turned again when he encountered two English ships near Barbados. He approached the smaller and signalled the captain to heave to, but instead it let fly a broadside and shortened sail to allow the second ship of twenty guns to catch up. With ten guns and a small crew, the *Fortune* was no match for both of them, and Roberts retreated, later to learn that they had been sent to take him by the governor of Barbados. Fleeing to the south, he heard at the Grenadines that the governor of Martinique had also sent out armed sloops, causing Roberts again to reverse course and follow the advance of spring into the north Atlantic. In June 1720 he arrived upon Newfoundland's Grand Banks, the rich, international fishing grounds where Kidd had taken his first prize.

In Trepassey and St Mary's bays he had good pickings, taking twenty-six ships and 150 boats. His tactic was simple, to terrify the fishermen into surrendering with as loud a show as he could muster: 'black Colours flying, Drums beating, and Trumpets sounding'.[13] Here they converted one of the prizes into their flagship and named it *Royal Fortune.* When he left the Banks late in July, it was with a hold full of plunder and a larger crew in an even finer flagship, a French prize of twenty-eight guns also named *Royal Fortune*. Roberts now cruised in New England water,s where he stopped several merchants including the rich *Samuel* out of London. His men were in high swagger aboard the *Samuel*, where they extracted the ship's wealth by brutally torturing the crew and told its captain 'they should accept of no Act of Grace; that the K— and P—t might be damned with the Acts of G— for them; neither would they go to *Hope-Point*, to be hang'd up a Sun drying, as *Kid*'s and *Braddish*'s Company were'. If cornered, they designed – like Blackbeard and Bonnet – to blow up the ship 'and go all merrily to Hell together'.[14]

The *Fortune* and *Royal Fortune* next appeared in Roberts's old hunting grounds, the Antilles. It was here that three of his crew who had been forced, including the navigator Harry Glasby, unsuccessfully attempted an escape. Charles Johnson takes this opportunity to report or imagine the kind of justice pirates might be capable of. Aside from the dark steerage of the flagship and the 'large Bowl of Rum Punch placed upon the table', he finds their proceedings to follow the course of British felony trials:

> The Prisoners were brought forth, and Articles of Indictment against them read; they were arraigned upon a Statute of their own making [article VII], and the Letter of the Law being strong against them, and the Fact plainly proved, they were about to pronounce Sentence...

'Here', Johnson comments, 'was the Form of Justice kept up, which is as much as can be said of several other Courts, that have more lawful Commissions for what they do'.[15]

> Here was no feeing of Council, and bribing of Witnesses was a custom not known among them; no packing of Juries, no torturing and wresting the Sense of the Law, for bye Ends and Purposes, no puzzling or perplexing the Cause with unintelligible canting Terms, and useless Distinctions; nor was their Sessions burthened with numberless Officers, the Ministers of Rapine and Extortion, with ill boding Aspects, enough to fright *Astrea* [goddess of justice] from the Court.[16]

Here, in this cramped and humble setting, the pirates are as 'noble sav-
ages' who preserve the spirit of their law in open and honourable
dealings.

The story now shifts gears and ends with the triumph of mercy
over the letter of the law. After the court had refused the people's
unanimous cry that the lives of the convicted be spared, a pirate in
good standing called Valentine Ashplant rose to speak:

> *By G—, Glasby shall not die; d—m me if he shall.* After this learned Speech,
> he sat down in his Place, and resumed his Pipe. This Motion was loudly
> opposed by all the rest of the Judges, in equivalent Terms; but *Ashplant,*
> who was resolute in his Opinion, made another pathetical speech in the
> following Manner. *G—d—n ye Gentlemen, I am as good a Man as the best of*
> *you; d—n me S—l if I ever turned my Back to any Man in my Life, or ever will,*
> *by G—; Glasby is an honest Fellow, notwithstanding this Misfortune, and I love*
> *him, D—l d—n me if I don't: I hope he'll live and repent of what he has done; but*
> *d—n me if he must die, I will die along with him.*

When this 'pathetical' rhetoric failed to convince, Ashplant turned to
another form of discourse,

> he pulled out a pair of Pistols, and presented them to some of the learned
> Judges upon the Bench; who, perceiving his Arguments so well sup-
> ported, thought it reasonable that *Glasby* should be acquitted; and so they
> all came over to his Opinion, and allowed it to be Law.[17]

Glasby actually was spared – although perhaps not in this manner –
later to become the star witness in a less whimsical piracy trial.

Roberts's arrival before Basseterre at St Kitt's caught the government by surprise. For a day or two, he terrorised harbour shipping
with little resistance from the depleted fort, but early next morning
his ships were hit by rounds from thirteen great guns that Lieutenant
Governor William Mathew had brought up in the night. The raiders
were forced to withdraw to tiny St Bartholomew's Island near Anguilla
where the French authorities allowed them to eat, drink and make
merry.

Late in October 1720, they were once more on the hunt off St Lucia in the Windwards. Usually merchants approached by Roberts surrendered quickly or fled to the land. He had taken about fifteen small ships with hardly a shot fired before entering St Lucia's harbour, but here he met one that would test his mettle, a Dutch slaver (*El Puerto del Principe*) with thirty guns mounted and a crew of ninety. Roberts's success at recruiting had swelled his force to 350 and together his two ships carried fifty guns. Anticipating a quick victory, they came in to board but were briskly repelled and forced to pound the immobilised prey with artillery and small arms. The Dutch kept up their own fire but had to submit at last even though they could expect no mercy from the enraged pirates. The offending crew were then slaughtered – some very painfully – out of revenge for dead pirates but also to maintain Roberts's valuable reputation for murdering resisters.

For sea rovers of this period, cunning was worth ten guns. Roberts soon devised a ruse that would humiliate an old foe and make a handsome profit. He had conceived a grudge against Barbados and Martinique for chasing him out of the West Indies in 1719–20; to lure the latter's residents into a trap, he sailed the restored *Puerto del Principe* before several Martinique ports to signal that it had slaves to sell. Fourteen planters took the bait, but when they came to St Lucia to buy, they were robbed, all but one of their sloops were burnt, and they were whipped, mutilated, or terrorised. After this most delicious victory, he designed two flags, variants on the Jolly Roger. One depicted him standing on a Barbadian's and a Martinician's skull, carrying in his hands a flaming sword and an hourglass; the second, an ensign in which he is shown in ghastly partnership with Death itself (see p. 199).

As Roberts lingered in the islands, he was presented with yet another opportunity to take revenge on his enemies. Early in 1721 near Hispaniola the *Royal Fortune* captured a French warship on which the governor of Martinique was a passenger. Roberts hanged him from his own yardarm and made the prize his flagship, renaming it the third *Royal Fortune*. Fearing that his recent atrocities would renew attempts to take him, he now proposed shifting operations to the coast of Africa. One of the reasons for Roberts's longevity at the 'sport' was his ability to sense when to pull out of an area; on this occasion as before, his judgement was unerring, for the governments of Barbados, Martinique and other French islands were at the very moment planning a coordinated attack against him while other governors were protesting the Royal Navy's failure to engage the pirates.

This was a time of peril for Roberts on the domestic front as well. At the beginning of April he had angered several of the crew by killing a drunken sailor who insulted him. When he was denounced by the victim's friend, he slashed him with his sword, but the enraged man went on to beat Roberts soundly. Friends of the dead sailor now joined forces with the crew of the consort *Good Fortune* who were piqued by the admiral's open disrespect for them. On the night of 20 April, the *Good Fortune* under Captain Thomas Anstis silently put to sea, bidding Roberts 'a soft Farewell' and depriving him of its twelve guns and 140 men.[18]

The loss of the *Good Fortune* was a blow – but not a fatal one – to Roberts's plans to descend in strength on the Slave Coast; the new *Royal Fortune* was still formidable with nearly 230 men and fifty-one light and heavy guns. It was June 1721 by the time he touched at Guinea, where he seized two French guard ships without a battle and heard that HMS *Swallow* and *Weymouth*, assigned to protect the trade of the Royal African Company, were cruising to the east. To stay clear of them, Roberts set up camp at the mouth of the Sierra Leone River until the warships should come west in December.

Before going out to hunt, he looked for something worth stealing at the Company's small fort on Bonthe (now Sherbro) Island. Johnson tells of his sending a messenger to ask the fort's governor Robert Plunkett 'if he could spare him any gold Dust, or Powder and Ball. Old *Plunkett* return'd him Word, that he had no Gold to spare; but as for Powder and Ball, he had some at Mr *Roberts*'s Service, if he would come for it'. This kind of mock-genteel discourse between predator and prey was a mainstay of contemporary stories of the pirates and recalls Morgan's interchange with the Viceroy of Panama. A very different kind of interchange ended the episode. The pirates had to bombard the fort for hours before they could take it, so that when the triumphant Roberts met Old Plunkett face to face, he assaulted him with a barrage of curses for his '*Irish* impudence'. The governor returned the curses 'as fast or faster than *Roberts*; which made the rest of the Pirates laugh heartily, desiring *Roberts* to sit down and hold his Peace'. For once, Roberts's established policy of severely punishing those who refused quarter was suspended, and 'by meer Dint of Cursing and Damning, Old *Plunkett*... saved his Life'.[19] (See Illustration 76)

Roberts's first great prize on the coast was the *Onslow*, a Royal African Company frigate he took early in August near the River Cess (modern Liberia). Stripped of fore and aft castles and mounted with forty guns, it replaced and took the name of his old, leaky flagship, *Royal Fortune* the third. Roberts sensed that many aboard the *Onslow* wished to join him and '[obliged] these fellows with a show of force' to give them cover should they ever come to trial.[20] (Judges and juries learnt to test the universal claim of being forced by inquiring whether the accused had participated vigourously in the actions of the pirates, had attempted to flee from them, and had received a share of their plunder. To buttress their claim, seamen would express disgust for pirate life to their mates or have released prisoners carry home protests of innocence for publication in newspapers, preferably the *London Gazette*.)

Believing that the *Swallow* and *Weymouth* had returned to Sierra Leone, Roberts sailed eastward in the autumn, seeking an area less crowded with fortified trading posts, and established a base on the Calabar River (Nigeria) some distance from the sea. From here he could send boarding parties to surprise ships that entered the river, and in October he began to reel them in. (See Illustration 77) After a violent confrontation with the natives, however, the pirates decamped for Cape Lopez (Gabon) to the south, where in mid-December they took the Dutch galley *Geertruyt*. But not finding the traffic they anticipated, the fleet provisioned at the small island of Annabon about 220 miles west of the Cape and then headed north-west back to the coast, their ultimate destination the busy slaving market of Whydah (or Ouidah in modern Benin).

On the way they took more slavers off Grand Lahou (Ivory Coast) in January 1722 – notably the *Tarleton* of Liverpool and the Royal African Company's *King Solomon*. Finding in the *Tarleton* a master that some of his own crew hated, Roberts dispensed with the forms of law and personally beat him viciously. The *King Solomon* was fully able to defeat the boatload of men Roberts sent against it, but the crew refused to take the risk and promptly surrendered. Such behaviour was a response to the pirates' terror campaign but also to the widespread reliance on ship insurance to protect the owners, a development that made captain as well as crew reluctant to fight. (If the war against the pirates was to be won, easy victories like this had to be stopped. The 1700 reform had offered merchant seamen payments for resisting the pirates, but it did not penalise those who gave up without a shot; one year after the taking of the *King Solomon*, Parliament corrected that omission by enacting 8 George 1, c.24.)

The pirates did not realise the danger they were in so close to the shore. A few hundred miles to the east lay the British men-of-war that they had avoided the year before. Roberts had been wrong about their location. Ravaged by disease, they had been incapable of returning west and had put in at Cape Coast (Ghana). Mercifully for everyone, the pirates went to sea before descending on Whydah and again missed a confrontation with them. When the pirate flotilla reached Whydah, up went the flags and ensigns announcing who they were so that their terror might work before they entered the harbour. (See Illustration 78) It worked so well that eleven ships of all nations struck to them without incident, and only the captain of a British slaver called the *Porcupine* refused to ransom his ship for eight pounds of gold dust. This refusal had horrible consequences. Against Roberts's orders, the *Porcupine* was set on fire before all the slaves could be removed, and eighty burnt to death, drowned, or were eaten by sharks. The pirates sailed out of the harbour on 13 January upon word that one of the King's ships was underway. Their plan was to water and provision at Annabon and withdraw to Brazil, where they would share out and disperse.

Now 'fit for the Sea', the *Swallow*, a third-rate battleship mounting sixty great guns, entered Whydah harbour two days after Roberts had left. Its captain, Chaloner Ogle, was only briefly disappointed. (See Illustration 79) His knowledge of the coast from Guinea to Gabon told him that Roberts would go east to careen, perhaps on the mainland in the Bight of Biafra, perhaps on an island such as Principe or Annabon.

On 17 January the *Swallow* sailed south-east by east towards the Niger River delta, entrance to the Bight; for the rest of January Ogle would search Roberts's old refuges. Meanwhile the *Royal Fortune* and its two consorts, *Little Ranger* and *Great Ranger,* had been blown to the east of their intended course and forced to put in again at Cape Lopez, unaware of the systematic search for them. Ogle picked up little useful information as he inched around the Bight so that late in January he stretched over to Principe, where in 1719 Howell Davis had died and Roberts risen to pirate chief. Slowly the paths of the hunter and his prey were converging.

When Principe proved a dead end, the *Swallow* zagged back to the coast and on 1 February began to search the estuary of the River Gabon. Finding nothing, it proceeded south towards Cape Lopez. Four days later, Ogle heard a gun sounding the break of dawn, and his spyglass revealed the probable source about twelve miles distant – three ships at anchor on the north side of the Cape. Surely this was Roberts's bloody fleet. It would take some luck to handle all three, but the forty-one-year-old commander was at the peak of his vigour and not about to withdraw.

Roberts saw that a ship was approaching and, reckoning it was a trader, an easy mark, called over to the *Great Ranger's* captain, 'There is sugar in the offing, have it brought in so that we may have no more mumbling'. It was a good thing to indulge his increasingly rebellious crew with strong, sweet punch. Captain Skyrme responded smartly, and the thirty-two-gun ship came out to speak with the stranger, 'English Colours and a black Flag at her Mizzen-Peek'.[21] Skyrme reckoned that he would soon be in cannon range if the trader's captain continued to shortsail his ship and tack so raggedly.

Although they were losing the race, spirits were high among the men of the *Swallow*. Ogle's plan was to draw the *Great Ranger* away from the other two vessels – far enough that they would not hear the sounds of an engagement – then turn about to fight, a tactic used by Kidd to trounce the Portuguese. It was nearly high noon when the two ships came within cannon range. Captain Skyrme opened with his chase guns, but the *Swallow* did not strike as expected. Instead, when his pursuer came within musket range, Ogle turned his ship

into its path, ran out his lower guns, and delivered a broadside 'both
alow and aloft'.[22] During the next four hours the ships exchanged
cannon and small arms fire, but casualties were mounting among the
pirates. Finally, when their main topmast was brought down and
attempts to board the *Swallow* disrupted, the pirates' discipline broke
and Skyrme asked for quarter. Twenty-six pirates had been killed or
badly wounded, some from an aborted attempt to blow up the ship
before surrendering. There were no fatalities aboard the King's ship.

It took the *Swallow* three days to return to Cape Lopez, but on 6
February Ogle spotted the *Royal Fortune* and *Little Ranger* at anchor
besides a new prize. At half-past ten the next morning, he approached
the bay and was happy to see the movement of men onto the largest
ship; he wanted the pirates to come out after him. The 152 men who
crowded into the forty-gun *Royal Fortune* included most of the *Little
Ranger*'s crew. Roberts was not fooled by the *Swallow*'s French ensign;
by now he knew the intruder to be one of the warships he had been
avoiding for more than seven months. Although he feared that the
company, largely drunk or hungover, were not up to such an
encounter, he bravely rallied them on.

According to Charles Johnson, he prepared himself for battle by
putting on

> a rich crimson Damask Wastcoat and Breeches, a red Feather in his Hat,
> a Gold Chain round his Neck, with a Diamond Cross hanging to it.

Flourishing 'a Sword in his Hand, and two Pair of Pistols hanging at
the End of a Silk Sling, slung over his Shoulders (according to the
Fashion of Pirates)', he climbed onto a gun-carriage to command and
inspire his troops.[23] The helmsman had been ordered to steer to within
pistol range of the *Swallow*, a daring tactic that would take the measure of the warships' gunners and perhaps give the pirate sea room to
escape.

Battle was joined when the *Swallow* hoisted its English ensign and
opened with a broadside. The *Royal Fortune* answered with one of its
own, but in his exposed position, Roberts was among the first to be
wounded. Hit in the neck by grapeshot, he fell across the cannon,

bleeding to death. His ship's initial charge had carried it past the *Swallow*; as its lead increased, the pirates lamented their great chief but began to hope that they could outrun the warship. Soon after they had thrown Roberts overboard, 'with his Arms and Ornaments on, according to the repeated Request he made in his Life-time', their hopes began to leak away.[24] The *Royal Fortune* had lost the wind. The *Swallow* took advantage of this blunder, closed quickly, and commenced firing at close range, its gunners hesitating until the ocean's swell raised the muzzles of their cannon, then sending balls and chain shot high into the enemy's rigging. Early in the encounter the *Royal Fortune*'s mizzen topmast had splintered and fallen; the last bombardment brought down the main topmast, leaving it at the *Swallow*'s mercy.

At two o'clock, after three-and-a-half hours of fighting, the *Royal Fortune* surrendered. No sooner had it struck to the *Swallow* than Joseph Mansfield, a former highwayman and perpetual drunk who had slept through the battle, came up on deck 'vapouring with a Cutlass, to know who would go on board the Prize; and it was some time before they could perswade him to the truth of their Condition'.[25] As they waited for the King's men to board, one James Phillips moved to ignite the magazine and 'send them all to H–l together',[26] but Harry Glasby and some of their captives overpowered Phillips and handed the pirate crew over to the mercies of the law. Ogle found alive aboard the *Ranger* and *Royal Fortune* seventy African slaves and 188 white men and learned that thirteen had been killed in battle. Holding the slaves innocent of piracy, he sent four prisoners to New York where all were convicted and three executed; the remaining 184 suspects he took into Cape Coast.[27] (See Illustration 80, 81)

The Royal African Company's fort at Cape Coast was an unusually remote site for the historic trials held there from 28 March to 19 April 1722, probably to save the expense of trials at London and provide a more effective deterrent in an area recently ravaged by the pirates. While the 1700 law had authorised vice-admiralty courts in 'Plantations, Dominions, Forts or Factories', mass trials had been rare outside of Britain's *bona fide* colonies. There were, however, two serious obstacles to prosecution. The 1700 law explicitly disallowed persons with interests in the plunder seized from pirate ships to sit as commissioners, a provision that excluded the *Swallow*'s officers. Moreover, the proper form of indictments, as promulgated in the instructions to colonial governors, required details of the alleged crime: time and place, name of the ship taken, owner of the ship, and the approximate value of the goods stolen, information lacking for many defendants. But charging the pirates solely with attacking HMS *Swallow* would solve both problems. Consequently, Mungo Herdman, captain of HMS *Weymouth*, was appointed president of the court and a combination of the *Weymouth*'s officers and the company's officials sat as jurors in all the trials. This arrangement respected one element of the law but ignored another in that the prosecution's evidence would come from the men of the *Swallow* who stood to share in the pirates' goods, not from 'indifferent' witnesses required under admiralty law. (See Illustration 82)

Initially, the court hoped to make fast work of the defendants by admitting solely the testimony of the *Swallow*'s lieutenant, mate and bosun. These men gave a brief account of the pirates' resistance to the warship and claimed to recognise all 165 prisoners (nineteen had died of their wounds before trial), an astonishing feat of memory no defence attorney would allow to stand unchallenged. According to the published trial report, however, not one defendant demanded to cross-examine any of the witnesses, but each assented to their account. Evidently, instead of following standard practice of inviting cross-examination and defence witnesses, the prosecutors went straight to the last part of the trial, asking the accused 'how they came to be on Board this Pyrate-ship, and the Reason of their audacious Resistance against the King's Colours'.[28] As in the trial of the turtle fishermen at Jamaica, the prosecution relied solely on presence in a pirate ship and on the shift of the burden of proof to the defendants. Of course, this was done to avoid a three-month trial, but such short cuts were fatal to the defence and not allowed under article six of the law.

Such an unfair procedure could not stand. A majority of the prisoners claimed to have been forced into the pirates' service and therefore to be innocent under the statute. In the face of solid evidence for several of these claims, the court decided to consider the defendants one at a time, no matter how long it took. But surmising that many veteran pirates whom Roberts had obliged with a show of force would evade justice by this procedure, the court came up with a compromise. In return for admitting exculpatory evidence, the court would also hear evidence of crimes not stipulated in the indictment. The court recognised it was on thin legal ice even as it tried to defend its 'merciful Resolution':

> that Circumstances of Burning, Sinking, or Robbery of any Ship in which any one of 'em was immediately concerned, tho' it was not particularly specified in the Indictment, would yet be a Conviction the Man or Men were Voluntiers in this, such Evidence, tho' it might want a Form, still carried the Reason of the Law with it.[29]

So the court would allow defence evidence it was bound by law to hear anyway in return for sanctioning evidence of prior bad acts contrary to the right of defendants to be told in the indictment what they were accused of. The court's ice was not only thin but in an advanced state of melt.

The 'reason of the law' referred to is the doctrine of 'felonious intent' under which their later piracies were used to convict Every's men of piratically taking the *Charles II*. Eighteenth-century criminal courts were, indeed, more tolerant of evidence of bad character or prior convictions than their modern counterparts, but there was a growing debate over this practice and an effort to restrict deliberations to the substance of the indictment. In 1696 Parliament passed 'an act for regulating trials in cases of treason' (7–8 William 3, c.3) by which 'no evidence is to be admitted or given of any overt act, that is not expressly laid in the indictment'.[30] The treason act sought to ban exactly the same prejudicial tactic introduced at Cape Coast. (Whenever judges and prosecutors of this period assure juries that their comments about the accused's prior or later bad acts are not meant to prove them guilty, they are probably attempting to deflect the ire of the reformers.)

The court's merciful resolution had to be applied in a haphazard manner given the limited availability of defence witnesses at Cape Coast. Worse yet, it let in hearsay, conjecture, and, in a few cases,

evidence from only one witness. Roger Scot, for example, was condemned on the strength of his own statement that he had been with
Roberts for nineteen months and of Charles Munjoy's testimony that
he drank and caroused with the rest of the pirates:'the Court thought,
that an old Offender [i.e. a previously convicted person] of his standing, must certainly be Guilty'. Hugh Harris received the same sentence in part because

> the Excuse he mentioned of being ill looked on by [the pirates], served
> only to aggravate his Crime with the Court; for a Man of his standing,
> must have very strong Inclinations to be a Rogue, to overcome the
> Disrespect and Contempt of being cut out of a half, and sometimes a
> third part of his Share, without Resentment, that is, trying to get away.

The trial report suggests that there was no cross-examination of witnesses hostile to the accused. In fairness, it must be noted that Scot's
and Harris's sentences were commuted, and the court acquitted sev-
enty-four, largely on the basis of their being forced or physically incapable of playing the pirate, including one who was 'decrepid and
ill-shapen, unfit for any purpose but Musick'.[31]

In fact, given its biases and false logic, the court made a noble effort
to find grounds for acquittal or mitigation of the death sentence; its
members had, after all, sworn a solemn oath to render impartial justice, and the Royal African Company could use all the qualified hands
it could find. Aside from those acquitted outright, seventeen prisoners
were sent to the Marshalsea, in anticipation of further evidence, and
twenty of the convicted – including Scot and Harris – were delivered
to the company for seven years involuntary servitude. On the dark
side, fifty-four men were sentenced to die, but the executions of two
were postponed pending the King's pleasure, a move that signalled the
court's preference for clemency. (See Illustration 83)

Convicted felons did not have the right to appeal before acts of
1873 (on matters of law) and 1907 (on matters of fact).[32] For most of
those condemned to death, the only hope was a pardon or reprieve
from the King, but it was easy for the authorities to avoid such pos-
sibilities by quick executions. The hangings at Cape Coast began on

3 April 1722, barely three days after the first convictions; six of the condemned – including the gunner and three pirate quartermasters – were executed 'without the Gates of the Castle, and... within the Flood-marks'.[33] On 9 April another six were hanged; thereafter, four groups of between four and fourteen were executed at intervals of two to four days until the last on 20 April.

The value of the pirate gold, cargo and ships was roughly £7,200, but after the cost of condemnation at Jamaica, the portion for the officers and men of the *Swallow* was reduced to £5,167 7s 4d. For his daring and skill, Captain Ogle's career advanced steadily after the battle. He became in 1723 the first navy commander to be knighted for a victory over pirates, and a coin was struck in his honour; in 1732 he was given command of Jamaica's armed forces and, seven years later, was made Rear-Admiral of the Blue. He rose to Admiral of the White in 1744 and ended his career as the navy's Commander-in-Chief. After his knighting, Sir Chaloner was, perhaps, too mindful of his elevation in the world to care properly for his old comrades-in-arms. He received the lion's share of the *Swallow*'s prize money, £3,147 7s 4d – about £376,450 in 2002 purchasing power – while the other officers and men had to share £1,940.[34] When the Admiralty pressed him to be more generous, he declined citing the additional expenses of his new state.

Despite this blemish, Ogle and his company could take justifiable pride in the significance of their victory. It was the most decisive of any military engagement in the war against the pirates, and one to silence criticism of the Royal Navy for reluctance to police the seas. With very little injury to ship or crew, they had captured a pirate squadron of 201 men, killed or wounded thirty-two, including the most effective captain of them all, and seized a handsome treasure. Such a glorious and profitable action would encourage post captains to emulate their brother. More importantly, the piracy trial at Cape Coast was the largest in modern times – certainly in admiralty history – and would help establish legal precedents for the second British empire. By setting up a court in Africa where persons of all nations might be tried for high crimes, Britain was planting the seeds for its future exercise of sovereignty.

8

Pirates and the Law

This book has attempted to sketch the lives of celebrated British pirates with an eye to the range of forces that made for their destruction as well as their success. Mariners were turned to outlawry by the forces of greed, poverty, suppressed ambition, resentment of abuse, and even political dissent. Ironically, the force of law itself also played a role in the rise of the pirates. Treaty law prior to 1670 wilfully allowed the Caribbean to become a perpetual cockpit of hostilities among the European powers, and it was under the legal framework of privateering that piracy was nurtured in the days of state-sponsored plundering of Spanish America. Indeed, the law of privateering greatly influenced how the pirates' cruise might be financed, what prey they would hunt, how they might entrap that prey, and how they would divide what they plundered from it.

The pirates were quick to take advantage of bitter divisions among Britain's colonies and the lack of uniformity among their legal systems. They could run for refuge from one colony with the authority and will to prosecute to another that had no such authority or that held trials expressly to acquit them. And they learnt to manipulate the colonial or central government's practice, born out of frustration, of offering pardons to reduce the threat of piracy. In the absence of a pardon, they might turn state's witness, trade a secret Spanish map, become a pirate hunter, or better yet a 'consultant' on the problem of piracy – contemporary forms of 'plea-bargaining'.

The turning point in the pirates' relation to the law came at the adoption of King William's piracy act of 1700. From important prosecutions held under that act, we have seen how well it was designed to clear away obstacles to the pirates' capture, trial and execution, obstacles ranging from community support for them in the colonies to legal protections of the accused previously held sacrosanct. While sweeping changes in trial procedure and judges' mastery of informal ways to control the jury – through their instruction, questions, personal opinions, summation of evidence, praise and reproof – helped to convict pirates, they also destroyed some against whom the evidence was weak or non-existent. Seeking to limit damage to the common-law trial by jury, Parliament set it to expire in a few years. But the toll it took on the enemies to trade caused it to be renewed periodically and made perpetual in 1719.[1]

Shrewd pirates and seamen in general would learn about the law as a matter of survival. Morgan's mastery of the rules of privateering, Dampier's recourse to the civil law, Every's ruse of giving a receipt for stolen provisions and his crewmen's acquittal by friendly juries in the Bahamas, Kidd's flag trick and concern for his French passes, and Blackbeard and Bonnet's wily acceptance of the King's pardon attest to the preoccupations of the pirates more than do the romantic myths that cling to them to this day. But knowledge, however invaluable, was not always enough. Pirates before 1700 might rise or fall according to their political savvy and their timing, as we have seen in the contrasting fates of pirateers such as Sir Henry Morgan and Captain William Kidd, and in William Dampier's rise from Campeche buccaneer to captain in the Royal Navy.

Morgan and Dampier were spared indictment for piracy because they were valuable men. Those who did enter homeland or colonial courts in shackles during the eighteenth century were subjected to a specie of justice that welded the interests of the merchants – especially the East India and Royal African Companies – and the court itself to that of the prosecution even more closely than in ordinary felony proceedings. We have seen that the 1700 law deprived the accused of important common-law protections, but also that the law itself was violated to achieve the state's ends. In London, the Bahamas, Jamaica,

Virginia and Ghana, exculpatory evidence was suppressed, or the system of piracy commissions was bypassed, or the rights to cross-examine the state's witnesses and call defence witnesses were denied. In certain cases, hearsay evidence was allowed upon which it should have been impossible to indict, much less to convict. Some of these violations resulted in the death of innocent men. If the justice system truly held with the Advocate General of Massachusetts 'that it is better that a guilty man pass Unpunished, than that an Innocent man should be Condemned', it failed repeatedly in piracy trials.[2] The conclusion is somewhat different if we take a wider view, however. We have seen that, on the whole, judges and juries, operating under either the 1536 or 1700 law, acquitted where there was significant evidence of the defendant's being forced. But even after conviction, it was the practice to spare defendants the death penalty if the evidence against them was less than solid, a merciful departure from the strict letter of the law. We have also seen that piracy trial procedure and the behaviour of admiralty judges were consistent with prevailing standards of decorum and beliefs about the courts' function in the community.

These standards and beliefs have changed dramatically in the last three centuries, so that today, when democratically elected governments seek to elevate national security above the individual's legal rights in the 'war against terrorism' – a position Sir Charles Hedges would have considered beyond reproach – many of their citizens feel anxious and disappointed. In their current dilemma, they find themselves uncomfortably reverting to the ethos of another age they like to deride as brutal. While there is encouragement in the fact that the piracy law did not impede but may even have hastened the acceptance of defence lawyers on matters of law and fact, of the neutrality of the bench, and, beginning in the late eighteenth century, of a modern code of evidence, it is disturbing that the most repugnant parts of this emergency legislation – those relating to trial procedure and the rights of the accused – remained in force for more than a century and a half, relics of real and spectral fears for the loss of England's trade and fledgling empire.[3]

Notes

Chapter 1. Introduction: Gentlemen of Fortune

1 A.T. Whateley, 'Historical Sketch of the Law of Piracy', *The Law Magazine and Review*, n.s., 3 (1874), 536.
2 Giles Jacob, *A New Law Dictionary* (London, 1729).
3 William Phillips's Confession, NA, SP 63/358/127–132.
4 E.A. Cruikshank, *The Life of Sir Henry Morgan* (Toronto, 1935), 24.
5 Condemnation entailed the legal transfer by a court of admiralty of property rights in a prize ship and its cargo to the investors in the privateering cruise or the officers and men of a naval ship.
6 Peter R. Galvin, *Patterns of Pillage: A Geography of Caribbean-Based Piracy in Spanish-America, 1536–1718* (New York, 1999), 31.
7 'Pirateer' is not in the *Oxford English Dictionary* but may have first appeared in a newsletter (*CSPD*, 1 July 1671, p.353); 'Pyrateering' is found in A.O. Exquemelin, *The Bucaniers of America*, 2 vols (London: W. Crooke, 1684–85), I, iii, 83 (hereafter, *Bucaniers*).
8 2nd edn (New York, 1998), 7.
9 Rubin, 10, 11, 21.
10 Rubin, 34.
11 Rubin, 56–57.
12 Instructions to colonial governors, NA, CO 37/5/108.
13 Matthew Hale quoted by Barbara J. Shapiro, *'Beyond Reasonable Doubt' and 'Probable Cause'* (Berkeley, 1991), 12.
14 Thomas A. Green, 'A Retrospective on the Criminal Trial Jury, *Twelve Good Men and True, The Criminal Trial Jury in England, 1200–1800*, ed. J.S. Cockburn and Thomas A. Green (Princeton, 1988), 360.
15 John H. Langbein, 'The Criminal Trial before the Lawyers', *University of*

Chicago Law Review 45 (1978), 285–298, 306–313.

16 Charles M. Andrews, *The Colonial Period of American History*, 4 vols (New Haven, 1938), IV, 226.

17 Robert Ritchie, *Captain Kidd and the War against the Pirates* (Cambridge, Mass., 1986), 143–153 (hereafter, Ritchie); the Company appointed an ad hoc committee on 5 February 1697 to assist Hedges (BL, OIOC, B/41/294–295).

18 Marcus Rediker, Villains of All Nations: Atlantic Pirates in the Golden Age (Boston, 2004), 148-69.

19 First published in *Bucaniers*.

20 My principal sources for the pirates' lives are Cruikshank, *Henry Morgan*; Ritchie, *Captain Kidd*; Nuala Zahedieh, 'Morgan, Sir Henry', *Dictionary of National Biography* (Oxford, 2004); Dudley Pope, *Harry Morgan's Way: The Biography of Sir Henry Morgan, 1635–1684* (London, 1977); Anton Gill, *The Devil's Mariner: William Dampier, Pirate and Explorer* (London, 1997); Robert E. Lee, *Blackbeard the Pirate: A Reappraisal of His Life and Times* (Winston-Salem, North Carolina, 1974); Stanley Richards, *Black Bart* (Llandybie, Carmarthenshire, 1966); and Lindley S. Butler, *Pirates, Privateers, and Rebels of the Carolina Coast* (Chapel Hill, 2000).

21 The attribution of the *General History* to Daniel Defoe was persuasively challenged by Philip Nicholas Furbank and W.R. Owens in *Defoe De-Attributions: A Critique of J.R. Moore's Checklist* (Rio Grande, Ohio, 1994).

Chapter 2. Henry Morgan: 'More Used to the Pike than the Book'

1   *CSPA*, 24 Feb 1680, no.1304.

2   Cruikshank, 8.

3   To estimate the current (2002) value of old money I have used the calculator at the Economic Services website, URL: http://www.eh.net/hmit/ppowerbp/.

4   *CSPA*, 28 April 1663, no.443.

5   *CSPA*, 1 March 1666, no.1142, i.

6   Ibid.

7   Pope, 115, 135.

8   Edward Long, *The History of Jamaica*, 2 vols (London, 1774), II, 140.

9   *CSPA*, 7–17 Jan, 1669, no.1, i.

10 Zahedieh.

11 *CSPA*, 7 Sept 1668, no.1838.

12 *Bucaniers*, I, tp.; II, [A4v].

13 *Bucaniers*, I, ii, 48.

14 *Bucaniers*, I, ii, 54.

15 *Bucaniers*, I, ii, 70.

16 *Bucaniers*, I, ii, 70. Sancho Panza in *Don Quixote* is conducted to his government wearing a Montera cap.

17 Long, II, 140.

BE Cruikshank, 123.

19 David Marley, *Pirates and Privateers of the Americas* (Santa Barbara, 1994), 349.

20 Cruikshank, 136; *CSPA*, 2 July 1670, no.212.

21 *CSPA*, 1 Aug 1670, no.226.

22 *CSPA*, 12 June 1670, no.194.

23 Pope, 227.

24 *CSPA*, 20 Apr 1671, no.504.

25 William Dampier, *Dampier's Voyages*, ed. John Masefield, 2 vols (London, 1906), II, 154.

26 Zahedieh; Long, II, 140.

27 Thomas Dalby, *An historical account of the Rise and Growth of the West-India Colonies* (London, 1690), 42.

28 George Berkeley, soon to be made 1st Earl of Berkeley, was one of the Lords of Trade, fellow of the Royal Society for the Promotion of Natural Knowledge and founding member of the Royal African Company; John Evelyn, *Diary*, ed. E.S. de Beer, 6 vols (Oxford, 1955), IV, 46.

29 Dalby, 42.

30 Long, I, 597.

31 J.S. Bromley, 'Outlaws at Sea, 1660–1720: Liberty, Equality and Fraternity among the Caribbean Freebooters', in *History from Below,* ed. Frederick Krantz (Quebec, 1985), 310.

32 Clennell Wilkinson, *Dampier: Explorer and Buccaneer* (New York, 1929), 57.

33 *CSPA*, 2 Aug. 1676, no.1129; Zahedieh.

34 *CSPA*, 15 Sept 1679, nos 1117-18

35 *CSPA*, 24 Feb 1680, no.1304.

36 *CSPA*, 27 Jan, no.15; 2 July 1681, no.159.

37 *CSPA*, 20 May, no.1361; 5 July 1680, no.1425.

38 *CSPA*, 24 Feb 1680, no. 1304 (soap anecdote); 20 May 1680, no. 1361; 12 May 1681, no.102; Thomas Southey, *Chronological History of the West Indies*, 3 vols (London, 1827), II, 122–23.

39 *CSPA*, 22 Feb 1683, no.938.

40 *Bucaniers* and *The History of the Bucaniers* (London: Thomas Malthus, 1684),

were both English translations of the Spanish translation (1681) of *De Americaensche Zee-Roovers.*

41 Bryan Edwards, *The History, Civil and Commercial, of the British West Indies,* 5th edn, 5 vols (London, 1819; reprinted New York, 1966), III, 136.

Chapter 3. William Dampier: 'That Old Pirateing Dog'

1 Cruikshank, 279.
2 Thus Samuel Taylor Coleridge eulogised Dampier *(Table Talk* in *The Collected Works of Samuel Taylor Coleridge,* 16 vols ([London, 1969–90], XIV, 268).
3 Dampier, *Voyages,* II, 52.
4 Dampier, *Voyages,* II, 114.
5 Dampier, *Voyages,* II, 151, 172, 163.
6 Dampier, *Voyages,* II, 179.
7 Dampier, *Voyages,* II, 211.
8 Marley, 90.
9 *Bucaniers,* II, iv, 30
10 Marley, 347.
11 Lionel Wafer, *A New Voyage and Description of the Isthmus of America* (1699), ed. George Parker Winship (New York, 1903), 39, 55.
12 Dampier, *Voyages,* I, 45, 47.
13 Derek Howse and Norman J.W. Thrower, eds, *A Buccaneer's Atlas: Basil Ringrose's South Sea Waggoner* (Berkeley, 1992), 7, 12, 262–264, 268.
14 Howse, 27–28, 31–32; James William Kelly, 'Bartholomew Sharp', *Dictionary of National Biography* (Oxford, 2004).
15 Gill, 143.
16 'The operation of heaving the ship down on one side, by the application of a strong purchase to her masts... [so] that her bottom, being elevated above it's surface on the other side, may be cleansed from any filth, which adheres to it' (William Falconer, *An Universal Dictionary of the Marine* [London, 1780], 78).
17 Gill, 148.
18 Gill, 294.
19 Dampier, *Voyages,* I, 114.
20 Dampier, *Voyages,* I, 151–152.
21 Dampier, *Voyages,* I, 180-181
22 Marley, 246-247; Dampier, *Voyages,* I, 228–229.
23 Dampier, *Voyages,* I, 242.
24 Dampier, *Voyages,* I, 296, 298.
25 Dampier, *Voyages,* I, 367.

26 Ibid.

27 William Dampier, *A New Voyage Round the World,* ed. Sir Albert Gray (New York: Dover, 1968), xli.

28 Dampier, *Voyages,* I, 399.

29 Dampier, *Voyages,* I, 448.

30 Dampier, *Voyages,* I, 450, 453–54.

31 Dampier, *Voyages,* I, 481.

32 Dampier, *Voyages,* I, 481–82.

33 Dampier, *Voyages,* I, 485–86, 487.

34 Joel Baer, 'William Dampier at the Crossroads: New Light on the "Missing Years", 1691–1697', *International Journal of Maritime History,* 8 (December 1996), 97–117; George F. Steckley, 'Litigious Mariners: Wage Cases in the Seventeenth-Century Admiralty Court', *The Historical Journal,* 42 (1999), 315–45.

35 Dampier, *Voyages,* II, 207 ; Dampier, *A Voyage to New Holland* (London, 1703) in *Voyages,* II, 342.

36 Evelyn, V, 295.

37 Joseph C. Shipman, *William Dampier: Seaman-Scientist* (Lawrence, Kansas, 1962), 30.

38 Dampier's testimony, NA, ADM 1/1692, 22 April 1699.

39 NA, ADM 33/202, 8 October 1701.

40 Dampier, *Voyages,* II, 604, 575.

41 *Captain Dampier's Vindication of his Voyage to the South Seas in the Ship 'St. George',* in Dampier, *Voyages,* II, 585.

42 Gill, 320.

43 Glyndwr Williams, *The Great South Sea: English Voyages and Encounters 1570–1750* (New Haven and London: Yale, 1997), 156.

44 B.M.H. Rogers, 'Woodes Rogers's Privateering Voyage of 1708–11', *Mariner's Mirror,* 19 (1933), 208.

Chapter 4. Henry Every: 'I am a Man of Fortune, and Must Seek my Fortune'

1 NA, HCA 13/81/337v.

2 Dampier, *Voyages,* I, 582. Since the fourteenth century, English sailors had referred to Coruña, a base for England's Atlantic fleet in times of peace with Spain, as the 'Groin'.

3 Petition of the seamen's wives, NA, CO 388/4/49. The Privy Council had reviewed this and other documents about the mutiny in 1694. See also NA, HCA 13/81, vols 335–338. Gibson replaced Strong, who died before the

ships reached Coruña.

4 Phillips.

5 NA, CO 388/4/49–62.

6 *GHP*, 422; Phillips.

7 Sir John Houblon is a prime example of William's new lords (see p. 107).

8 Edward Barlow, *Barlow's Journal of his Life at Sea*, ed. Basil Lubbock, 2 vols (London, 1934), I, 162.

9 *The Tryals of Joseph Dawson* [et al.] *at the Old Bailey, for Felony and Piracy* (London, 1696), in *A Complete Collection of State Trials*, ed. T.B. Howell, 33 vols (London, 1816–26), XIII, cols 451–83 (hereafter, *Tryals*).

10 *A Copy of Verses, Composed by Captain Henry Every, Lately Gone to Sea to seek his Fortune* (London [1694]), (hereafter, *Verses*).

11 *Tryals*, cols 469, 467. English law permitted this practice only if the crew with the food were not themselves left to starve.

12 *Tryals*, col. 469.

13 I am indebted to Christopher J. Ware, formerly of the National Maritime Museum, for suggesting how the *Fancy* may have been altered.

14 Examination of Peter Claus, 15 Aug, 1698, NA, CO 323/2/324.

15 Phillips; *Tryals*, cols 467, 470.

16 Deposition of John Elston, Oxford University, Bodleian Library, Rawlinson A 272.

17 BL, OIOC E/3/50/5981 (354).

18 Douglas Botting, *The Pirates* (Alexandria, Virginia, 1978), 82.

19 *Tryals*, cols 467, 470; Elston.

20 *CSPA*, 18 December 1696, no.517i; 25 May 1700, no.466 xi.

21 Phillips; Lady Alice Archer Houblon, *The Houblon Family*, 2 vols (London, 1907), I, 298.

22 Phillips.

23 Ashin Das Gupta, *Indian Merchants and the Decline of Surat: c.1700–1750* (Wiesbaden, 1979), 94, 73; Philip Baldæus, *A Description of the Coasts of Malabar and Coromandel* (Amsterdam, 1672), in Awnsham Churchill, *A Collection of Voyages and Travels*, 4 vols (London, 1704), III, 575–76.

24 Deposition of John Dann, NA, CO 323/2/25iv; Elston; Houblon, I, 298.

25 Phillips; Elston; Information of John Dann, NA, HCA 1/53/10.

26 Muhammad Hâshim Khâfi Khân, *Khâfi Khân's History of 'Alamgir'*, trans. by S. Moinul Haq (Karachi, 1975), 420; Phillips.

27 Phillips.

28 Khan, 420; Jadunath Sarkar, *History of Aurangzib*, 5 vols (Bombay, 1972–1974), V, 343–344.

29 Khan, 420; John Franklin Jameson, *Privateering and Piracy in the Colonial Period: Illustrative Documents* (New York, 1923), 159.

30 BL, OIOC, H/Misc/36, 199 (hereafter, Middleton).

31 *Tryals*, col. 471.

32 Ritchie, 110, 114.

33 Dann.

34 Dann.

35 Case of Nicholas Trott, NA, CO 5/1257/37.

36 Ibid; Dann.

37 Adams came to Ireland with a woman he had probably met and married in New Providence.

38 East India Company Court Minutes, BL, 010C, B/41, 174, 262; H/MISC./36, 201-204.

39 Dann. The reward published by the government on 18 July 1696 was later doubled by the Company's contribution of 4,000 rupees (Narcissus Luttrell, *A Brief Historical Relation of State Affairs*, 6 vols [Oxford University Press, 1857], IV, 86; John Bruce, *Annals of the Honourable East-India Company 1600 to 1707–08*, 3 vols [London, 1810], III, 203–04).

40 Dann. The sequin or chequin was 'a Venetian or Turkish coin worth about nine shillings' (Jameson, 171, note 30).

41 *CSPA*, 20 September 1697, no.1,331; Cyrus Karraker, *Piracy was a Business* (Rindge, New Hampshire, 1953), 75.

42 *Tryals*, col. 482; Jonathan Swift, *Gulliver's Travels*, ed. Herbert Davis (Oxford, 1965), I, vii, 73.

43 *An Exact Narrative of the Tryals of the Pyrates... held in the Old Bayly... 7th and 9th of Jan. 1674/5* (London, 1675), 4.

44 *Tryals*, col. 464.

45 Joel Baer, '"Captain John Avery" and the Anatomy of a Mutiny', *Eighteenth-Century Life*, 18 (1994): 5, 17, 25; *Post Man*, 17–20 Oct. 1696.

46 *Tryals*, cols 455–57.

47 *Tryals*, cols 460–61. Jurors of the period might hear several cases during the course of a session.

48 Langbein, 282; *Tryals*, col. 463.

49 *Tryals*, cols 454–55.

50 *Tryals*, cols 459, 467, 471.

51 *Tryals*, cols 480–81.

52 *Tryals*, cols 475–76.

53 Baer, 'Anatomy', 9–11.

54 Henry Slesser, *The Administration of the Law* (London, [1948]), 101.

55 *Tryals*, cols 477–78.

56 *Tryals*, col. 480.

57 *Tryals*, col. 480.

58 Shapiro, 8–12 ; Langbein, 266.

59 *Account of the Behaviour, Dying Speeches, and Execution of Mr. John Murphey...* (London, 1696).

60 Anthony Farrington, *A Biographical Index of East India Company Maritime Service Officers 1600–1834* (London, 1999); Anthony Farrington, *Catalogue of East India Company Ships' Journals and Logs 1600–1834* (London, 1999).

61 'Villany Rewarded', *The Pepys Ballads*, ed. by Hyder Rollins, 8 vols (Cambridge, Mass., 1929–32), VII, 243–44. Broadsides were printed on large sheets, frequently adorned with musical notation and woodcuts, and sold on the street.

62 *Verses*; Joel Baer, 'Bold Captain Avery in the Privy Council: Early Variants of a Broadside Ballad from the Pepys Collection', *Folk Music Journal*, 7 (1995), 4–26.

63 *The Successful Pyrate* (London, 1713), 22.

Chapter 5. William Kidd: 'Because I Would Not Turn Pirate, You Rogues, You Would Make Me One'

1 Ritchie, 197.

2 *The Tryal of Capt. William Kidd*, ed. Don C. Seitz (New York, 1936), 64 (hereafter, *Seitz*).

3 Seitz, 64–66.

4 Kidd would not have lied about events in which his correspondent had participated; a New York acquaintance, Colonel Hewson, testified that Kidd told him at the time of Bellomont's pressure (Seitz, 191).

5 Seitz, 7.

6 Ritchie, 54–55. Such grants were rare, the last being made to Sir Robert Holmes in 1687 but never used.

7 Seitz, 23.

8 Ritchie, 93.

9 Barlow, II, 484. A plain red or black flag meant that no mercy or 'quarter' would be given to ships that resist. The jolly roger was the pirate version of this traditional signal.

10 Although the ownership of the vessel, not its passes, determined the legality of the capture, a taking disallowed in court was rarely considered piracy.

11 Ritchie, 102; Seitz, 117.

12 *Trial of Captain Kidd*, ed. Graham Brooks (Edinburgh: William Hodge, 1930), 195 (hereafter, *Brooks*).

13 Seitz, 43.

14 Seitz, 86, 87, 89, 91.

15 Seitz, 118.

16 Ritchie, 108. In 1696, the East India Company valued the rupee at 2s 6d.

17 Seitz, 44, 174.

18 'Kidd's own Narrative of His Voyage,' Brooks, 194, 197; Seitz, 62.

19 Ritchie, 137.

20 Seitz, 45.

21 Seitz, 46.

22 Seitz, 31ff., 56; Ritchie, 178, 285, note 62.

23 Ritchie, 179, 231–232, 232, note 17; Seitz, 63.

24 Two years later Kidd was convinced that 'my Lord Bellomont haveing sold his Share of my Ship, and in ye Adventure, thought it his Interest to make me a pirate, whereby he could Claim a Share of my Cargo' (NA, HCA 1/29/285).

25 Seitz, 20.

26 Ritchie, 205.

27 Ritchie, 196

28 Seitz, 75.

29 Seitz, 77.

30 NA, HCA 1/29/285.

31 Seitz, 79.

32 The appearance of lawyers in capital cases was a lively topic at this time. Defendants in treason cases were first allowed counsel by an act of 1696 (Langbein, 267).

33 Seitz, 79–80. *Peine fort et dure*, the pressing to death of defendants who stand 'mute by malice', was still available in 1701, but Kidd's judges followed a provision of the 1700 piracy law mandating a guilty plea for such defendants. Pressing was outlawed in 1772, and by 7–8 George 4, c.28 (1827), a plea of 'not guilty' was automatically recorded for *all* recalcitrant defendants.

34 Seitz, 85. A defendant subject to the death penalty had thirty-six 'peremptory' challenges. The prosecution had none but it could delay the sitting of any juror until the entire panel had been canvassed (J.H. Baker, 'Criminal Courts and Procedure at Common Law 1550–1800', in J.S. Cockburn, ed., *Crime in England 1550–1800* [Princeton, 1977], 36).

35 Cf. the jury list in *Tryals*, col. 452, with that in Seitz, 85.

36 Admittedly, jury pools were relatively small at this time, and many individuals served on juries for years.

37 Seitz, 87, 101.

38 Seitz, 98.

39 Seitz, 90.

40 Seitz, 98.

41 Slesser, 19; Seitz, 98; Langbein, 313.

42 Shapiro, 21–22. Shapiro suggests that the first use in court of the phrase 'guilty beyond a reasonable doubt' may have been in the 1770 trial of British soldiers accused in the Boston Massacre. It did not supplant the *moral certainty* or *satisfied belief* standard but was a clearer way to express it.

43 Seitz, 90, 96, 98.

44 Such severity was not mandatory. Other Madagascar pirates had been allowed to surrender to officials not named in the pardon proclamation (Ritchie, 217).

45 If there were a plot to pack the jury for Kidd, it didn't work, perhaps because the charge was murder, not disruption of Indian Ocean trade, and because merchant resentment against the East India Company had abated since the breaking of its monopoly in 1698.

46 Seitz, 111, 113.

47 Ritchie, 209; Seitz, pp. 85, 150.

48 Ritchie, 218.

49 Seitz, 153, 155.

50 Langbein, 301–302.

51 Seitz, 177, 182, 218.

52 Kidd's point was largely rhetorical, for the evidence of defence witnesses 'seems to have been given the same weight as if it had been sworn, though if it turned out more favourable to the Crown an oath was hurriedly administered' (Baker, 38). The 1700 piracy law explicitly required that defense witnesses in colonial trials be administered the oath (Rubin, 402).

53 Seitz, 195.

54 Brooks, 47.

55 Seitz, 225, 226.

56 Seitz, 221.

57 Green, *Verdict*, chapters 3 and 4.

58 *The Ordinary of Newgate his account of the behaviour confessions and dying words of Captain William Kidd...* (London, 1701; reprinted in Brooks), 49.

59 *A True Account of the Behaviour, Confession, and Last Dying Speeches of Captain William Kidd, and the Rest of the Pirates... Executed at Execution Dock... the 23rd of May 1701*, reprinted in Brooks, 220.

60 Brooks, 221.

61 Brooks, 50.

62 Symbolic of Admiralty court and civil law jurisdiction over affairs at sea unto the first bridge upriver.

63 Seitz, 227, 228.

64 Swift, I, vii, 67.

Chapter 6. Blackbeard and the Pirates of the Bahamas: 'They Shall Plant No Colony in Our Dominions'

1 'Private revenue cutters used to enforce the Spanish trading monopoly in the Caribbean' *(GHP*, 667, note 12).

2 *An Essay on the East-India Trade* (London, 1697; reprinted in *The Political and Commercial Works of... Charles D'Avenant*, ed. by Charles Whitworth, 5 vols, London, 1771), V, 89. See above, chapter 1, note 17.

3 Lauren Benton, 'Oceans of Law: Piracy and the Legal Geography of the Seventeenth-Century Seas', paper presented at the American Bar Foundation colloquium, Chicago, 8 April 2002.

4 Rubin, 400–402.

5 Rubin, 401.

6 Rubin, 405–06; *CSPA*, 12 May 1698, no. 451.

7 Rubin, 403.

8 *GHP*, 71.

9 Butler, 57.

10 Butler, 35.

11 *Boston News-Letter*, 30 June–7 July 1718.

12 *GHP*, 84–85.

13 Butler, 32.

14 Butler, 41.

15 *The Tryals of Major Stede Bonnet, and other Pirates* (London, 1719), 13.

16 *Tryals of Bonnet*, 5.

17 William Searle Holdsworth, *A History of English Law*, 6th edn, 17 vols (London, 1938), IV, 531

18 *Tryals of Bonnet*, 10.

19 *Tryals of Bonnet*, 15, 16, 17, 39, 40.

20 *Tryals of Bonnet*, 15.

21 *Tryals of Bonnet*, 34.

22 *GHP*, 112.

23 *GHP*, 292–294.

24 Lee, 129–125.

25 *GHP*, 80.

26 *GHP*, 81–82.

27 Lee, 123–125.

28 NA, CO 137/114/24.

29 *GHP*, 142; *Romances and Narratives by Daniel Defoe*, ed. by George A. Aitken, 16 vols (London, 1895), II, 47.

30 *GHP*, 643–44.

31 NA, CO 23/1/74.

32 NA, CO 23/1/79–80.

33 *GHP*, 149.

34 *GHP*, 150.

35 See above, chapter 1, note 12.

36 *The Tryals of Captain John Rackam, and other Pirates* (Jamaica, 1721), 31.

37 *Tryals of Rackam*, 33; *GHP*, 152.

38 *Tryals of Rackam*, 18–19.

39 Ibid.

40 Richard Clark, 'The history of judicial hanging in Britain', Capital Punishment Resource Centre, URL: www.geocities.com/CapitolHill/6142/timeline.html.

41 Dianne Dugaw, *Warrior Women and Popular Balladry, 1650–1850* (Cambridge, 1989).

42 *The Three Penny Opera*, translated by John Willett and Ralph Manheim, in *Bertolt Brecht Plays: One* (London, 1987), 83.

Chapter 7. Bartholomew Roberts: 'No, A Merry Life and a Short One Shall be my Motto'

1 Ritchie, 114.

2 Richards, 23.

3 *GHP*, 205.

4 *GHP*, 211–12.

5 *GHP*, 210.

6 *The Tryals of the Pyrates Lately Taken by His Britannick Majesty's Ship the Swallow* (London, 1723), 16 (hereafter, *Swallow*).

7 *GHP*, 343.

8 *Swallow*, 21, 26, 43, 62, 74.

9 Joel Baer, '"The Complicated Plot of Piracy": Aspects of English Criminal Law and the Image of the Pirate in Defoe', *The Eighteenth Century*, 23 (1982), 23.

10 Reprinted in *The History of the Buccaneers of America* (Boston, 1853), 'Preface'.

11 *Mist's Weekly Journal*, 23 May 1724.

12 Baer, 'Complicated Plot', 22.

13 NA, CO 194/6/83; *GHP*, 216.

14 *GHP*, 217. Joseph Bradish was arrested in Massachusetts and sent to London in the same ship as Kidd and James Kelley. Bradish and Kelley were tried and hanged one year before Kidd's trials, their bodies 'exhibited in chains at Hope Dock near Gravesend' (Marley, *Pirates and Privateers*, 60).

15 *GHP*, 222; 'form' was sometimes used during the eighteenth century to mean 'expression of the essence' as in Bacon's phrase, 'the soul or essential form of the universe' (Samuel Johnson, *Dictionary*).

16 *GHP*, 222.

17 *GHP*, 222–23.

18 *GHP*, 225.

19 William Smith, *A New Voyage to Guinea*, 2nd edn (London, 1745), 42–43.

20 Richards, 66.

21 *Swallow*, v.

22 *Swallow*, 5.

23 *GHP*, 243.

24 *GHP*, 244.

25 *Swallow*, 51.

26 *GHP*, 267.

27 BL, Egerton ch.8197. I follow the accounting of the captured in *Swallow*, which differs slightly from that given by Ogle (David Cordingly, *Under the Black Flag* [New York, 1996], 247).

28 *Swallow*, 8.

29 *Swallow*, 5–6.

30 *State Trials*, XIII, col. 495. See also the colloquy on the restricted admissibility of evidence under this law (cols 495–500).

31 *Swallow*, 19, 20, 68.

32 Edward Jenks, *A Short History of English Law* (Boston, 1912), 342. Appeals were sometimes heard before the King's Bench, with permission of the Attorney General, on technical errors in the proceedings. Convictions could also be reviewed before the session's panel of judges upon the request of the trial judge (Baker, 45–48).

33 *Swallow*, 24.

34 BL, Egerton ch.8197.

8. Pirates and the Law

1 6 George 1, c.19.
2 *The Trials of Eight Persons Indicted for Piracy* (Boston, 1718), 18.
3 The articles concerning trial procedure were repealed by the Statute Review Act of 1867.

Bibliography

The reader is referred to the table of abbreviations on p. 6.

Primary Sources, Manuscript

British Library

Egerton MSS, ch. 8197
OIOC, Court Minutes, B/41; Home Miscellaneous Series, H/misc/36;
    Original Correspondence, E/3/50
Sloane MSS, 3236

National Archives

ADM 33/202
CO 5/1257; 23/1; 37/6; 137/114; 152/13; 194/6; 323/2; 388/4
HCA 1/14; 1/29; 13/81
SP 63/358

Cornwall Record Office

Instructions for finding Every's treasure, J 2277

Primary Sources, Printed

Account of the Behaviour, Dying Speeches, and Execution of Mr. John Murphey...
    (London, 1696)
Baldæus, Philip, *A Description of the Coasts of Malabar and Coromandel* (1672;

reprinted in Awnsham Churchill, ed., *A Collection of Voyages and Travels*, 4 vols [London, 1704])

Barlow, Edward, *Barlow's Journal of his Life at Sea*, ed. by Basil Lubbock, 2 vols (London, 1934)

Calendar of State Papers, Colonial Series, America and West Indies (London: Her Majesty's Stationery Office, 1860)

Calendar of State Papers, Domestic Series, of the Reign of Charles II, 28 vols (London, 1860–1939)

Coleridge, Samuel Taylor, *Table Talk*, in *The Collected Works of Samuel Taylor Coleridge,* 16 vols ([London], 1969–90) 16 vols

A Copy of Verses, Composed by Captain Henry Every, Lately Gone to Sea to seek his Fortune (London, [1694])

Dalby, Thomas, *An Historical Account of the Rise and Growth of the West India Colonies* (London, 1690)

Dampier, William, *Dampier's Voyages*, ed. by John Masefield, 2 vols (London, 1906)

Dampier, William, *A New Voyage Round the World*, repr. with an introduction by Sir Albert Gray (New York, Dover, 1968)

Davenant, Charles, *An Essay on the East-India Trade* (London, 1697; repr. in *The Political and Commercial Works of... Charles D'Avenant*, ed. by Charles Whitworth, 5 vols, London, 1771)

Defoe, Daniel, *Romances and Narratives*, ed. by George A. Aitken, 16 vols (London: J.M. Dent, 1895)

Evelyn, John, *Diary*, ed. by E.S. de Beer, 6 vols (Oxford, 1955)

An Exact Narrative of the Tryals of the Pyrate... held in the Old Bayly... 7th, and 9th of Jan. 1674/5 (London, 1675)

Exquemelin, Alexander Oliver, *Bucaniers of America*, 2nd ed., 2 vols (London: William Crooke, 1684–85)

Falconer, William, *An Universal Dictionary of the Marine* (London, 1780)

Jacob, Giles, *A New Law Dictionary* (London, 1729)

Jameson, John Franklin, ed., *Privateering and Piracy in the Colonial Period: Illustrative Documents* (New York, 1923)

Johnson, Captain Charles [attributed to Daniel Defoe], *A General History of the Pyrates* (London, 1724–28; ed. by Manuel Schonhorn, Minneola, New York, Dover, 1999)

Johnson, Charles, *The Successful Pyrate* (London, 1713)

Johnson, Samuel, *A Dictionary of the English Language* (London, 1755)

The Life and Adventures of Capt. John Avery grown from a cabin boy to a King
(London, [1709])

Khâfi Khân, Muhammad Hâshim, *Khâfi Khân's History of 'Alamgir'*, translated by
S. Moinul Haq (Karachi, 1975)

[Kidd, William] *The Ordinary of Newgate, his Account of the Behaviour, Confessions,
and Dying-Words of Captain W. Kidd, and Other Pirates* (London, 1701; repr. in
Trial of Captain Kidd, ed. by Brooks, 48–50)

[Kidd, William] *Trial of Captain Kidd* (London, 1701; ed. by Graham Brooks,
Edinburgh, William Hodge, 1930)

[Kidd, William] *A True Account of the Behaviour, Confession, and Last Dying
Speeches of Captain William Kidd* (London, 1701; repr. in *Trial of Captain Kidd*,
ed. by Brooks, 220–221)

[Kidd, William] *The Tryal of Capt. William Kidd for Murther & Piracy* (London,
1701; repr. by Don C. Seitz, New York, Rufus Rockwell Wilson, 1936)

Leslie, Charles, *A New History of Jamaica* (London, 1740)

Long, Edward, *The History of Jamaica*, 2 vols (London, 1774)

Luttrell, Narcissus, *A Brief Historical Relation of State Affairs*, 6 vols (Oxford
University Press, 1857)

Ovington, John, *Voyage to Suratt in the Year 1689* (London, 1696)

The Pepys Ballads, ed. by Hyder Rollins (Cambridge, Mass., 1929–32)

Smith, William, *A New Voyage to Guinea*, 2nd edn, 2 vols (London, 1745)

[State Trials] *A Complete Collection of State Trials*, ed. by T.B. Howell, 33 vols
(London, 1816-26)

Swift, Jonathan, *Gulliver's Travels* (London, 1726; ed. by Herbert Davis, Oxford,
Basil Blackwell, 1965)

The Trials of Eight Persons Indicted for Piracy (Boston, 1718)

The Tryals of Captain John Rackam, and other Pirates (Jamaica, 1721)

The Tryals of Joseph Dawson [et al.] at the Old Bailey, for Felony and Piracy
(London, 1696; in *A Complete Collection of State Trials*)

The Tryals of the Pyrates Lately Taken by His Britannick Majesty's Ship the Swallow
(London, 1723)

Wafer, Lionel, *A New Voyage and Description of the Isthmus of America* (London,
1699; ed. George Parker Winship, New York, Burt Franklin, 1903)

Primary Sources, Newspapers

Boston News Letter, 1718
Mist's Weekly Journal, 1724
Post Man, 1696

Secondary Sources, Printed

Baer, Joel, 'Bold Captain Avery in the Privy Council: Early Variants of a Broadside
    Ballad from the Pepys Collection', *Folk Music Journal*, 7 (1995), 4–26

Baer, Joel, '"The Complicated Plot of Piracy": Aspects of English Criminal Law
    and the Image of the Pirate in Defoe', *The Eighteenth Century*, 23 (1982), 3–26

Baer, Joel, '"Captain John Avery" and the Anatomy of a Mutiny', *Eighteenth-
    Century Life*, 18 (1994), 1–26.

Baer, Joel, 'William Dampier at the Crossroads: New Light on the "Missing
    Years", 1691–1697', *International Journal of Maritime History*, 8 (December
    1996), 97–117

Baker, J.H., 'Criminal Courts and Procedure at Common Law 1550–1800', in
    J.S. Cockburn, ed., *Crime in England 1550–1800* (Princeton: Princeton
    University Press, 1977), 15–48

Benton, Lauren, 'Oceans of Law: Piracy and the Legal Geography of the
    Seventeenth Century Seas', paper presented at the American Bar Foundation
    colloquium, Chicago, April 8, 2002

Botting, Douglas, *The Pirates* (Alexandria, Virginia: Time-Life Books, 1978)

Brecht, Bertolt, *The Three Penny Opera,* translated by John Willett and Ralph
    Manheim, in *Bertolt Brecht Plays: One* (London: Methuen, 1987), 63–141

Bromley, J.S., 'Outlaws at Sea, 1660–1720: Liberty, Equality and Fraternity
    among the Caribbean Freebooters', in Frederick Krantz, ed., *History from
    Below* (Quebec: Concordia University Press, 1985), 301–320

Bruce, John, *Annals of the Honourable East-India Company 1600 to 1707–08*, 3 vols
    (London, 1810)

Butler, Lindley S., *Pirates, Privateers, and Rebels of the Carolina Coast* (Chapel Hill:
    University of North Carolina Press, 2000)

Clark, Richard, 'The history of judicial hanging in Britain', Capital Punishment
    Resource Centre, URL:
    www.geocities.com/CapitolHill/6142/hanging1.html, and
    www.geocities.com/CapitolHill/6142/timeline.html

David Cordingly, *Under the Black Flag* (New York, 1996)

Cruikshank, E.A., *The Life of Sir Henry Morgan* (Toronto, 1935)

Das Gupta, Ashin, *Indian Merchants and the Decline of Surat: c.1700–1750* (Wiesbaden: Franz Steiner, 1979)

Dugaw, Dianne, *Warrior Women and Popular Balladry, 1650–1850* (Cambridge, 1989)

Economic History Services, 'How much is that?', URL: www.eh.net/hmit/ppowerbp/

Edwards, Bryan, *The History, Civil and Commercial, of the British West Indies*, 5th edn, 5 vols (London, 1819; repr. New York, AMS Press, 1966)

Farrington, Anthony, *A Biographical Index of East India Company Maritime Service Officers 1600–1834* (London, 1999)

Farrington, Anthony, *Catalogue of East India Company Ships' Journals and Logs 1600–1834* (London: British Library, 1999)

Furbank, Philip Nicholas and Owens, W.R., *Defoe De-attributions: A Critique of J.R. Moore's Checklist* (Rio Grande, Ohio: Hambledon Press, 1994).

Galvin, Peter, *Patterns of Pillage: A Geography of Caribbean-Based Piracy in Spanish-America, 1536–1718* (New York, 1999)

Gill, Anton, *The Devil's Mariner: William Dampier, Pirate and Explorer* (London, 1997)

Green, Thomas A., 'A Retrospective on the Criminal Trial Jury, 1200–1800', in *Twelve Good Men and True, The Criminal Trial Jury in England, 1200–1800*, ed. by J.S. Cockburn and Thomas A. Green (Princeton: Princeton University Press, 1988), 358–99

Green, Thomas A., *Verdict According to Conscience: Perspectives on the English Criminal Trial Jury 1200–1800* (Chicago, 1985)

Holdsworth, William Searle, *A History of English Law*, 6th ed., 17 vols (London, 1938)

Houblon, Lady Alice Archer, *The Houblon Family*, 2 vols (London, 1907)

Howse, Derek and Thrower, Norman J.W., eds, *A Buccaneer's Atlas: Basil Ringrose's South Sea Waggoner* (Berkeley, 1992)

Jenks, Edward, *A Short History of English Law* (Boston, 1912)

Karraker, Cyrus, *Piracy was a Business* (Rindge, New Hampshire, 1953)

Kelly, James William, 'Bartholomew Sharp', *Dictionary of National Biography*, 60 vols (Oxford, 2004)

Langbein, John H., 'The Criminal Trial before the Lawyers', *University of Chicago Law Review*, 45 (1978), 263–316

Lee, Robert E., *Blackbeard the Pirate* (Winston-Salem, North Carolina: John F. Blair, 1974)

Marley, David, *Pirates and Privateers of the Americas* (Santa Barbara, 1994)

Pope, Dudley, *Harry Morgan's Way: the Biography of Sir Henry Morgan, 1635–1684* (London, 1977)

Richards, Stanley, *Black Bart* (Llandybie, Carmarthenshire, 1966)

Ritchie, Robert, *Captain Kidd and the War against the Pirates* (Cambridge, Mass., 1986)

Rogers, B.M.H., 'Woodes Rogers's Privateering Voyage of 1708–11', *Mariner's Mirror*, 19 (1933), 196–211

Rollins, Hyder ed., *The Pepys Ballads*, 8 vols (Cambridge, Mass.: Harvard UP, 1929–32)

Rubin, Alfred P., *The Law of Piracy*, 2nd edn (New York, Transnational Publishers, 1998)

Sarkar, Jadunath Sarkar, *History of Aurangzib* (Bombay, 1972–74)

Shapiro, Barbara J., *'Beyond Reasonable Doubt' and 'Probable Cause'* (Berkeley, 1991)

Shipman, Joseph C., *William Dampier: Seaman-Scientist* (Lawrence, Kansas, 1962)

Slesser, Henry, *The Administration of the Law* (London, [1948])

Southey, Thomas, *Chronological History of the West Indies* (London, 1827)

Steckley, George F., 'Litigious Mariners: Wage Cases in the Seventeenth-Century Admiralty Court', *The Historical Journal*, 42 (1999), 315–45

Wilkinson, Clennell, *Dampier: Explorer and Buccaneer* (New York, 1929)

Williams, Glyndwr, *The Great South Sea: English Voyages and Encounters 1570–1750* (New Haven and London, 1997)

Zahedieh, Nuala, 'Morgan, Sir Henry', *Dictionary of National Biography*, 60 vols (Oxford, Oxford University Press, 2004)

List of Illustrations

41 The government-sanctioned report of the trials of Every's men. Law Library, University of Minnesota.

42 Captain Avery's encounter with the Emperor's granddaughter, a twentieth-century rendering. G.H. Maynadier, ed., *The Works of Daniel Defoe* (New York: Jenson Society, 1905). Wilson Library, University of Minnesota.

43 'John Avery', King of Madagascar. Captain Charles Johnson, *General History of the Pirates* (London: Midwinter, 1725). Library of Congress.

44 Avery's buried treasure, a nineteenth-century hoax. Cornwall Record Office J 2277.

45 The *Charles Galley*, a ship that resembles Kidd's *Adventure*. Willem van der Velde (1676). National Maritime Museum, Greenwich.

46 Kidd buries his bible and joins the Devil's party. Charles Ellms, *The Pirates' Own Book* (Portland, Maine, 1837). Library of Congress.

47 Kidd's French pass from the *Quedah Merchant*. National Archives, London.

48 Arms of the New East India Company established by Parliament in 1698. George Birdwood, ed., *Report on the Old Records of the India Office* (London, 1891). Ames Library, University of Minnesota.

49 Entrance to Newgate Prison in 1672. Charles Gordon, *The Old Bailey and Newgate* (London, 1902). Wilson Library, University of Minnesota.

50 The Old Bailey, where Every's men and Kidd were tried. Guildhall Library, Corporation of London.

51 Kidd explains his refusal to plead in a letter to a lord, *c.*1701. National Archives, London.

52 The taking of testimony in the Old Bailey. Charles Gordon, *The Old Bailey and Newgate* (London, 1902). Wilson Library, University of Minnesota.

53 Hanging of a pirate at Execution Dock, Wapping, after 1747. Guildhall Library, Corporation of London.

54 The Thames near Execution Dock in 1746. John Roque, *A Plan of the Cities of London and Westminster* (London, 1747). Anderson Library, University of Minnesota.

55 The execution of the idle apprentice. William Hogarth, 'Industry and Idleness' (1747) in *The Works of William Hogarth* (London [1806]). Anderson Library, University of Minnesota.

56 The bodies of hanged pirates placed between high water and low, a woodcut in use since 1639. *Villany Rewarded, or, the Pirates Last Farewel* (London, 1696). Pepys Library, Magdalene College, Cambridge.

57 Set of giblet chains with skull. Courtesy of the Corporation and Council of Rye.

58 Captain Kidd hanging in chains at Tilbury Point, a nineteenth-century depiction. Charles Ellms, *The Pirates' Own Book* (Portland, Maine, 1837). Library of Congress.

59 The piracy act of 1700, 11–12 William III, c.7.

60 Instructions to colonial governors for the trying of pirates under 11–12 William III, c.7. National Archives, London.

61 Copy of the trials of John Augur and his crew (1718) sent from the Bahamas to the High Court of Admiralty. National Archives, London.

62 Thatch of the terrible eyes. Alexander Smith, *General History of the Highwayman and Pirates* (London, 1734). Princeton University Library.

63 Captain Charles Vane. Captain Charles Johnson, *History and Lives of the Pyrates* (London: Midwinter, 1725). Library of Congress.

64 'The crews of Blackbeard's and Vane's vessels carousing on coast of Carolina'. Charles Ellms, *The Pirates' Own Book* (Portland, Maine, 1837). Library of Congress.

Maps

Index